DIPLOMATIC EPISODES
IN MEXICO
BELGIUM AND CHILE

DIPLOMATIC EPISODES
IN MEXICO

BELGIUM AND CHILE

By

HENRY LANE WILSON

Ambassador to Mexico
Minister to Belgium, Minister to Chile
1897-1914

GARDEN CITY   NEW YORK
DOUBLEDAY, PAGE & COMPANY
1927

DEDICATED TO
ALICE
FAITHFUL COMPANION OF
EVENTFUL YEARS

PREFACE

THIS book is written in the hope that it may be useful in an historical way. It aims to delineate in their true colours the characters of some eminent men; to correct misleading accounts of important events; to furnish an intimate picture of the history and life of the peoples of three countries; to give a silhouette sketch of life inside the diplomatic corps.

The official documents which are printed are used with authority and no confidences have been abused. My purpose in publishing the book is to render useful service and not to do harm.

CONTENTS

CHAPTER I

CONTENTS

CHAPTER VII

CHAPTER VIII

CHAPTER IX

CHAPTER X

CHAPTER XI

CHAPTER XII

[x]

CHAPTER XXIX

CHAPTER XXX

CHAPTER XXXI

CHAPTER XXXII

CHAPTER XXXIII

CHAPTER XXXIV

CHAPTER XXXV

CONTENTS

CHAPTER XL

CHAPTER XLI

CHAPTER XLII

CHAPTER XLIII

CHAPTER XLIV

CONTENTS

CHAPTER XLV

CHAPTER XLVI

CHAPTER XLVII

DIPLOMATIC EPISODES IN MEXICO, BELGIUM, AND CHILE

CHAPTER I

Appointment preliminaries—McKinley—Mark Hanna—Department of State

THE political campaign of 1896—spectacular, intense, and sensational—culminated in the triumphant election of William McKinley. In compliance with the request of Mr. McKinley, I had borne an active part in this campaign, performing extensive work over a section of our country in which the Republican party was temporarily unpopular and discredited. We obtained few victories but we preserved our organizations intact and through them eventually redeemed the lost electorates.

I had known William McKinley for many years. Our friendship dated back to the Blaine campaign in which as a young spell-binder I accompanied him for some part of his Indiana campaign. Removal to the State of Washington had not weakened the ties which existed between us, and it was largely because of my respect and affection for McKinley that I took such active part in the St. Louis convention, where I was a delegate-at-large, and in the subsequent campaign.

Soon after the close of the campaign I visited Mr.

McKinley at Canton and during my stay he expressed his desire to have me attached to his administration in some capacity.

I remarked that I believed I could be more useful in the diplomatic service than elsewhere.

"Precisely what I had in mind," he replied, "but I haven't the matter fully worked out yet, and we will let it go over until after the inaugural."

This promise was not forgotten. I was asked to be present at the inaugural but during the event I was taken ill, and for some time after was an inmate of the Garfield Hospital in Washington. During my illness the President showed his usual kindness, making frequent inquiries and remembering me with gifts of flowers. As I approached complete convalescence he sent word that he had decided to appoint me as minister to Japan.

Some days after this, being almost restored to health, I visited my friend, Senator Mark Hanna, to discuss some affairs which he had placed in my hands. At the close of the interview Senator Hanna said: "I hope you are going to take office under this administration and, if so, I should like to be of service." I replied that I supposed he already knew of the President's intention to appoint me to the Japanese mission. The Senator seemed very much surprised at this and said: "I am afraid you will be disappointed, as I am sure the President has forgotten that he is committed in the matter of the Japanese mission and cannot, without violating obligations of a sacred character, appoint you to the place." This was rather embarrassing and I limited myself to the statement that I believed the President was fully aware of his obligations and that, as the offer to me was entirely spontaneous, I must leave the matter in his hands. Almost immediately after this interview, not desiring to be drawn into an undignified contest, I left Washington, placing my affairs in the hands of my friend Senator Cushman K. Davis of Minnesota.

Some days passed before a letter came from Senator Davis saying that he had just had an interview with the President, who confessed to being in an awkward position; that in the early stages of the campaign his political managers had promised the mission to Japan to Judge Buck of Georgia; that he felt chagrined that such a situation should have developed, realizing that he was bound by his own spontaneous expressions to appoint me but that he left the matter in my hands.

There was only one conceivable answer to be made to such a gracious and tactful message and I immediately sent a telegram saying that I wished the President to have a free hand in the matter and that whatever course he might take would be satisfactory to me. This telegram pleased the President and, in his characteristic way, he said to Senator Davis, "Now, that was very sweet of him and I intend that he shall not suffer in consequence. He may have any diplomatic post which has not been filled with the exception of Russia, which is too expensive for him, and if you will give me a memorandum of three posts in the order in which they are desired, I will immediately designate him to one of the three and most likely to the first named on the list."

At that time the posts in Europe still vacant were Holland, Belgium, Switzerland, and I believe Sweden, Norway, and Denmark; in Asia, China; and in South America, Brazil, the Argentine, Chile, and Peru. After some discussion it was decided, for one consideration and another, to eliminate Europe and Asia entirely, and I then handed in a memorandum with the names of Brazil, Argentine, and Chile. This order of preference my brother, Senator John L. Wilson, who was opposed to my going to Brazil on account of the climate and to the Argentine on account of the expensiveness of the post, changed to Chile, the Argentine, and Brazil. When the memorandum was handed to the President he immediately said: "The appointment to Chile is definitely settled and the announcement may be given to the press at any time."

On the 8th of June, 1897, my name was sent to the Senate, together with that of Mr. Leishman, later our ambassador to Turkey, who was then appointed to Switzerland, and an hour after its reception by the Senate it was confirmed.

Upon receipt of the notice of my appointment I went to Washington to take my instructions and pay an official visit to the President. Mr. John Sherman, Secretary of State, was absent, and Mr. Day, who afterward became secretary, was acting secretary. After some talk with Mr. Day he passed me on for more explicit instructions to one of the assistant secretaries whom I found dispensing wisdom and advice to a crop of embryonic diplomats whom the political lottery had launched upon new careers. This assistant secretary apparently had the wisdom of forty appellate judges. I think he looked upon me—and perhaps upon all other new appointees— as an unpleasant evidence of the "spoils system," for he consumed the time, which should have been given to sensible and minute instructions concerning the scope and nature of my duties, in pessimistic prophecies concerning my diplomatic future, coupled with extravagant eulogiums of my predecessor.

After finishing my duties at the State Department I went to the White House to pay my respects to the President.

It was always a real pleasure to come into the presence of McKinley; to feel the friendly grasp of his sympathetic hand; to see the kindly light in his great expressive eyes, and to rest under the charm of his courtly manners and magnetic personality. There were many points of resemblance between McKinley and Harding, who followed him in office nearly a quarter of a century later. There was the same personal magnetism, the same genial disposition, and a striking resemblance in personal demeanour and charm of manner. The two men possessed identic high ideals and equally high conception of the dignity of the presidential office. McKinley adhered to his ideals more closely than Harding. Harding sometimes appointed unfit men to office, perhaps blinded to their demerits by his affection for them; McKinley never knowingly put an unfit man into public office. Intimate contact with the inner workings of public affairs brought Harding at the close of his career in the White House to about the same level reached by McKinley on the day of his inaugural.

On this particular day events had evidently been moving to his satisfaction for his face beamed with happiness and his manner was genial. I started to go through the formalities supposed to be observed on occasions of this kind, but he quickly interrupted me, saying, "My dear boy, leave that out. It is a pleasure to appoint you and I am sure that you will render good account of your-

[5]

self and make it possible and proper for me to send you higher. . . . Take this rose," and he removed the one he wore in his buttonhole, "and go to your work in happiness and peace."

What could have been more gracious, more kindly, and how little it all cost! Yet the memory of it and of the kind heart that inspired the utterance to me, as it did to hundreds of others, still lingers.

Immediately after this I joined my family at New York, where we made our preparations for the long voyage as diligently as the pressure of social affairs would permit.

CHAPTER II.

WE SAILED out of New York in a blinding and gloomy mist, which had settled down upon all the earth like a mantle of desolation, the great skyscrapers looming like spectral shadows, and toward the sea, nothing but impenetrable darkness and gloom.

For days we struggled along, tossed by the waves, blown by the winds, and drenched by the pelting rains, without a ray of sunshine or a vestige of sea life. The first harbinger of better weather and kindlier elements came as we stood far off from Hatteras. Here the sun broke through the clouds and far away to the shore our eyes rested upon the historic spot which in years past was called the "sailors' graveyard"—a terror to navigators of all climes. Advancing civilization and the necessities of modern commerce have robbed Hatteras of its former terrors and now ships of the most insignificant size as well as the great ocean greyhounds ride safely and defiantly close to its grizzly rocks. Yet the seas thereabout are storied seas, and what a tale they could unfold from their vast depths! Beneath these waters lies the Spanish *conquistador* and the gold which lured him on to destruction. Here lie the buccaneer who preyed all the way from Nova Scotia to La Guayra, the hardy tar from New England, and adventurous spirits of all nations.

[7]

Leaving Hatteras we were again enveloped in clouds and darkness, riding on mountainous waves for two days, when upon our right we sighted Watling's Island. Watling's Island! What a travesty of history! Who would recognize in this tiny speck of land now dressed in the nomenclature of a respectable British citizen, the world-famed San Salvador, where Columbus first set foot upon American soil and, kneeling in the sands, invoked the blessings of the most High God upon his enterprise. Watling's Island—the dust of immortal Cæsar come to fill a bunghole—what irony of fate is here expressed! The vast empire which the great navigator added to the diadem of Spain has passed away little by little, until naught but the memory of better things remains.

Passing on in our voyage we rounded, under the light of a tropical moon, the southern coast of Cuba—Cuba for three hundred years the plaything, purse, and curse of Spain, but soon to come up out of her years of desolation into a purer atmosphere with her feet planted on the firm soil of constitutional liberty.

Then came the smell of the tropics borne upon sultry winds and the ship took on the air of a summer resort. White duck suits, iced drinks, and siestas on the shady side of the deck were the order of the day.

Seven days out from New York, and we approached shores covered with tropical verdure, and before the sun had reached its meridian we landed at Colon amid an indescribable babel of tongues frantically chattering English but in queer and weird accents. In those days the population was composed mostly of Jamaica Negroes whom an unkindly fate had brought to these shores, and one heard the camp-song notes and the shouts of glee so familiar in the cotton fields of the South. A glimpse of the wood-built city amid clustering palms, a bird's-eye view of the castle of De Lesseps, whose far-seeing vision was later to be realized through the genius and masterful statesmanship of Roosevelt, and then we sped away over the mountains toward the Pacific. A vision of palms, banana trees, and a vast accumulation of rusting machinery—the only remaining assets of the great financial bubble of the last century; a quick ascent and descent and our eyes rested upon the same gorgeous panorama, with the background of the calm Pacific, upon which Balboa gazed more than four hundred years ago—Panama, ancient, picturesque, and filthy.

Here Pizarro, the king of freebooters, set out for his conquests of the land of the Incas; here Morgan, the Welsh sea king, seized, plundered, and ravished. A city great in history, with vast but unfulfilled possibilities, it lay dormant awaiting the hand of the builder.

Panama is not merely the connecting link between North and South America; it is the gateway to the north, the east, and the south, and its commercial possibilities leap beyond the bounds of imagination. Through it may be unlocked the commercial treasure houses not only of the Far East but of all of Latin America. The commercial empire of Latin America is in itself no mean thing. Extending from the Rio Grande River to the furthermost point of Cape Horn and including in its sweep the West Indies and the islands of the Pacific, Latin America contains a total area of 10,350,000 square miles. This vast stretch of territory is traversed by great rivers, draining and enriching the encircling valleys, and crowned by chains of mountains feeding the plains and valleys with the life-giving moisture. Within this far-flung area are found all climates, unlimited agricultural and mineral resources, and arboreal supplies sufficient to meet the needs of the world. Chile produces nitrates, copper, and wine; the Argentine Republic, cattle, wheat, and sugar; Brazil, coffee, sugar, medicinal plants, and lumber; Peru, sugar, copper, and gold, Ecuador, lumber, copper, chocolate, and tropical fruits; Colombia, silver, gold, copper, and oil; Venezuela, coffee, sugar, oil, and lumber; Costa Rica, coffee and tropical fruits; Salvador, coffee, sugar, indigo, rice, and tropical fruits; Honduras, cattle, sugar, and rich woods; Nicaragua, cattle, sugar, coffee, and minerals; Mexico, coffee, sugar, tobacco, cattle, and the precious metals; the West Indies, tropical fruits, coffee, sugar, tobacco, and medicinal plants.

The significance of this varied production lies in the circumstance that it enters unappreciably or not at all into competition with our raw products. Great staples of the temperate zones will find here, save in the case of the Argentine Republic, a wide and unchallenged market. Over the same territory—for these are exclusively an agricultural people—the output of our factories will find easy routes and markets.

In all Latin America there is a population of not more than 100,000,000 of people, differing in origin but with nearly identic speech implanted by European pioneers; only in Chile and the Argentine Republic do composite types exist. Elsewhere the line is sharply drawn between the pure-blooded European races and those of mixed or indigenous origin, the latter preponderating numerically but yielding in influence, position, and wealth to the former.

Here is a sparse population scattered over a vast area which at the present time is carrying on a considerable trade with the world and with which our own commercial exchanges are growing by leaps and bounds; an area capable of sustaining ten times its present population and of multiplying its trade with the world, by the adoption and development of modern methods, more than twenty times; while at the same time almost every European country is suffering from the press of population, the menace of unemployment, and the difficult problem of trade routes and outlets. Under these circumstances it is easy to foresee Latin America populated by a billion souls, immigrants from Europe and their descendants, escaping from European conditions.

The plain inference of this simple statement is that our diplomacy and our commercial expansion should be steadily directed to the south and that all the aids and encouragement possible for the procurement of healthy and growing trade relations should be given by our government. Diplomatic clashes, unfriendly acts, or failures of courtesy should be carefully avoided not only by government representatives but by the agents of American commerce. The attitude of superiority and super-wisdom sometimes affected by crude diplomacy, but oftener by commercial agents, should have no place in our relations with Latin America.

A sympathetic understanding of racial psychology aids materially in the maintenance of amicable relations with all peoples. It were an error to measure the Chilean or the Argentine with traditions inherited from the Guadalquivir or the slopes of the Pyrenees, by the austere standards of Puritan morals, or a Mexican or a Brazilian by the inelastic codes of a twentieth-century philosophy. Of whatever origin he may be the Latin-American has in common his prejudices, his traditions, his habits of thought and living, and to these he stubbornly adheres in spite of the changing modes of life and thought created by inventive genius and the tremendous stride of the Anglo-Saxon energy. The Anglo-Saxon world moves with rapid steps; the Latin-American moves slowly into new fields; the Anglo-Saxon reaches out for everything that is new; the Latin-American instinctively clings tenaciously to the old; the one exhausts his energies in ceaseless mental and physical strife; the other maintains his primitive vigour by adhering to ancient faiths and hoary legends. We may not hope, we should not wish, to take from him the world in which he and his forefathers have lived. We should rather try to assimilate and join in a semblance of euphonious whole the apparent discordant elements.

The Latin-American states should be our best customers and our best friends, unafraid and unsuspicious of the tendency of our foreign policies, and our loyal allies in the event of international difficulties.

Leaving Panama behind us we sailed for four days through calm seas caressed by tropical breezes, gazing often over the taffrail into the depths of crystal-blue waters, swarming with varied types of the finny tribe. Then again came the land. Under the light of the Southern Cross we passed into one of the loveliest bays in the world and by it on into the Guayas River, a stream of majestic width and swift current whose banks were glorified with all the vivid hues of the wild and untrained tropics.

Then Guayaquil, a painted city upon painted waters,

low, picturesque, and dirty, abounding in noxious vapours and yielding abundant crops of mosquitoes.

Away again, down the rockbound coast of Peru to the Bay of Callao, abandoned and rat-infested; only the counterfeit presentment of great entrepôt of other days. A flight through sunny fields and we were in Lima, the "City of the Kings"—not a great or imposing city, and one hardly knows why it rejoices in this imposing title. Perhaps because a hundred of those royal plunderers called viceroys lived and robbed here. Much of Lima's glory had then departed. The hand of the hardy Chilean invader was laid upon her and she had sickened nigh into death.

An amusing incident occurred as we were about to land at Callao. It seems that the Peruvian government thought that the new American minister to Peru was on board the ship and they prepared, in consequence, to render the usual courtesies connected with the arrival of a diplomat. The government's tugboat came off to the steamer and a gorgeously arrayed official presented himself at my cabin, addressing me in Spanish, with profound bows and great deference. I returned the bows in kind and even amplified their impressiveness. But I was totally unable to understand the gentleman and therefore totally unable to respond. So, in the absence of explanations, I was taken on shore with my family in the government's tug and a private car to Lima was assigned to me. Before we arrived at Lima, however, the mistake had been discovered, resulting in a considerable cooling of official courtesy.

It perhaps should be explained that at the time of this incident relations between Chile and Peru were greatly strained. The war of the Pacific and the humiliating

[13]

defeat of Peru by Chile coloured and exaggerated all phases of social, official, and political life. It left lasting resentments in Peru, irreconcilable hatreds in Bolivia, and implanted in the minds of the Chilean people a profound suspicion of the motives of their trans-Andean neighbour, the Argentine republic. This war, through which Chile triumphed over Peru and her other South American enemies, is now almost forgotten by the world, though one of its aftermaths, the treaty of Ancon, which established a *modus vivendi* for disposition of the provinces of Tacna and Arica, recently troubled the waters of diplomacy at Washington. Whether Chile was the aggressor or was simply defending her own rights against a secret alliance of the three South American powers is a question for the historian. The important fact is that as a result of the war Chile took from Bolivia and Peru the provinces of Atacama and Tarapacá, thus cutting off Bolivia from all communication with the seas, and provisionally added to this rich copper and nitrate territory the adjoining Peruvian provinces of Tacna and Arica, their fate finally to be decided by a plebiscite of their residents.[1]

After leaving Lima, our next stop was at the first Chilean port Arica, where three hundred years ago the first expedition for the conquest of Chile was organized by Pedro Valdivia. Arica is in the territory supposed to be taken care of by the treaty of Ancon, but is yet in dispute between Peru and Chile. It is the oasis of the nitrate plains which, from thence, stretch south for 450 miles to the privince of Atacama. These nitrate fields constitute the chief riches of Chile and their development has made a

---

[1]This was written before the attempt to hold the plebiscite as provided for by the arbitration of President Coolidge.

great industrial centre. The crude nitrates, in strata some four or five feet thick and lying close to the surface, are found on lifeless, elevated plains, extending from the coast to a distance of twenty-five or thirty miles into the interior. In its raw state it is white and soft as cheese and, after being subjected to chemical processes to eliminate deleterious matter, it emerges in the form of infinitely small white crystals, and so is shipped to the market. The nitrates have been a great staple of commercial exchange with Europe for many years and recently with the United States, and at times the total annual shipments have approximated to a value of $100,000,000.

Notwithstanding their barren and bleak character, the nitrate plains have their romance. George Smith, an impecunious and wandering Scotsman, in tending his small garden in the village of Pica, discovered the value of the nitrates as a fertilizer. Smith died as poor as he was born, but his discovery passing into other hands created vast fortunes. North, a mechanic out of Leeds, England, an inventive genius, originated and applied the mechanical and chemical processes which gave to the discovery its practical value. North and others made vast fortunes and built great palaces, but the pioneers of the industry vanished into the unknown. Once within the memory of man, in 1892, the tradition of the sterility and barrenness of the nitrate plains was upset. Variations of the isothermic lines, coincidentally with the same phenomena in the Antarctic and Gulf Stream currents, transformed these sun-scorched sands into veritable gardens with green grass, flowers, and plants, interspersed with blooming poppies; the picture came and vanished not to reappear in this generation.

[15]

From Arica we continued our journey, spending a day each at the ports of Iquique, Antofagasta, Parral, and Coquimbo, and arrived early one morning in September at the harbour of Valparaiso, having been thirty-five days at sea and having travelled something like six thousand miles.

CHAPTER III

*Some observations on the physical aspects of Chile—Its history, political
structure, and contributions to literature and art—Racial elements*

THE republic of Chile extends from latitude 18 to
latitude 56 south, is 2,600 miles long, varies in
width from 110 to 40 miles, and contains a total
area equal to that of the German Empire before
the war. It possesses all climates from the tropical to the
arctic, so that while the Chilean of the north is toiling
under a burning sun, his brother in the south is struggling
to protect himself from the intemperate winds of the frigid
zone.

From the northern limits for more than 500 miles
stretches an unbroken desert over which no bird flies and
where neither water flows nor living things grow. This
vast desert, however, is stored with treasures of minerals,
like nitrates, silver, gold, and copper, which to-day constitute the chief source of the wealth and revenues of
Chile.

From the terminal point to the river Bio Bio, on the
south, a distance of 760 miles, extends the most densely
populated and cultivated part of the country, spanned
and intersected in every direction by modern railways
and waterways. Here three fourths of the population
lives in cities and great country estates; and here are produced the breadstuffs, the wine, the wool, the fruits of all
climes but the tropical, and almost every known product

depending upon a salubrious climate and a rich soil. Toward the east spreads the eternal vista of the snow-capped Andes and to the west lies the calm Pacific, its surface unbroken to the shores of Asia. Beautiful rivers here run with rapid steps to the sea through vineyards rich with purpling fruit and fields smiling with fragrant and luxurious plenty.

From the river Bio Bio south extend vast forests whose dim aisles have never been trodden by the foot of man, traversed by rivers of unknown sources bringing vast volumes of water to the sea. Then comes the Straits of Magellan—the land of ice—Tierra del Fuego—the land of fire—and finally Cape Horn, the most southern point of this hemisphere, beyond which lie the immense and silent wastes of the antarctic regions.

The country which is now called the republic of Chile was first made known to the world by that Almagró who Prescott tells us was the companion and aid of Cortes in the ruthless extermination of the Aztec empire; eventually his restless craving for adventure and wealth led him to Peru to become one of the chief actors with Pizarro in the overthrow of the ancient kingdom of the Incas. In due time the pursuit of gold led this Launcelot of Spanish romance to the south of Peru and thence, in company with some hundreds of kindred spirits, he finally reached Chile by a circuitous route across the cordillera and made a devastating march to the river Maule. From there he retired again into Peru without having established any foothold or colony to mark his inglorious campaign.

In 1540, Pedro Valdivia, an officer in the army of Pizarro, invaded Chile and, after subduing the whole north of the country, founded the capital Santiago and other important cities. Valdivia, an enterprising and ambitious spirit, extended his conquests for a very considerable distance into the Araucanian country but finally died an ignominious death at the hands of the brave native races.

After Valdivia followed two hundred and fifty years of Spanish governors and of constant and desolating war with the Araucanian Indians, the Spanish civilization, nevertheless, making steady progress, and eventually becoming dominant from the northern limits to the river Bio Bio.

Beyond the river Bio Bio the Spaniards never established empire though they expended vast treasures and thousands of lives in the effort. The brave race which in these gloomy forests battled so valiantly for their liberties really sounded the first knell of Spanish dominion in the new world.

With the overthrow of the Bourbon dynasty in Spain came the revolution of its Latin-American colonies; and after a few years of struggle under the leadership of the Argentinian, San Martin, and of the Chilean O'Higgins, the republic of Chile finally emerged to take its place among the nations of the world, receiving its first recognition as an independent power from the government of the United States.

*   *   *

For many years the Spaniards who came into Chile were soldiers from Aragon, generally an inferior class of people, having among them many outlaws and criminals. After nearly two hundred years there resulted from a mixture of races the lower classes commonly called the Chilean *roto* and the Chilean *huaso* or yeomen of a somewhat higher social standing than the *roto:* to these classes belong two thirds of the Chilean nation.

The mixed-blood or lower-class Chilean leads a patriarchal life upon the hills and plains, yielding unquestioning obedience and devotion to the *patron* or master, which is usually repaid with solicitude for his welfare and a paternal interest in his affairs. He rides like a centaur, is industrious in the field, ingenious and inventive, happy in disposition, possessed of a genial humour, and ready wit and repartee almost Celtic.

The women of this class have high-strung and poetic natures which find expression in the lavish use of flowers and the trilling of old songs and forgotten airs; upon festal days the poorest peasant woman carries flowers upon her bosom and songs upon her lips. Types of extraordinary beauty and grace are not infrequently found among them, and their affections are strong and enduring.

The ruling class is of pure Spanish blood and origin. Early in the eighteenth century the mixed Chilean population began to be reinforced by a strong tide of immigration out of Catalonia and the Basque provinces, whence, from time immemorial, has come the most virile and progressive blood in Spain. Possibly a million Chileans are of this blood; they hold the wealth of the country, and its lands; they make its laws, elect its magistrates, command its armies and fleets, and create its literature and art.

The higher-class Chilean is a modern person with just enough of the flavour coming down from Castilian days to enrich and soften the severe outlines of modern times. Highly educated, courteous, hospitable, generous, and romantic, if he were dressed in the habiliments of yore one might easily imagine the old cavalier come to life—the type that Velasquez and Rubens have handed down on priceless canvas. But disenchantment is very easy, and with a change of scene we find the Chilean a modern man of the world, more like the American than any other people in this hemisphere; hard and practical in business affairs, sure in reading character, clever in diplomacy, and abounding in oratory. He possesses all of the patriotism of the Chilean of the lower class; that egotistical patriotism which is no mean element in the making of a nation.

The Chilean constitution is modelled rather upon the British than the American plan.

The government is popular and representative—every registered Chilean twenty-one years of age, who can read and write, holding the right of suffrage—with centralized powers lodged in the hands of Congress, the Executive, and the Supreme Court.

The President is elected for a term of five years, and possesses the power of appointment, by and with the consent of the Senate, of all public officials, save municipal, but is not commander of the army and navy as is the President of the United States. While by the theory of the constitution he is clothed with very limited powers, the possession of the right to make all appointments renders the position of a bold and discreet executive one of supreme importance and authority. As the parliamentary system prevails, he does not govern directly but through ministers who retain office so long only as they are able to count upon the support of a majority of Congress.

Chile has been very fortunate in her choice of presi-

[21]

dents. Nearly all of them have been men of sincere patriotism and some have displayed great abilities and foreseeing statesmanship. Bulnes, Montt, Santa Maria, Pinto, and Balmaceda were all men of strong characters and pronounced gifts for governing, and their administrations achieved lasting benefits for the country. The power of the Chilean executive has always been the surest safeguard of the rights of the people, and the moving force in progress.

The English parliamentary system has not been a success in Chile. It has resulted in too-frequent changes in administration, in obstruction, and in a vast waste of time. The demand for a system more rational and better adapted is almost general.

It is perhaps the remoteness of Chile from the great world centres which imparts to domestic politics such absorbing interest. Be that as it may, every educated Chilean is well instructed in public affairs and fluent and eloquent in their discussion. The Chilean legislator, therefore, begins his career well equipped for his duties, and able at once to participate in debate. The discussions in Congress are orderly, dignified and, as far as the rules of an antiquated system will permit, expeditious. Not infrequently the debates abound in eloquence, pungent wit, and sharp logic.

* * *

There are more than 5,028 miles of railway in Chile, of which 2,000 were built by, and belong to, the government. The government subsidizes and fosters a line of steamships, the best on the Pacific coast, which navigates from Valparaiso to San Francisco; has built thousands of miles of public highways; spent millions for educational and benevolent institutions; constructed floating docks and an elaborate system of coast defense; organized and maintained what I believe to be the strongest land and sea fighting force in South America; has had a war with Peru and Bolivia, and a savage domestic revolution, and yet her foreign and internal debt to-day is barely $250,000,000, upon which she has never defaulted a day in the payment of interest or principal. She exports $162,000,000 worth of products of all kinds, and her imports reach $139,000,000, thus maintaining that unvarying balance of trade which our American economists think so essential to a nation's welfare. The government receipts from exports and imports are $74,000,000 per annum,[1] the larger part of which comes from export duties on nitrate; and the expenditures rarely create a deficit.

No branch of the government of Chile is maintained upon a higher plane, or has yielded better results, than its system of national defense. Nearly forty years ago the government inaugurated the plan of employing German officers and placing them at the head of its military schools and important commands. This policy was adhered to with the result that the army, when put to the test, has always acquitted itself in a highly creditable way. The system implanted by the Germans still exercises a preponderating influence in military circles, making the Chilean army to-day, in the opinion of some high authorities, by far the most excellent in *esprit de corps* and thoroughness in South America, and one of the best relatively in the world.

The Chilean *roto* makes one of the finest soldiers in the

---

[1] These were the statistics of 1923.

[23]

world, just such a one as would have marched with Napoleon to Egypt or Moscow—quick to take on the bearing and habits of a soldier, docile to his superiors, having great powers of endurance and a reckless and headlong bravery. He is intensely patriotic, and loves the panoply and glory of war, the stirring march and the midnight bivouac.

Chile's chief defense, however, and one to maintain which she hesitates at no sacrifice, is her navy.

There is nothing so closely connected with the pride of the Chilean people and the policy of the government as the maintenance of this navy at the highest standard compatible with national resources. When one considers the vast length of the country and the vital importance of the control of the Straits of Magellan, the reason for this is apparent. Undoubtedly, if Chilean preëminence and prestige in South America are to be maintained at the present point, it must be through the efficiency, thoroughness, and preponderance of her naval establishment. This, I believe, to be fully comprehended by her statesmen, and it may be readily understood that their efforts will be constantly directed to the increase of the sea power and coast defenses of the country.

Even in the early days of the republic, during the war of independence, the Chileans were distinguished among all the nations of South America as sailors and lovers of the sea. Lord Cochran, who commanded the Chilean naval forces during the revolutionary struggle, said that the world produced no better seaman or braver man than the Chilean sailor.

The first Chilean navy was the creation of Cochran and O'Higgins, the first president of Chile. For years Chilean ships were officered by Englishmen, and the system which they implanted, though accommodating itself to changing conditions, has been constantly maintained.

*   *   *

Considering Chile as a new country, as she essentially is in all that concerns growth and development, her contributions to literature and art have been prolific and of high order.

Although the colonial period, owing to severe governmental restrictions, was comparatively barren of contributions to literature, there were two brilliant exceptions: "The Coming of the Messiah," by Manuel Lacunza, a work rich in religious fervour and imagination, which has passed into all languages as one of the ornaments of a purely Roman Catholic literature, and the geographical and natural history works of the great savant Juan Ignacio Molina, whose statue one sees to-day in the streets of Bologna, Italy.

But it was not until the democratic movement had fully taken hold of the country that the intellectual movement began—a movement which has constantly gathered impetus, until to-day Chilean literature makes brilliant pages in history, science, philosophy, and verse.

At the head of a galaxy of writers stands Andrés Bello, perhaps the most eminent authority on jurisprudence in Latin America and widely read throughout the world. Not only eminent in jurisprudence, the later years of his life were devoted to the compilation of higher textbooks, which for fifty years have remained the standards in the universities and colleges of Chile.   He is the author of the Chilean Civil Code as it exists to-day, and his works on

[25]

Roman and international law constitute the best contributions from Latin America.

Another of the founders of Chilean literature is Miguel Luis Amunátegui—a distinguished scholar and author of many valuable works on modern and American history. Upon all historical questions relating to Latin America, he is perhaps to-day the highest authority. We Americans owe him much for his unexcelled translations of the works of Prescott and Irving, the rich beauty of these graceful writers passing unsullied through his hands into sonorous Spanish.

The historical and poetical works of Benjamin Vicuna MacKenna, widely read and popular, the historical works of Diego Barros Arana—volumes representing enormous research and authoritative upon Latin-American biological questions—the fiction of Alberto Blest Gana—admirable pictures of Chilean life and customs—the classic and graceful verses of the lyric poet Eduardo de la Barra, and the translations and patriotic songs of the lamented Carlos Morla Vicuna, are all worthy of serious reading and doubtless one day will find their way into the English language.

There is such a thing as Chilean art, too.

Visitors to the Pan-American Exposition were doubtless surprised to find in the Chilean pavilion the evidences of a meritorious school of art, especially in painting and design. Seventy years ago there was no such thing as Chilean art; but in 1860, Kirchbach, a German painter of great talent, founded the modern Chilean art cult, the influences of which have been most potent. At the present time, the number of Chilean painters of eminence is considerable, and there are many works worthy of the highest praise. "Independence" by Campo, the "Death of Christopher Columbus," "Labor," and "Philip II" by Lira; the "Death of Pedro Valdivia," the "Sinking of the *Esmeralda,*" and "Balmaceda's Reply" by Guzmán; the "Sampson and Delilah" by San Martin; and the many creditable productions of Molina, Lynch, and Swinburne are doing much toward the formation of a distinct Chilean school and the attainment of a national culture of the beautiful.

CHAPTER IV

Arrival at Santiago—Personnel of the legation—Michaels—Official presentation and incidents

AFTER a brief stay at Valparaiso we left by an evening train for the capital, Santiago, and on our arrival there went directly to the legation. We accepted this, our future home, with some doubts but in a spirit of philosophy, deeming it better to endure a magnitude of evil with a modicum of comfort and dignity. The house was not prepossessing in any way and was far and away from being a proper residence for the diplomatic representative of the United States. I took over the lease and purchased the furniture of my predecessor, and thus established our domestic and official environment for the next four years.

The official staff of the legation consisted of a minister and a secretary. There was also a clerk who was paid partly from the legation contingent fund and partly by the minister. The secretary, Mr. D———, a Harvard graduate, had many agreeable qualities, but as he was independently rich he did not take his duties too seriously. He had been appointed to the service at the request of my predecessor who had been his tutor at Harvard, and his duties prior to my arrival had consisted mostly in the superintendence of his chief's bachelor dinners, the arrangement of little evening parties, and the fabrication of various alluring but potent cocktails, supposedly of American origin, which contributed in some measure to the popularity of the legation but not especially to its prestige.

Michaels, the clerk, was one of the odd characters that occasionally emerge out of bohemian life to take some part in the serious affairs of the world. He was altogether grotesque in history, character, and appearance. Running his thread of existence back to its source it was found that he was a native of Cologne, Germany, of very respectable parentage, and had been educated thoroughly in languages. Thence in early manhood he passed into England where he lived for some years, while employed on a London newspaper. His next move was to New York, where he became a reporter on the New York *World* and took out and completed American citizenship papers. Tiring of New York and moved by the migratory spirit, he in some way reached Peru, where he abandoned his benedictine state and joined in matrimony with a Peruvian lady. Eventually he reached Chile and Santiago with this Peruvian spouse and a brood of children of uncertain nationality and confused patriotism. There in some way he became identified with the American legation and his connection survived through at least twelve years of fitful and erratic performance of duty and regular essays in the speculative world which invariably ended in financial embarrassment and probably in an acute stringency of the domestic budget.

Michaels was somewhere between six and seven feet in height, with enormous hands and feet, and a generally awkward movement of the body. He was invariably dressed in a frock coat, crowned by a rusty stove-pipe hat which had the appearance of having left the hands of its maker in the era of Louis Napoleon and of having afterward run the gauntlet of a Donnybrook fair. On feast days or special occasions these habiliments were supplemented by gloves and cane so that when the band played and the *vivas* mounted, our clerk presented an altogether imposing and distinguished appearance. Let it not be inferred, however, that Michaels was not a useful and loyal clerk; he was all of that and sometimes more. He took my dictation, transcribed the records, coded and decoded the cablegrams, translated from Spanish into English and vice versa, taught the entire family Spanish, advised Mrs. Wilson in her marketing and shopping, and by way of recreation instructed various Chilean families in the English language and played the organ at two churches.

This would betoken an industrious life; but Michaels was not always faithful to his obligations. His lapses were frequent, unexpected, and sometimes annoying, but he weathered the storm invariably, beaming with good nature and a solicitude which disarmed severe criticism. His American patriotism was undiluted and exuberant. Upon one occasion the priest of the church, where Michaels presided at the organ, in the course of his remarks broke out into a furious denunciation of the government of the United States for its supposed attitude toward the Vatican. The priest's violent outburst made a very marked impression on the audience but as it was dispersing, Michaels, who was seated at the organ, lifted up to the rafters the soul-stirring strains of the "Star-Spangled Banner." My affection for Michaels increased with years and I cultivated broad toleration for his shortcomings and an enormous appreciation of his virtues.

In the latter days of our association he was swept momentarily out of his accustomed environment and engaged in speculative adventures somewhere in southern Chile.

For weeks and months we knew no Michaels and then he finally reappeared shabbier, more cheerful and insinuating than ever, ready for drudgery, dancing, or drams. He was reinstated in his accustomed duties with all ceremony and when I left Santiago for the last time he was still vacillating between devotion to duty and the call of the wild.

Immediately after my arrival I dispatched the usual note to the Minister of Foreign Affairs, asking for an audience with the President to present my letters of credence. On the day designated the government's gala coach, with liveried footmen and six military outriders, was dispatched to the legation, and accompanied by the secretary (referred to as "official suite") I was conducted to the Moneda (Government Palace) where, after passing through a file of soldiers, I was met by the Minister of Foreign Affairs, Señor Silva Cruz, and immediately ushered into the presence of the first magistrate of the republic, Don Federico Errazuriz. Without further ado I read my address and presented my credentials with the letter of recall of my predecessor. The President read a reply, expressing appreciation of the cordial sentiments and the reciprocal good wishes of the government of Chile.

After these formalities were concluded the President, inviting me to take a seat at his side, made a very commendable endeavour to engage me in light conversation, an effort which was not crowned with perfect success, owing to my limited acquaintance with the Spanish language and his lack of familiarity with the hardy Anglo-Saxon tongue. I judged him, however, to be saying a number of agreeable things to which from time to time with safe accuracy, if with questionable expansiveness, I replied: "Si, Señor," and occasionally, when I thought some de-

[31]

parture was needed, by "mucho" or "poco á poco," linguistic flights which exhausted my vocabulary but left me otherwise undisturbed and confident. Parenthetically it may be said that my shortcomings in the Spanish language were soon repaired and that I eventually obtained considerable fluency in its use.

The President, Don Federico Errazuriz, was a little man with sharp olive-tinted features, sparkling with native intelligence, and was possessed of that humour and spontaneous wit which is so characteristic of the Latin-American of Basque origin. He made an active, intelligent executive, and maintained the government during his administration upon the high plane of dignity in the performance of its international and national obligations which has made Chile from its foundation preëminent among the republics of South America. I had pleasantly intimate relations with him during his term of office and when I left for a visit home, near the end of his term, he sent for me, being then affected by an incurable disease, and talked to me in the most intimate and affectionate manner; when I said farewell I found he was moved to tears. His death, after complete mental collapse, followed soon after my departure, and the remainder of his term was filled by the vicepresident, Señor Zanartu, who retained the office until the election of Jerman Riesco.

Jerman Riesco, the succeeding President, was a man of exceptionally high character and dignified deportment. He was not brilliant but he did prove to be a very wise and conservative executive, keenly alive to his responsibilities to all classes and conditions of people. In most ways his administration was a success though his personal following was small and his political connections negligible.

CHAPTER V

The diplomatic corps at Santiago—Some odd personalities

OUR first official duties at Santiago were social ones: visits to the members of the cabinet, the wife of the President, all the diplomatic corps, and some distinguished Chilenos to whom I had letters of introduction. With some few exceptions the diplomatic corps was not interesting or exciting, except as their eccentricities contributed to the gaiety of the hour.

The dean of the corps, Señor José Arrieta, the minister of Uruguay, was a wealthy old gentleman who had been discharging his functions for more than eighteen years. He lived in a most gorgeous palace and gave entertainments which for brilliancy and spectacular effects I have never seen equalled. One went away from them with the feeling of having participated in a court levee of Ferdinand and Isabella. He was a kindly intentioned old person and if he is still living I hope he is passing his declining days in peace and happiness.

The British minister at this time was Sir John Kennedy, who had been stationed in Chile for nine years and whose anxiety for a transfer to another post was equalled only by his government's lack of enthusiasm in according it. He was an eccentric person and rather made a point of utilizing his eccentricities for the purpose of escaping functions and duties not agreeable to him. One of his peculiarities **was** to criticize the table and the food of whatever host and hostess happened to be entertaining him. He would handle everything that came upon the table with an eye of suspicion and sometimes he would say in English *soto voce*, "Looks damn bad, tastes damn bad." These little peculiarities, it may be imagined, did not contribute to his popularity, though his charming wife, Lady Kennedy, saved his position from absolute wreckage. After years of service in Chile he was transferred, greatly to his satisfaction, to Roumania. His son, A. L. Kennedy, was to be known to fame in later years as the author of the brilliant and instructive work, "Old Diplomacy and New."

Another peculiar colleague was the Brazilian minister, who, in his youth, in an adventurous spirit, drank a bottle of ink in a wager with some other gay bloods and in consequence went about the world the balance of his life with a stomach which refused to perform its proper digestive functions. He went through a course dinner with the air of a stoic, his food and drink consisting of water only.

One of the odd diplomatic characters was Mr. R ————, representative of one of the Central European governments, who, after years of faithful service as archivist in the foreign office of his country, had been given this post for the purpose of enabling him to accumulate a sufficient fortune to ease the declining years of his life and those of his spouse. These two made a very systematic business of the economies, and their entertainments were ample evidence of thought and prudence. The few dinners they gave during the year were all given in the same week and it was rumoured that the viands that were put before the later guests had passed through various stages of banqueting before reaching the final eclipse, and that after the season of carnival had finished, the good couple fared sumptuously the coming week upon the remnants of their expensive dissipation. This poor man finally died at his post just as he was preparing to go home to enjoy the fruits of his spartan official life. His widow, however, though profoundly affected by his death, still inflexibly maintained her long-practised system of economy and, when the government offered the customary public funeral, she intimated that she preferred to have the cash and dispense with it. In his last testament the minister bequeathed his head to some scientific society and it was supposed that his remains would be shipped home, but Madame, with an exemplary spirit of fidelity to his specific instructions, caused the head to be severed from the body and dispatched it to its destination, where no doubt it enriches the collection of the society to which it was bequeathed, while the body rests in Chilean soil.

The German government was represented by the Count C ——— R ———, a man of distinguished lineage and connections, but who, the story ran, had been banished to this remote part of the world by the Emperor in punishment for various escapades and delinquencies repugnant to the strict conventions of the courts of western Europe. When I first knew this unhappy individual, his extremely eccentric manner, spasmodic contortions, and inconsequent remarks aroused in me the suspicion that he was a child of the "delirium tremens" and something of a bore; this opinion was confirmed by future experiences. For some time the volcano did not break out, but in the second year of his stay the promenaders and habitués at the afternoon concerts on the Plaza de Armas were frequently edified by the spectacle of the representative of the German Empire marching at the head of the band and performing,

[35]

with various antics, the self-conferred office of drum-major. These performances usually culminated in fright-ful debauches, with all their attendant horrors. He was a most pitiful spectacle and, although the thing was in every way disgraceful, the man himself was perfectly harmless and inoffensive and his death, after one of these prolonged affairs, was a shock to all. He was buried with great pomp and, in representation of the diplomatic corps, I delivered his funeral address, a copy of which was after-ward requested by Emperor William, who took the deep-est interest in the affairs of this, his far-away and erring relative.

I served with two other German colleagues in Chile, Mr. Von Steubel and Mr. Von Reichenau, both highly capable and industrious men. Von Steubel was called home soon after his arrival to take charge of the German Colonies Office and his subsequent history there was stormy and strenuous, ending in his retirement from public life. His successor, Von Reichenau, was quite up to the standards of German diplomacy. He was young, fluent, well educated, speaking with facility French, English, and Spanish, and he had, moreover, that very essential attribute of diplo-macy in these days, an American wife. We were very intimate with the Von Reichenau family and still carry with us the most agreeable impressions of them. Von Reichenau went later to Brazil and Roumania but I have lost sight of him in these days.

The Italian minister, during the greater part of the time I was in Chile, was the Count Antonio Grippi, a man of charming manners and interesting personality. His death, about 1900, caused wide-spread sorrow in Santiago, where he was much beloved not only by the large Italian colony but throughout Chilean society. Upon the occasion of his funeral I was designated to represent the diplomatic corps in pronouncing the funeral discourse.

Grippi was succeeded by Count Cucchi Boassa, who principally distinguished himself during his brief stay by protesting in the most positive and public way against the offensive remarks made by the officiating priest against the government of Italy on the occasion of the funeral ceremonies in honour of Pope Leo XIII. The offensive remarks were uttered in the presence of the entire diplomatic corps and were directed not only at the Italian government but at the German, French, and English. Boassa rose from his place in the middle of the sermon and marched in full uniform out of the church. He would have been followed by the German, French, and British ministers but unfortunately their knowledge of Spanish was not sufficiently accurate to enable them to judge the measure of the offence which had been committed. After the service there were some animated meetings which resulted in the Chilean government addressing notes of apology to the representatives of all of the offended governments.

My Spanish colleague, during the greater part of my stay in Chile, was L——— G———, a gentleman of the old Spanish school, of bland and engaging manners but doubtful morals. His diplomatic career was terminated abruptly by his government on a charge of misappropriation of trust funds, and he was sent home to Spain in irons to be tried on these charges. He was eventually found guilty but was pardoned on account of his advanced years. Notwithstanding his agreeable exterior and pleasant qualities, he had very vague ideas of steady morality and honesty.

After his departure the Spanish government sent over Don José de Llaberia, a man of excellent character but weak constitution, who was obliged to devote most of his energies to keeping alive. I believe he was afterward transferred to Morocco and was in charge of the mission there during the difficulties between Germany and France.

CHAPTER VI

Santiago and its beauties—The Alameda—The hill of Santa Lucia—Social aspects and life—Adherence to old customs—Chilean political affairs.

THE city of Santiago, where we were to live for eight pleasant years, lies between high ranges of the Cordillera and the coast range. The lower inclines of the Cordillera reach almost to the limits of the city and one may enjoy a full view of snow-capped peaks while experiencing all the rigours of summer heat.

From the central railway station the magnificent Alameda extends through the city to the foot of the hill of Santa Lucia. The Alameda is one of the most impressive avenues in the world; through its centre for the entire distance, with driveways on each side, runs the great promenade lined with beautiful trees and resting places. Alongside the driveways are the handsome residences of wealthy and distinguished Chileans, and on Sundays and feast days the avenue is crowded with people of all degrees.

The hill of Santa Lucia is a very curious rocky elevation which some freak of nature has thrown up within the limits of the city; originally it was sheer and precipitous, but solid winding roads have been gashed into its rocky sides and artificial gardens have been implanted in trailing beauty on each side of the steeply winding ascent. From the summit of this hanging garden of nature one obtains a wide and charming view of the valley of Santiago. On the largest projecting arm of the hill there is a public theatre, where plays and operas are regularly produced in the summer season, and a restaurant, well managed and greatly frequented. Scattered over the hill are many beautiful monuments and statues of Chileans distinguished in religion, politics, and art. Here one might revert to an historical incident of interest. In the days of Spanish control, religious intolerance had sway in Chile; not only was the practice of Protestant religion prohibited by law, but communicants of any Protestant church, if they happened to die in the country, were denied official sepulture. In consequence all Protestant burials were made in secret places and unmarked except as private records of them were kept. After the revolution, when complete freedom of religious worship was proclaimed by O'Higgins, the first President of Chile, who though a Catholic was devoid of religious prejudice, he gathered together, as far as he could from obtainable records, the bones of all of these neglected dead and placed them under one monument alongside the public driveway on the slopes of Santa Lucia and erected a monument inscribed with these words: *A los hombres expulsados de la tierra y del cielo.* After O'Higgins, Protestants were never again denied freedom of worship in Chile. The eighteenth century was a century of intolerance—an intolerance not by any means confined to Roman Catholic countries.

Scattered throughout the city there are numerous parks, a very creditable number of public buildings, and military schools. The Cousino Park is extensive and beautiful; the botanical and agricultural gardens on the west side of the city are greatly celebrated. In the centre of the city there is the Plaza de Armas where the splendid military band of Santiago plays during pleasant weather. The Plaza was in some ways the centre of Chilean life and society and on certain evenings of the week everybody was found there promenading to the strains of the band. There courtships were begun, marriages arranged, and political questions discussed.

The homes of Santiago are above the average found in cities of similar size and many of them are really imposing and lofty. The prevailing architecture is the old Spanish patio style of house which the Spanish inherited from the Moors and which the Moors got from the ancient sons of the desert. Every house of any importance has its interior garden, luxuriant and colourful. From the environs of Santiago the great country estates commence and these extend without break to Coquimbo on the north and to the river Bio Bio on the south. The river Maipu takes its winding course through the city, sometimes flooded with water and at other times absolutely dry.

Santiago society in all its aspects is quite comparable with that of any other city; it is hospitable, open-handed, generous, and kind, and to strangers who are sympathetic and appreciative there is an unending flow of attention and entertainment.

In the first days of our residence we were received with courtesy, it is true, but with that caution which marks the initial stages of social recognition in every well-ordered society. But as our circle of acquaintance widened and as we became better known, and perhaps better understood, the conventional restraint disappeared and a really warm-hearted and friendly attitude took its place.

The Chileans of the upper class travel extensively and possess that high measure of culture which usually accompanies family distinction and wealth. Most of the younger generation are educated either in France, Spain, or the United States, and it is not an uncommon thing to find them speaking French and English fluently. Of course the old Spanish conventions still control the relations between sexes. Young women are not permitted to go about unchaperoned, and they receive company only in the presence of some member of the family. Dinners on an extensive scale are the rule rather than the exception; it is a frequent occurrence for a Chilean host to sit down to dinner two or three times a week with from fifteen to twenty guests who are entertained lavishly and with complete absence of formality.

Among the socially prominent families in our time were the Conchas, the Ossas, the Errazurizes, the Astaburragas, the Undurragas, the Irarrazavals, the Aldunates, the Tocoknals, the McClures, the Edwardses, the Montts.

The Chileans entertain on their extensive estates as liberally as in the city. Visits to the country places were void of formality and we usually enjoyed them. At some of the larger haciendas it was not unusual for as many as fifty guests to sit down to a dinner; after dinner there was generally entertainment at cards and dancing. During the day there was complete freedom for every one; guests usually occupied themselves in riding about the estate, in hunting, or fishing.

Balls, receptions, weddings, and the races formed agreeable diversions, and the annual exodus to Vina del Mar, the Chilean summer resort, furnished an agreeable relaxation from the social activities of the winter. In this season the Chilean government, headed by the President, moves in a body to Valparaiso, with the records of the foreign office, making it convenient for members of the diplomatic corps to establish residence and chancellery there.

While we were in Chile we spent three summers at Vina del Mar, which lies in the environs of Valparaiso. There was an especially nice and numerous British colony which contributed generously to the social activities, and there was always golf, tennis, and riding; our children throve in the bracing atmosphere and outdoor life and we all grew to be very much attached to the pleasant informal life.

There were a number of excellent theatres in Santiago, but the greatest attraction was the magnificent opera house where during the winter season Chilean society was regaled with grand opera of the best kind. Usually these operatic companies were sent directly from Milan and included the promising young stars just rising on the horizon and eager to make their *ballon d' asai;* here I first heard Tetrazzini and Scotti, both then unknown to fame. The opera on gala nights presented a most brilliant appearance with elaborate toilets and profuse display of jewellery.

The home life of the Chileans adheres closely to old Spanish customs and traditions. Often three generations are found living under the same roof in apparent, if not real, peace; all rendering the profoundest respect and deference to the head of the family and all manifesting in their intercourse with one another real affection and demonstrative attachment. The women of Chile, especially after marriage, seem to become entirely absorbed by their home life and are extremely domestic; the rearing of

[43]

children, household affairs, and other domestic duties seem to absorb a large part of their daily existence. Scandals, lapses from the strict path of virtue are extremely rare; devotion to home, husband, and family are the first considerations; usually they have fine figures, beautiful eyes, hair, and complexion, and bear themselves with an air of distinction and grace; they are vivacious, witty, and alluring, but withal possess an abundance of dignity and reserve.

Chilean political affairs absorbed my attention for the first few months. In government the parliamentary system prevailed but it did not work smoothly. What were termed ministerial crises occurred with great frequency. It happened in this way that changes in the personnel of the cabinet were so frequent as to demand great mental activity in remembering who was his excellency and who was his ex-excellency. One of the advantages derived from these rapid changes was that in our residence of eight years we became more or less acquainted with every public man in Chile.

At first I took these crises seriously and dispatched the information hurriedly to the Washington government, but after some experience I decided that the slower medium of the mails would serve. One of my Chilean friends credited me with having said that I had ascertained that these crises simply meant another favourite indoor sport.

When we arrived in Chile, Federico Errazuriz, the President, had about him a very brilliant cabinet drawn from the ranks of the conservative party. At the conclusion of his term of office, however, the government had ceased to be wholly conservative and nearly all shades of political opinion were represented in the cabinet.

[44]

The men most prominent in public life at that time were Carlos Aldunate, Pedro Montt, Antonio Valdes Cuevas, Ismiel Tocornal, Jerman Riesco, Augustine Edwards, Francisco Huidibro, Rafael Errazuriz. These were all men of marked ability and high character, filling posts of great distinction and usefulness. There were many others, but these names are fairly representative.

The government of Chile during my time was generally conservative; but the tendencies were constantly in the direction of liberalism and some of the ablest men belonged to the radical party, which many years after I left achieved political triumph in the election of Arturo Alessandri. There was not a great deal of difference between the liberal and conservative parties; both were supporters of the Chilean constitution and of the land-holding class. The radical party, however, advocated many things which to the Chilean mind appeared to be revolutionary. Radical victories may occur from time to time but the preponderating sentiment of the country is conservative and inclines reluctantly to rapid or extreme changes.

CHAPTER VII

The Spanish language—Some experiences and incidents—The war with Spain and public sentiment in Santiago—Lilliputian battles—The plot against the American battleship "Oregon" and its frustration.

I HAVE often wondered why it was given to the Spaniards, the most impracticable of the Aryan races, to produce the most sensible and practical, as well as the most sonorous and beautiful, of all languages. The eccentricities of Spanish are few and its rules of pronunciation and orthography follow the ear rather than the imagination or fancy of lexicographers.

Our early experiences with the language under the tutelage of Michaels, the clerk of the legation, were somewhat baffling; it seemed simple, and yet we were being constantly involved in ridiculous incidents brought about by that quality of courage which is usually attributed to the foolish rather than to angels. Eventually we acquired the language so as to speak it with fluency, if not with elegance, but the earlier periods of our apprenticeship were painful ones. Some of our mistakes were ludicrous. After about three months of residence I established the rule that only Spanish could be spoken at the family table. This rule inflicted no hardship on the children but became a burden to the adults. The butler, Amador, a person of some years' connection with the legation, was possessed of great dignity in the discharge of his functions. He usually, as is the case with all Chileans, managed to keep a straight face when blunders in the language occurred, but when he found it impossible to do so, he retired behind the serving screen for relaxation. This was usually the signal for my children to exclaim, "Papa, Amador has gone behind the screen."

Upon another occasion, which happened to be a dinner given to us by my Chilean friend, Don Ruperto Vergara, most of the guests invited were English-speaking, out of supposed consideration for us. Mrs. Wilson was seated at the right hand of Antonio Valdes Cuevas, the Chilean prime minister. As the dinner progressed Mr. Valdes Cuevas, who spoke no English, said to me across the table, "*Pero la señora habla muy bien el Español.*" Desiring to come to Mrs. Wilson's rescue and at the same time to show my own superior accomplishments in the language, I replied in the midst of a profound silence: "*Si, la señora habla bastante bien, pero ella podria hablar mucho mejor si no tenia medias.*" The error was in the word "*medias*" which means stockings and the word which should have been used was "*miedo,*" which means fear. What I really said was that Mrs. Wilson would have spoken better Spanish had she worn no stockings. It was a long time before I heard the last of this.

The children, however, acquired the language with marvellous rapidity and before long frequently assisted me in my somewhat distressing interviews with people who spoke only the Spanish language.

Soon after our arrival in Chile the Spanish-American War broke out and the legation immediately became involved in the discussion of the various questions which always arise between belligerents and neutrals in time of war.

The recollection of the *Baltimore* incident,[1] which occurred in the harbour of Valparaiso, was still fresh in the minds of the Chilean people. Memory of this affair and perhaps natural tendencies of race and religion put Chilean sympathies very strongly behind Spain in her contest with *El Coloso del Norte*. Public opinion in Santiago ran strongly in favour of the Spanish cause and the defeat of the Americans was confidently predicted. The press was so vigorous in its denunciations and abounded in such savage attacks on the American government and people that patient endurance became difficult. Sometimes there were popular demonstrations on the streets and public places; when such demonstrations occurred at night the servants of the legation always urged me not to go upon the streets. Although I knew their advice to be good, I, nevertheless, persisted in going openly to the Plaza in the evenings and never varied an instant from my daily habits.

The situation had an amusing side, too. My eldest son, John, who was then about ten years of age, became the object of a combined hostile attack on the part of the small boys in the neighbourhood of the legation who sympathized with the Spanish cause, and he was frequently obliged to retreat hastily to the precincts of the legation. I found him one day, after a rather severe encounter with these young ruffians, badly bruised up. Inquiry divulged the fact that a number of boys had beset him about half a block from the legation and had

[1]Sailors and marines from the U. S. battleship *Baltimore* went ashore at Valparaiso at a time when relations between the United States and Chile were somewhat strained. They were attacked in the streets, perhaps not without provocation, by a Chilean mob. Many were wounded and some were killed. Our government demanded and received from the Chilean government compensatory damage, but the affair led to a profound resentment in Chile which endured many years.

[48]

vindicated the cause of Spain by unitedly and cheerfully pounding him about the body and the head, while he was obeying my injunction to avoid any difficulties. I immediately released him from his obligations to keep the peace and directed him to make a devastating war in the enemy's country. This he did so effectually that he established a genuine terror among the Chilean boys of the neighbourhood, which finally led to their parents calling upon the police for protection.

About the time the wave of public opinion had reached its crest came a cablegram announcing the proposed trip of the American warship *Oregon* from San Francisco to Cuba, with stops at Lima, Valparaiso, and other points. On April 5th, following this announcement, Mr. Caples, our consul at Valparaiso, advised me that the news of the expected arrival of the *Oregon* with the gunboat *Marietta* had stirred up some activity and bitterness among the Spanish residents of the port and that dangerous talk was being indulged in. Upon receipt of this news I immediately went to Valparaiso for a consultation with our consul. Mr. Caples informed me that two Chilean citizens of the highest social and political standing had made known to him that there existed among the Spanish residents of Valparaiso a secret but well-organized plot to destroy the *Oregon* and the *Marietta* while they were at anchor in the harbour. The story, bearing the evidence of truth, demanded prompt action.

As it was a holiday, communication with the Department of Foreign Relations at Santiago was impossible. Determined upon some action, in company with Mr. Caples, I called upon the Intendente of Valparaiso, Señor Cabezon Jordon, and put him in possession of the information which had reached me. He immediately put detectives on the case and on the following day called to say that the information we had given him had been fully confirmed and that the plot existed. He added that to avoid delay he had brought the matter to the attention of the President and had received instructions from him to exercise rigid police control in the harbour and allow no boats, except those of the Chilean government, to approach the *Oregon* or the *Marietta*.

In the meantime I had telegraphed to Lima and to Antofagasta recommending that the *Oregon* should not enter the harbour of Valparaiso but should proceed directly to the port of Coronel. As a result of these steps the *Marietta* alone came into the port of Valparaiso, the *Oregon* proceeding to the port of Coronel. While the *Marietta* remained at anchorage she was made the object of a quiet but strict system of patrol by the Chilean navy and on the 9th, having completed her repairs and coaled, she sailed for Punta Arenas to join the *Oregon*.

Coincident with the departure of the *Marietta* I addressed a letter to our minister in Montevideo advising him of what had transpired in Valparaiso and urging him to adopt similar precautions when the *Oregon* should enter the port of Montevideo. The *Oregon* incident demonstrated the necessity of some method of rapid communication between American diplomatic and consular offices in South America, and with the permission of the Department of State I established a code system of communication for that purpose. This code system was found of great value during the further progress of the war in maintaining surveillance of ships of all nationalities entering South American ports.

As the war between Spain and the United States continued and American victories followed one another in rapid succession and overwhelming measure, public sympathies in Chile veered completely to the American side, and by the end of the war many Chileans were claiming descent from Araucanian Indians in preference to Spanish grandees.

CHAPTER VIII

*A trip to a Chilean country estate—Festivities and humorous incidents
—Arrival of new British colleague—Some of his peculiarities—Incident
at official dinner to American and British naval officers.*

IN THE month of October of this year my friend,
Francisco Undurraga, invited me to spend a week
at his country place of Las Aranas, an estate about
a hundred miles from Santiago. The experiences
of this trip are fairly illustrative of Chilean rural life.

After a seventy-mile rail journey we arrived at Consti-
tucion, where we were met by a two-horse vehicle of the
Spanish type—with outriders—and were carried off like a
shot to a halfway point. Here the horses were changed
for fresh ones and we proceeded on our way, reaching Las
Aranas, a trip of forty-five miles, in precisely three hours.

On the outskirts of the estate we were met by a procession of probably a thousand of the tenantry and escorted
to the family mansion for luncheon. The menu was primitive but unique: the first shoots of celery and onions, but-
ter made at the door five minutes before it was eaten, fish
from the ocean near by, and turkey, washed down with
homemade wine, made a sufficiently palatable meal.

After a siesta we visited the central village of the estate, where the post office is located, the supply depots,
and the houses of many of the tenants. Here a large
crowd was assembled for the double purpose of seeing the
Yankee minister and of hearing Don Francisco, who was
a candidate for the Chilean House of Deputies, make a

political speech. As there was a considerable sprinkling of qualified voters among the tenants, I had an opportunity of contrasting the Chilean campaign methods with ours. They do not greatly differ; there was the same appeal to patriotism; the same abundance of promises and the same exchanges of badinage and humour which so frequently mark the progress of our own campaign. As the district in which Don Francisco was a candidate was largely covered by estates owned by branches of his family or intimate friends, there was little chance of his opponent's success.

Chilean country life is still very patriarchal; the owners of the great haciendas look upon their tenants as so many children and they provide for their necessities and comforts with real benevolence. On the other hand, the tenants as a rule have a very profound affection and reverence for the *patron*.

After the meeting at the village was concluded we were taken to a rodeo which had been prepared for my entertainment. The rodeo, be it understood, is the Chilean process of putting cattle in fit condition; numbers of them are herded into a circular enclosure and are driven about at a great rate of speed which results in hair shedding and cleansing of the blood. Upon this occasion some novel features in honour of my visit were introduced. At one end of the rodeo circle a platform for distinguished guests had been erected; it was occupied by Don Francisco, the postmaster of the village, the chief vaquero, and the American minister. Four of the best riders on the estate were brought forward and four of the fiercest cattle were driven into a small pen adjoining the ring. At an appointed moment one of the beasts was led out and saddled and, after the practice of considerable strategy, one of the *huasos* was placed astride him.

The scene which resulted was indescribably ludicrous but nevertheless exciting. The first, second, and third *huasos*, after spectacular careers in the air, were brought to the ground, one of them in a senseless condition. The fiercest of the animals and the best rider had been reserved for the last, and what occurred at this stage equalled any similar exhibition I have ever witnessed. The man was finally dismounted and dragged about the arena in a manner and with a violence which would have made short shift with the life of any being less tough than a Chilean *huaso*. It looked for a moment as though he might be killed and, when his foot finally broke from stirrup, after he had been twice dragged around the ring, my platform colleagues, abandoning me, rushed down to ascertain his condition. While they were busily attempting to restore him to consciousness, the liberated animal, which had been totally forgotten in the scrimmage, made a charge on the party from the rear. Shrill cries of warning went up from the assembled crowd, and rescuers immediately broke for cover; not soon enough, however, for one of them was assisted over the hedge by the enraged animal, which then remained sole master of the situation. As there were no enemies in sight the active attention of the animal was turned to the platform on which I was sitting and, exhibiting an appalling intelligence, it began to raise the boards of the platform with its horns. This performance was not down on the programme, and with that prudence which is the better part of valour I threw dignity to the winds and quickly climbed a tree which grew inside the platform. This episode afforded vast amusement to the rustic audience, and the story of my hurried climb to safety was afterward told with generous amplification all over Chile, and I was sometimes referred to as *el altisimo ministro*—"the most high minister."

That night Don Francisco gave a dinner followed by a dance for the tenants. The dinner was attended by the local celebrities and was not especially exciting. The postmaster, whose name was Don Henrico, was a mute but respectful auditor. At one point, however, he went astray. I was engaged in explaining to Don Francisco the benefits which Chile would derive from the construction of the Panama Canal. Don Henrico endeavoured to follow the conversation but got hopelessly befogged. He finally interrupted with the questions: "*que es el canal de Panama? Es un canal de regamiento?*" (What is the Panama Canal? Is it an irrigation canal?)

The ball was an event; the tenants gathered from all parts of the estate, bringing their own musicians who filled the air with melody as they approached; then, upon an extemporized platform, they danced the *cueca*, the *zemi cueca*, the tarantella, dances peculiar to Spain and Chile. We finally joined in the festivities, but as I had not at that time learned the Chilean dances, I instructed some of the young women in the waltz, which, after the trial, they dubbed "*la revolucion.*"

During the five remaining days at Las Aranas there were repetitions of the same programme—visits all over the estate on horseback by day, music of the guitar and flute in the evening, and then a blessed sleep in a quiet corner of the great house, looking out through the windows upon the starlit southern skies.

[55]

In the latter part of this summer the diplomatic corps was enlarged by the arrival of the new British minister, Sir Audley Gosling, with his interesting family. Gosling was a fine-looking man of the florid British type, hospitable and kindly to everyone, but disinclined to excessive labour and very much dissatisfied with his residence in Chile. He had married a Swedish Countess, one of the best and kindest women I have met in my diplomatic experience. She was an unfailing source of help and strength to her husband and an excellent mother to a large family of children.

Sir Audley had one amusing peculiarity, which was a never-failing source of entertainment to those who knew him well. He was fond of diagnosing all kinds of diseases, and upon the least hint or suggestion of an ailment among any of his friends he would immediately discover its exact cause and provide the remedy. I remember very well his great excitement upon one occasion when he thought that a nasal trouble of mine was due to the existence of polypi, and in spite of my protests, he haled me off to a physician and had me examined and operated upon, though I am quite sure nothing whatever was the matter. He was obsessed with the belief that pestilential microbes were everywhere present and when with him one was not permitted to grasp railings or straps or to sit down. This obsession became a perfect mania with him and he not only observed a most rigid discipline but compelled everyone within the radius of his friendships to do the same.

One of Gosling's antipathies was the British Consul General at Valparaiso, Sir Barry Cusack-Smith, with whom he had frequent and amusing passages at arms. Upon one occasion, when Mrs. Wilson and I were visiting

Sir Audley and Lady Gosling at their summer home near Valparaiso, an amusing incident occurred between these two representatives of the British government. At that time the American fleet, returning from the Spanish-American War under the command of Admiral Barker, was lying at anchor in the harbour of Valparaiso; alongside of same, British war-vessels anchored there also.

Gosling conceived the idea of having a "hands-across-the-sea" dinner and invited the British and American officers and the British and American consuls at Valparaiso. During the afternoon the American officers inquired whether or not they should come to dinner in uniform. I told them that a uniform would not be appropriate as I knew Sir Audley detested his uniform above all things and would certainly appear in evening dress. In the meantime, the British Consul General had advised our officers to come in uniform and they, being somewhat confused, informed him of my advice. Sir Barry then telephoned to Gosling saying: "Am I or am I not to come in my breeches?" Gosling, who never lost an opportunity to be rude to the "Jubilee Knight" as he called him, said: "I think Lady Gosling would not be pleased to see you without your breeches." But what was meant as a sarcasm was accepted as an instruction and the British officers and Consul turned up at the dinner in full uniform, while the American officers, the British minister, and I were in simple evening dress. The effect which was produced was somewhat ludicrous and especially embarrassing to those in uniform.

During one of Gosling's long leaves of absence his faithful wife passed away and he refused to return to Chile and eventually left the service.

[57]

CHAPTER IX

Differences between Chile and the Argentine republic over boundary limitations—Friendly American intervention—Return to the United States on leave of absence—Visit to the President and his request that I return immediately to Chile—Imposing banquet given me upon my arrival in Santiago—Attempts to soften differences between the Argentine and Chile.

IN 1899 serious differences arose between the Argentine and Chile relative to the so-called *Puna de Atacama* boundary delimitation on the northern part of their frontier line. As time went on the situation developed alarming possibilities and an armed conflict appeared to be inevitable; the press was exceedingly bitter and provocative and the attitude of both governments appeared to be irreconcilable. At this juncture friendly diplomatic activities were initiated. The governments of the United States and Great Britain were deeply concerned at the threatened interruption of peaceful relations between the two republics and instructed their diplomatic representatives at Buenos Aires and Santiago to use all proper efforts to prevent a complete break.

Intervening quietly in this delicate situation, I suggested—whether under instruction or not I do not now recall—that the differences, in the event of the failure of the two governments to come to an agreement, should be submitted to the arbitration of a commission headed by the Honourable William Buchanan, our minister at

Buenos Aires, with whom should be associated one Chilean and one Argentine delegate. After numerous diplomatic exchanges and consultations the Chilean government, with some misgivings, I think, accepted this plan of settlement and Mr. Buchanan, as chairman of the commission, immediately entered upon his duties, discharging them with commendable zeal, promptitude and, as I thought, fairness. The award, unfortunately, was not favourably received in Chile and lessened to some extent the growing feeling of confidence in the friendly attitude of our government. However, war had been averted and to that extent our friendly intervention had been successful.

About this time I received a personal letter from President McKinley intimating that my transfer to another post was about to be made and advising me to apply for a leave of absence and return home. Supposing my departure from Chile to be final, I surrendered our house, disposed of our furniture, and removing the legation to offices in the commodious Equitable Building sailed, with my family, for the United States.

On my arrival at Washington I found a note advising me that the President desired to see me, with Mrs. Wilson, that evening at nine o'clock. We found the President, Mrs. McKinley, and Mrs. Fred Grant in the President's reception room, where, later, refreshments were served. During the evening the President took me aside and asked me if I had visited the Department of State since my arrival. I told him that I had found his note upon my arrival at three o'clock and under the circumstances supposed it was my first duty to visit him. He then said that troubles in regard to the southern part of the boun-

[59]

dary line between the Argentine and Chile had broken out and that the situation was very alarming. He gave me some details, which I recognized as being significant in character, and asked me if I did not think it advisable to return at once to Chile where my supposed popularity might be of some avail in tempering the threatened storm.

I had then been absent from home some four years and was, of course, reluctant to abandon the plans I had made for a pleasant vacation with family and friends. I said as much to the President but added that if in his judgment it was my duty to return immediately I would yield to the official necessities but must go alone. He replied, "You know that I am the last person in the world to separate a man from his wife and family without having good reasons for doing so. Your course in Chile meets with my warm approval and I had expected to give you an honourable promotion at this time. It appears to me that your duty lies at the post where you can do the most good." I reluctantly said farewell to my family the next day and went to New York to take passage on the first available steamer. I expected to be gone but a brief time and then to return for the promised vacation and promotion. As events turned out, I remained alone in Chile about a year and I never saw William McKinley again in life.

During my brief stay in the United States I had an opportunity to explain in some measure to the press the political situation in the southern part of the hemisphere and to say some things about the Chilean attitude in international affairs which apparently were favourably received in Chile.

In confirmation of this pleasant appreciation I learned

on my way down the coast that elaborate preparations were being made for my reception and that they were to take the form of a personal testimonial by the government, public, and press. Arriving in Chile, I found the Chilo-Argentine controversy raging furiously. The public mind was absorbed with various phases of the boundary question and was extremely pessimistic of a peaceful outcome.

The government was busily engaged in preparation for war; the Chilean warships had been repainted in the nebulous fighting colours and were being made ready for serious business. Although occupied with this intense situation the Chilean press signalled my return by most cordial comments and the general public prepared for the great banquet which was to be the expression of appreciation of Chilean society. The event was celebrated at the Club de la Union and was the most pretentious affair of the kind which occurred during my residence of eight years in Chile. The concurrence was enormous and distinguished; the profusion and display imposing. The Chilean cabinet attended in a body and the Minister of Foreign Affairs, Mr. Martino, presided. The address of the evening was delivered by Don Marcial Martinez, the most venerable and distinguished diplomat and statesman in Chile, whose references to me were exceedingly complimentary and seemed to sound a note of real sympathy and kindness in the attitude of the Chilean people. I responded in kind and, with the purpose of influencing the strained relations which existed between Chile and Argentina, I extolled in the highest terms the character and history of the Chilean people with expressions of confidence in Chile's future growth and power through peaceful development.

The banquet was a great success and was a subject of favourable comment by the press and public for some days. I believe my speech influenced in some measure the critical situation existing between Chile and the Argentine and I immediately followed it up in coöperation with the British minister, Mr. Gerald Lowther, with as much energy as could be employed commensurately with dignity. My personal instructions from President McKinley gave me a rather free hand in the premises and, as this was known on both sides of the Cordillera, a very distinct gain was made for peaceful diplomacy. Vigorous diplomatic activities had the effect of moderating the menacing tone of the press of the two countries; if the relations did not become positively better, they at least did not become worse, in that they became intricate and prolonged rather than acute.

CHAPTER X

Trip through the south as the guest of the Chilean government—Talca—Chillan—Concepcion—Lota—Coronel—Development of southern Chile—Araucanian country.

IN THE temporary lull of agitation which followed our initial friendly intervention in trans-Andean affairs, the Chilean government invited me to make a trip of observation through southern Chile to the temporary terminal of the railway extension. This excursion was a part of Chile's programme of commercial expansion and the government wished me to have an opportunity to see the development and resources of the central valley of Chile and to follow with a trip to the settled portion of southern Chile.

A specially equipped train, decorated with American and Chilean flags, was provided by the government and placed under the personal direction of the three directors of the railways, Señores Valdes, Vial, and Bernales. My three Chilean friends, Francisco Irarrazaval, Francisco Undurraga, and Anibal Pinto, and the American Consul at Valparaiso, Mr. Mansfield, were invited to go along.

Leaving the railway station on Sunday morning, we dashed through the villas and country seats which environ Santiago and about noon arrived at Graneros, the beautiful estate of my friend, Francisco Irarrazaval, where we were to make our first stop and to have luncheon with the accomplished wife of Mr. Irarrazaval, Elena Irarrazaval de Concha.

[63]

The Irarrazaval mansion is very imposing, modelled somewhat on the plan of the White House at Washington; it is set among magnificent trees and flowering shrubs and from the tops of two rugged hills there is a surpassing view of all the rich extent of garden lands stretching to the foot of the Cordillera.

In the middle of the afternoon we resumed our trip south and after a brief stay at Talca, a well-ordered city of about twenty thousand people, we went on to Chillan, arriving there early Monday morning.

Chillan is an English-built, modern-looking city, set in the midst of a fertile valley, and is noted in an historical way as having been for many years the advanced outpost of the Spaniards in their wars with the Araucanian Indians.

After having been officially and agreeably entertained at this place, we pursued our course along the banks of the beautiful Laja River to its junction with the Bio Bio—the latter renowned in history as the scene of the border warfare between the Spanish invaders and the Araucanian Indians. It is an imposing stream, reminding one of the Ohio, the banks on either side receding in regular slopes covered with verdure. Near the junction of these two rivers lies Concepcion, a city of sixty thousand inhabitants, and the most important in the southern part of central Chile. This bustling modern city was quite a revelation. Its streets are wide and spacious, lined with modern buildings, giving it more the appearance of an American city. Concepcion is an illustration of what is called peaceful penetration; its business is almost entirely in the hands of foreigners—Germans and French predominating. One may walk from end to end of the principal avenue and see nothing but German and French names, with now and then a sprinkling of Italian and English on the windows.

At Concepcion we were officially received by the Intendente of the Province who was to accompany us to Talcahuano (the port of Concepcion), lying six miles farther down at the junction of the Bio Bio with the sea. A special train, under charge of a committee of citizens, had been provided and we went on our way followed by the usual military pomp and inevitable band of music. Admiral Perez, in command at Talcahuano, met our party at the station and conducted us through the docks and arsenals which the government of Chile, at a cost of more than five million dollars, has constructed. When one views the system of docks built in the open sea, the ships in process of repair or construction, and the army of workmen maintained at a great expense, it is easy to understand why Chile successfully maintains her position as the chief sea power of South America, indomitable, virile, pugnacious nation hesitating at no sacrifices of men or money to preserve the position of the most formidable and influential power on the southern continent.

Later in the day we were entertained at what was called a tea, but which was really a banquet, at the summer hotel which Mr. Augustine Ross had recently erected. In addition to our party there were present thirty-five citizens of Concepcion and Talcahuano, and the occasion was enlivened by toasts for Chile and the United States. The day was rounded out by a banquet given by the citizens of Concepcion.

Early the next morning we crossed the Bio Bio River by the three-mile bridge of the English railway which spans it at Concepcion and took our course due south to

[65]

Arauco, running almost constantly in sight of the sea, through beetling and picturesque cliffs.

Passing through Coronel we arrived at Arauco, the terminal point of the English railway, where we were regaled with an elaborate luncheon—a feast that would have done justice to a New York caterer—oysters and fish fresh from the sea, small game from the neighbouring hills, and English-made bread and sweets—all prepared and served with perfect taste, a novel experience in this remote part of the world. The Englishman carries his bathtub, his cookery, and his whiskey with him wherever he goes. He carries many other things with him which serve to make the world a better place to live in; some of these become eroded by foreign contact, but never the whiskey, the bathtub, and the cookery.

In the afternoon we stopped at Lota, the coal-producing and manufacturing centre of Chile, and were met at the station by Mr. Perry, the English manager of the Cousino properties, and taken in carriages through a charming drive, past mines and factories, into what is perhaps the most extensive private estate in South America. By winding paths, shaded by trees of almost every known variety, getting an occasional glimpse of the blue expanse of the sea, we approached the portals of a mansion so strikingly English in appearance that for the moment we might have thought ourselves in Sussex or Kent. Within all was flowers, and elegance, and comfort, and that night I slept in the most commodious room and comfortable bed I had occupied in South America.

Rising with the dawn, we followed the winding paths of the estate through grottoes and past statues, passing now and then along the edge of steep precipices which run sheer to the sea, covered with trailing vines and flowering roses. Lota is a dream of beauty—a small paradise set down in this remote part of the world—the eloquent evidence of what diligence, taste, and the unstinted use of money can accomplish in beautifying nature.

After this we saw the practical picture—the coal mines far down under the waters of the sea, and the factories where iron, stone, and earth were being wrought into useful forms by hundreds of clever Chilean workmen.

Noon of the next day found us across the Bio Bio with stops at Traiguen and Angol, where we were received with the usual ceremonies by the Intendente and General Lopez, commanding the third military zone. Our stay at the latter place, aside from the usual ceremonies, was made interesting by an exhibition drill of the Bulnes Grenadiers, and we witnessed with admiration the perfect evolutions of two thousand soldiers who had been only three months enlisted.

The Chilean is a native-born soldier and takes to his gun and his military step as a duck does to water. Tireless, docile, fearless, and vigorous, with strong strains of Araucanian blood running in his veins, he is the embodiment of Chilean patriotism, and with the Chilean sailor, makes the name of Chile respected and dreaded all the way from Panama to Cape Horn.

After the exhibition drill we were driven six miles into the country and hospitably entertained at breakfast at the home of Señor Vargas, a Chilean senator—an American-built house, with broad porticoes and French windows, elevated upon a sloping hill, with a charming vista in every direction.

The country through which we now were passing is, in

[67]

some respects, the most attractive part of Chile; the soil is rich, producing abundant crops of alfalfa, wheat, and hops. It is a new country, modern in appearance, with evidences of thrift everywhere. The German, the Yankee, and the Englishman are in evidence; American machinery makes cheerful music in nearly every field; all the way from the river Bio Bio to the beginning of the heavily timbered land at Victoria, there is visible that progress and energy which at some time will make it the commercial centre of Chile. The scenery, too, is beautiful. Rivers like the Malleco and the Tolton whirl their waters through deep gorges to the sea. The hills rise domelike in every direction, dressed and panoplied in the greenest of green verdure, diversified with luxuriant and richly coloured foliage. Valleys, peaceful and picturesque, stretch away in sinewy curves, running races with the rivers to the sea. Here, too, one finds bird life, and the familiar music, which had not fallen upon our ears before in all this continent, greeted us in a melody of song. Altogether, it is a charming country where one might live and wax fat in comfort.

Still moving toward the south we passed through Lautaro, where the famous Araucanian chief of that name, whom history has surrounded with romantic legend, lies buried.

Lautaro was a picturesque figure who, if historians tell the truth, performed acts of incredible bravery and heroism. He lies sleeping here to-day—the people of his race banished though not forgotten—and around his resting place modern civilization is moving its forces.

[68]

CHAPTER XI

The story of the Araucanians—Their customs and history

THE Araucanians were a people widely different from the effeminate and emasculated races to the north who had so meekly bowed the knee to the Spanish invader. Not only were they a virile people, loving and understanding liberty, but in many ways they were civilized and virtuous.

They manufactured beautiful woollen cloths and embroidered them in a highly artistic manner; they wrought edged tools of many kinds from the metals which they knew how to wrest from their hiding places in the hills; they made fixed dyes, rich as the Tyrian purple, and beautiful ornaments and utensils from marble and wood, painting and decorating them in an ingenious and artistic fashion. This people worshipped God through the symbol of the sun; their morals were severe and their living cleanly. Their laws were few in number, as are the laws of all primitive peoples, but they were modelled on democratic forms and executed with Draconian severity. In a rude form they possessed the essence of a republic, since all questions affecting the general welfare were settled in open council by a majority of votes, the execution of decisions being delayed three days before being carried into effect.

Physically, the Araucanians are a splendid race—hence the legend of the Patagonian giants—loving war as the

[69]

ancient Germans and preferring like them annihilation to slavery.

Their education was not unlike that of the primitive Germans; war-like tastes were cultivated from childhood and those who adopted the profession of arms enjoyed special privileges, among others, exemption from all menial work; the children competed for prizes in races, barefoot along narrow, steep, and rocky paths, some of them becoming fleet as deer. Among the elders, prizes appropriate for warriors were awarded to successful competitors in athletic sports and tests of strength. A warrior never attempted to train himself in the use of more than one weapon, in the choice of which he was permitted to follow his own inclinations. Their arms were pikes, halberds, long lances, hatchets, darts, arrows, bludgeons, and catapults; to protect the head and trunk of the body they wore corselets of such tough leather that only swords of the finest steel could cut through them. Advancement in the army was attained through merit and no favouritism was shown on account of birth or position. The skill of the Araucanian in war enlisted the admiration of their Spanish foes, who were loud in praise of their discipline, order, and intelligent strategy. Forming in columns of about a hundred men each, the archers attacked from a distance, while the pikers advanced to engage in hand-to-hand encounters with the enemy; if a column failed, another immediately took its place in perfect order and silence, while the defeated column reorganized in the rear. In their engagements with the Spaniards it was a common occurrence for the boldest, sometimes numbering thirty or forty, to leave the ranks and advance toward the enemy, offering challenge to single combat.

The Araucanians had great leaders; Colocolo, a sagacious and prudent chieftain, shaped their policy and moved their passionate patriotism with profound and subtle eloquence; Lincoyan, a giant of the heroic ages, raged in the storm of battle, gigantic in stature and courage; Caupolican, a hero of staunch heart and swift decision, displayed qualities which among other peoples would have crowned his savage brow with the olive-green chaplet. Lautaro, who, from having been a slave in the house of Valdivia, became the leader of his people, defeated the Spaniards upon many battlefields but finally fell, a victim of his own adventurous courage, leaving the war to be carried on by Colocolo. The death of Lautaro was a severe blow to the Araucanians. He was able, brave, and patriotic, and has, not without reason, been described as the most valiant defender of American soil from California to Cape Horn.

After the loss of Lautaro, Caupolican and the sagacious Colocolo, with their sons and their sons' sons, carried on the Araucanian war until imperial Spain recognized Araucanian independence and received Araucanian ambassadors at the court of the viceroy at Santiago. When Chile shook off the rule of Spain the Araucanian problem remained, but the wisdom and diplomacy of Chilean statesmen finally accomplished the practical assimilation of the Araucanian race.

At Temuco we entered the Indian country. Here the Araucanian Indians, stalwart, picturesque, and proud, still abide, practising their ancient customs and speaking their beautiful language over a stretch of country between Temuco and Valdivia.

On our way from Temuco we passed through a densely wooded country to Petrufuquen, the last station on the state railway and the farthermost point south in the world to which a railway has been constructed, and where workmen were busily building a bridge to span the Tongoy River, the boundary between the provinces of Cautin and Valdivia.

The Tongoy River was our *ultima thule*, and from thence we returned to the Indian town Temuco and spent the evening making purchases from the Indians. The beautiful shawls and rugs which they manufacture are not surpassed anywhere, and the prices for which they may be purchased are ridiculously low. These shawls and rugs never wear out and retain their colour and fibre for years.

Early the next morning we took the train for Santiago, arriving there on Monday morning, having been absent eight days.

CHAPTER XII

*Arrival of the American fleet under Admiral Casey and banquet—
Final solution of Argentine and Chilean difficulties—Popular demonstration of approval given me—The death of McKinley—Memorial
services in Santiago—Estimate of McKinley.*

IN THE month of August, 1900, when the difficulties
between Chile and the Argentine had become intensi-
fied, an American fleet under the command of Admiral
Casey arrived at the harbour of Valparaiso. The
arrival of the fleet was interpreted by Chilean public
opinion as evidence that American sympathies were with
Chile and its advent was welcomed with manifestations of
great satisfaction. A deluge of banquets, receptions, and
official visits followed. Conspicuous among these affairs
was a banquet given by the officers of the American navy
at which speeches were made by officers of the Chilean,
American, and British navies and by the British and
American ministers.

Soon after these events the negotiations between the
Argentine and Chilean governments, earnestly supported
by the British and American legations, took a more favourable turn; all of the differences were finally composed
and the basis of what has proven to be a permanent peace
between the two countries was established. Under the
terms of the agreement all disputed questions were to be
submitted to the arbitration of his majesty, King Edward
VII. This led to the creation of a boundary commission,
which was instructed not only to determine the line of

division on the southern boundary but to fix it and mark it so that further discussion might be made possible. The findings of this commission were later embodied in the formal arbitral decision of King Edward VII, and thus the boundary question which had disturbed the peace of these two otherwise friendly nations came to an end.

To celebrate the peaceful solution of their difficulties the two countries erected on the highest peak of the Cordillera a heroic statue of Christ. There was, however, a trans-Andean note of discord when the question of placing the statue in position came up for decision, the Argentines contending that the Redeemer of the world should turn His face toward the rising sun and the Chileans asserting, with an apparently equal show of reason, that as the Son of Man came from the east, His statue must necessarily be represented as facing the west. A happy compromise was finally effected by which the statue was so located as to face the north with its right eye on the smiling plains of the Argentine and its left on the purpling hills of Chile. After this arrangement perfect peace reigned.

The opening of the New Year, 1901, after peace had been preserved, was celebrated by the Chileans with great enthusiasm. I went that night to the Club de la Union with my friends, Francisco Undurraga and Anibal Pinto, to watch the old year out. The club was jammed with people who were there apparently for the purpose of accelerating the passing of the old year in a very earnest way. During the evening there were some informal toasts and talks and, in obedience to a demonstrative demand, I made some informal congratulatory remarks bearing on the final termination of the differences between Chile and the Argentine. As I was concluding my remarks the first hour of the New Year struck and, to my great surprise, the demonstration took on the form of a testimonial to me, and I was finally borne in undignified triumph on the shoulders of the enthusiastic youth of Santiago through the long streets amidst *vivas* to *el señor ministro*, interspersed with similar *vivas* for the *Iowa* and *Wisconsin*. Arriving at the American Legation, I was permitted to retire to my apartments after a few brief remarks. This demonstration, while apparently paid to me, was really a token of recognition of the impartial and friendly attitude of the government of the United States in the difficult situation which had existed so long between Chile and the Argentine.

In the month of September, 1901, while I was preparing to return to the United States, came the dreadful news of the shooting and death of William McKinley. This untoward event aroused the deepest sympathy among the Chilean people, and the long hours of agony and the final inspiring death were watched with profound interest. So universal and so unusual were the expressions of sympathy emanating from the representatives of the various governments that I decided that a funeral ceremony worthy of the distinguished dead and creditable to the American nation ought to be observed. The active cooperation of the American colony in Santiago was enlisted, and the government tendered its services to the legation. At the appointed hour a crack regiment entered the public theatre, where the exercises were to be held, first, and soldiers were stationed at the heads of all aisles, around the improvised bier, in a solid line around the walls, in the galleries, and at the back of the stage.

American ushers, clad in black frock coats, white gloves, and carrying wands, to which were attached three ribbons, red, white, and blue, were in charge of the interior. Then the procession, under the escort of two additional regiments, began to march, the President and his cabinet entering the building first, followed by the diplomatic corps, provincial and municipal officers and other public functionaries. The hall was then thrown open to the general public, which quickly filled all available space. The stage was set in floral decorations interlaced with the McKinley red colours screening a full orchestra, which rendered specially selected music throughout the exercises. The opening prayer and reading of the text were by Rev. Ira Le Fetra, president of the Santiago College, and the sermon was preached by the Rev. William Lester of the Presbyterian church. The great Italian singer, Grazzi, who had volunteered to sing two numbers during the ceremony, sang Gounod's "Ave Maria" and a Wagnerian selection with a pathos which profoundly moved the audience. The services closed impressively, and echoing military commands and the strains of military bands paid to a great man the last testimonial of respect at one of the extreme points of the world.

The events which have passed in endless procession across the stage of the world have not effaced my affectionate remembrance of William McKinley. His sturdy patriotism, his keen sense of justic, his ready and demonstrative sympathy, his genuine and constant kindness of heart and soul made an impress which has not been obliterated in these more strenuous hours.

McKinley had a genius for political leadership. His personal appearance was striking and commanding. Hand-

[76]

some in figure and face and always faultlessly attired, his advent on the platform made an instantaneous impression, which endured throughout his masterly and convincing discourse. Warmth, vigour, honesty, and patriotism were breathed into every word he uttered, and a spirit of kindness and comradery passed from him into the great audiences which he held under the magic spell of his eloquence and unusual power of clear reasoning. He was an orator and a statesman and he looked the parts, and those who hung upon his words carried away conviction in their hearts. His manner of dealing with people on or off the stage was admirable. He knew how to say kind things and to sound encouraging notes, and trouble vanished before the all-pervading impression of helpfulness and genuine interest. There was nothing assumed or fictitious about this. His sympathy was real and his interest was sincere. He never forgot his friends but followed them in affectionate remembrance across continents and seas, holding them ever in gentle memory. Yet he was not always gentle nor persistently patient. Wrongdoing, disloyalty, lack of fidelity to public or private trust aroused in him the profoundest indignation and called forth the severest denunciation. He could be firm, severe, or resentful to those who stood nearest to him and to those who exercised the greatest influence and power in political affairs. His deep religious spirit, his tender and affectionate care for his afflicted wife, and his constant reverence and thoughtfulness for his aged mother, were beautiful traits of character which appealed strongly to the sentimental side of the American people and which after his death enshrined him in the hearts of all.

[77]

CHAPTER XIII

Leave of absence—Crossing the Andes—Buenos Aires—Rio de Janeiro—Charles Page Bryan—Seeing the city with Mr. Bryan—Completion of trip by the way of Europe and arrival at New York.

IN THE month of May, 1902, I obtained a leave of absence to return to the United States and determined to go by the European route, which offered the advantage not only of greater comfort but of more useful and interesting experiences. The Chilean government very kindly placed a car at my disposal to the termination of the Chilean railway in the Andes, and I invited to accompany me on the trip the American consul at Valparaiso, Mr. Mansfield, and John Brunet, a young Cuban-American then living in Chile.

Boarding our train, we passed rapidly through the fields and vineyards up as far as Los Andes, the last town of any importance on the Chilean side. There we dined delightfully under a crescent moon which flooded the valley and mountains with light. At ten o'clock we reached a point called El Salto del Soldado, where trans-Andean passengers usually passed the night, or rather that part of the night allotted for sleep, before making the final ascent to the summit.

About four-thirty in the morning the entire party was aroused from slumber and, without further ado, mounted mules which were in readiness and, as this final lap was that part of the trip which was frequently interrupted by

[78]

brigands, we also prepared our arms and began climbing up the face of Mt. Aconcagua. The panoramic scene that spread out in every direction was weird but gloomily majestic. The moon was still in the heavens and its rays fell upon mountain crags stretching away for miles and miles. Off in the distance might be seen innumerable waterfalls apparently of diminutive size but really containing considerable volumes of water. Shadows made by the mountains took on gigantic shapes, and as we went silently on our way the winds blew stronger and stronger. Here we were at a height of 15,000 feet, and as we approached the summit we retained our seats on mule back with the greatest difficulty.

At the actual summit—"*las mas ultimas cumbres de la cordillera*"—our Chilean guards saluted and retired and their places were taken by Argentine guards who were to escort us down the Argentine incline of the mountain. After we had proceeded about three or four miles we were dismounted and put on board a little mountain railway which brought us down to the Inca Baths—so called because in the days before the Spaniards came it was the custom of the Inca king and his suite to come hither once a year to take the cure, supposed to exist in the waters of these springs. After refreshing ourselves with a dip in the boiling water of these springs we resumed our trip down the mountainside, arriving in a few hours at the prosperous Argentine town of Mendoza. Thence we took the overland train reaching, after a night-and-day trip, a rolling stretch of country resembling the plains of the Dakotas, the city of Buenos Aires. The difficulties and dangers of crossing the Cordillera have now been eliminated by the construction of the trans-Andean tunnel through which passengers from Santiago to Buenos Aires now go without interruption in trains as well equipped as any in Europe or in the United States.

The stay in Buenos Aires was made enjoyable by drives about its handsome environs and boulevards and by a dinner given by my friend, the Chilean minister at Buenos Aires, Mr. Carlos Concha. The dinner was followed by a gondola ride through the canals of the marvellous park which lies in the centre of the city. An enlivening feature of the evening's entertainment was a formal introduction to the presiding genius of the great restaurant, an American, whose sole business was to manufacture American cocktails for a salary of five thousand dollars a year. Devotion to the material things of life sometimes brings better rewards than does consecration to those things which are spiritual.

Leaving my pleasant Argentine and Chilean friends in Buenos Aires I took passage on the Royal Main Steamship *Pernambuco*, crossed over the river Plate to Montevideo —a replica in appearance of the city of Lisbon—where we were hospitably entertained by the American minister.

When we anchored in the harbour of Rio de Janeiro I was somewhat thrilled to see, approaching the steamer, a large steam launch decorated with American flags and carrying the American minister, Mr. Charles Page Bryan, and some prominent residents of Rio de Janeiro who had come out to welcome and invite me to a dinner to be given that night on the hills overhanging the city. In spite of the intensely sultry weather, these gentlemen were all attired in frock coats and top hats and Mr. Bryan intimated that I should array myself in a similar manner. This I courteously but firmly declined to do and, although

Mr. Bryan felt apprehensive at the supposed violation of Brazilian etiquette, I visited the Brazilian Minister of Foreign Affairs in white duck and a straw hat. I was not disappointed to find his Brazilian Excellency coatless and otherwise attired in harmony with Brazilian climatic exigencies.

The demands of official etiquette complied with, we took a promenade through the steaming streets of Rio de Janeiro, a task I accomplished with unwilted linen, but my colleague, who was a rather full-blooded person, shed vast torrents of perspiration and under the deluge his collars quickly collapsed. However, Mr. Bryan, who evidently was a thoughtful man in such emergencies, had established first-aid hospitals about four blocks apart where he always kept a fresh supply of collars and other requisites. Thus on the way down the principal avenue of Rio de Janeiro, our march was interrupted by frequent pauses while His Excellency, the American minister, readjusted his frontal attire, retiring in disorder and reappearing in excellent formation. As we continued on our way Mr. Bryan's face grew redder with each step; what would have happened if our travels had been further prolonged can only be imagined.

Mr. Bryan was afterward appointed minister to Portugal and eventually came from there to succeed me in Belgium. From Belgium he was promoted to be ambassador to Japan, but remained at the last post but a very short time. After his retirement from the diplomatic service he lived in Washington City where he became a liberal and constant host to a large circle of visiting friends and diplomats.

From Pernambuco, the last port in Brazil, our steamer

took a direct course to Lisbon, where I landed, and after a brief visit with the American minister, Mr. Francis B. Loomis, proceeded through Spain to Paris, spending some days with our ambassador, General Horace Porter, a unique and impressive figure in American diplomacy, possessing that quite common American faculty of combining in one personality many apparently dissimilar traits of character—lawyer, general, statesman, and diplomat. He shone as a star of the first magnitude in the diplomacy of western Europe and his influence and popularity seemed almost unlimited.

After some pleasant days in London, with Ambassador Choate, I took passage for New York, arriving there in the month of June, about one year after I had been abruptly ordered back to Chile, to find new political forces in control and with considerable uncertainty as to my own future.

CHAPTER XIV

I WENT to Washington with considerable misgiving and with the half-formed intention of concluding my connection with the diplomatic service. The record I had made in Chile I knew was satisfactory to the Department of State and especially to Secretary Hay, with whom my relations were then, and until his death, very close, but I was not sanguine about President Roosevelt's attitude toward me; prior to this visit I had only met him once and then rather casually. I was received very cordially by Secretary Hay, who told me that the President was greatly pleased with my work in Chile and advised me to go directly to him and to express my views without reserve.

While in Washington I passed some intimate hours with Secretary Hay who, when free from the restraints of his official character, was a delightful companion. His conversation was charged with a flood of reminiscence, philosophy, and humour which added a charm of novelty to his shrewd comments and gentle criticism. His *bête noir* was the United States Senate, and his estimate of that body was not high. "A senator," he quaintly said, "is a person with a conscience wholly apart and distinct from that of the great body of citizenry. Let a man be ever

[83]

so modest, simple, and retiring, once he becomes a United States senator, a complete transformation of character takes place and we at once have an overweening, dominant figure, rude and abrupt in speech, with a parochial vision and utterly oblivious of the larger aspects of national life." He said of Roosevelt, then just come into the presidency: "He is unchained energy, ferocious in the pursuit of his objects, undeterred by the considerations which ordinarily influence men. He is willing that the Almighty shall do His fair share in the direction of human affairs but the leavings must fall to him. He is and has been a tremendous power for good and is capable of doing great things, yet I am always fearful that his courage may overleap his wisdom. He is a lovable character and no one can be about him without feeling an excess of devotion."

Though not an old man at the time of his death, John Hay spanned in his activities a succession of great epochs. His public career extended all the way from Lincoln to Roosevelt; from the great drama of the Civil War to the Portsmouth treaty; from the birth of a nation to the apogee of its power. He was a friend of Lincoln, a trusted adviser of Grant, Garfield, and McKinley, and again, at the close of his career, a friend and intimate adviser of Roosevelt. The remarkable versatility and adaptability of the man is revealed in his ability to gain and hold the confidence and esteem of these greatly contrasting personages and in the circumstance that his wisdom and tact, transmuted through them, brought great and lasting results. Hay was the real creator of our modern diplomacy; before him we had policies but no diplomacy; after him came a very distinct type of Ameri-

can diplomacy which, with some setbacks and interruptions, has endured. The impression made by Mr.
Hay upon the chancelleries and rulers of Europe was so
great and lasting that it may be said to have been epochal
and its influence survives to this day.

After leaving Secretary Hay I asked at the White House
office for an appointment with the President. My note
was acknowledged with an invitation to Mrs. Wilson and
to me to meet Mrs. Roosevelt and the President at tea
on the following day. While we were engaged in conversation with Mrs. Roosevelt, the President came in,
followed by his brood of children, making a riot of noise
in an animated discussion which they were carrying on.
After an introduction to Mrs. Wilson he excused himself,
making a further appointment with me for nine o'clock
that evening. Meeting him informally at that hour,
he broke without ceremony into a discussion of the political situation in southern South America and asked me
for a detailed story of the events which had recently occurred there. This I gave as accurately and as clearly
as I could, the President manifesting marked interest and
understanding, and interrupting me only twice during the
long statement I made. When this was finished I changed
the conversation and said to him that I had come home
with the intention of tendering my resignation. He immediately replied in his impetuous way: "I don't want
your resignation. I want you to remain in the diplomatic
service. Both Mr. Hay and I greatly appreciate the work
you have done in Chile and I think you deserve a high
measure of credit. If you will remain in the service and I
remain here sufficiently long, I will send you to the head."
I was surprised to find that the President had such an

excellent opinion of my work, and his words had the effect of changing my attitude toward continuation in the diplomatic service. Very much gratified, I replied: "If you feel that way about it, Mr. President, I shall be glad to go on, but I hope that I may be transferred to a new post when a proper vacancy occurs." He said: "I can assure you that you may look forward to a transfer, which will be in the nature of a promotion, as soon as an opportunity presents itself."

I left the White House delighted with the compliments paid me by the President. Human beings are very much alike all over the world; the satisfaction that one derives from the performance of a good deed or many good deeds is not quite sufficient payment. There is always something wanting until someone "higher up" sounds a note of approval.

My first acquaintance with Theodore Roosevelt dates from the Republican National Convention of 1884 at Chicago, whither he went as a delegate from the State of New York. At that convention, he was a strenuous supporter, along with George William Curtis, of the candidacy of George F. Edmonds. What impressed me then was his youthful appearance and apparent earnestness in the cause which he had espoused. I had some talk with him at that time but did not see him again until he became Assistant Secretary of the Navy under President McKinley. This was in 1897, just after the President had appointed me minister to Chile. I then called upon him in connection with some official matters and was immensely entertained by the originality and vigour of his views on public questions, revealed with perfect frankness and with absolute disregard of caution. From that day my relations with him were more or less intimate. While in office we clashed a number of times but I think he never took umbrage at my independence, seeming to be rather amused and entertained by it. On one of these occasions he went over the head of the Secretary of State and in private letters instructed me to take a course which in my judgment was irregular and unwise. I evaded direct refusal but did not conform to the course he suggested. He must have been very much irritated, but the irregularity of his own procedure made it impossible for him to make complaint. Let it be well understood that his instructions in these matters were intended to accomplish good results; the fault was in the method and not in the objective.

Roosevelt was an unleashed berserker when pursuing a great object under difficult circumstances; his mental reservoirs were deep, rich, and varied, and he drew upon them with unceasing energy. His physical equipment was marvellous in its strength, virility, and endurance; he had a sound mind and a sound body, undaunted courage, superb ambition, and laudable patriotism. Fate and fortune treated him handsomely in the battle of life, but without the aid of either he would have gone far. An aristocrat at heart, nourished in the lap of luxury, highly educated, and highly endowed, he yet became the prophet of democracy and sounded the depths of public opinion with a keener insight and with a readier response to signals than perhaps any other president. The country came to know him as a fighter and as one who fought in the interest of the people, and it followed him not only when he was right but when he erred.

He was an absolutely just man, unmistakably an honest

[87]

one, undoubtedly a patriotic one. His whole life was a battle for principle. He was not, however, overly nice in the selection of the instruments through which he accomplished his ends nor was he, when he believed a public interest could be served or injury to a public interest prevented, a stickler for the niceties of veracity. He once said to me that he regarded the presidency as "a great pulpit from which a man of courage and ability could influence and move the affairs and fortunes of the world. That is why I like the job." His greatest errors came at the last of his career, but they were born of the heat and passion of a tremendous political intrigue into which he had been led by unwise friends. I know from his own lips that he was conscious of the mistakes he had committed and that had he lived again to fill the office of President, his course would have been everything that might have been desired by the friends of constitutional and conservative government.

His quarrel with President Taft was a sad mistake. Taft adored Roosevelt and would have sacrificed anything short of the dignity and independence of the presidential office to preserve his affection. When, in the campaign of 1918, at the close of the World War, President Wilson issued his statement that only Democrats ought to be elected to Congress, I telegraphed Mr. Hays, the able and active chairman of the Republican National Committee, urging him to invite Roosevelt and Taft to speak from the same platform in common repudiation of the un-American attitude of Wilson. They were so invited, as the world knows, and became formally, and I hope sincerely, reunited.

Roosevelt had a profound contempt for Woodrow Wilson, whom he described as a person wholly unequal to the demands of critical emergencies, with "a vision like a person looking through wire netting at a far-distant landscape." He said to me just before he sailed for Brazil: "I thought the administration of Taft about the last word in blundering and ineptitude, but since the advent of the Wilson administration, I am disposed to think of the Taft administration as having been eminently respectable."

If Roosevelt had lived he would have been nominated and elected President in 1920 and I am sure that this would have been a great blessing to the country, as he had the qualities of mind and heart to inspire the confidence of the people, an enormous aid in the solution of the great problems left by the war, and to regain many things lost by the instability, narrowness, and prejudice of the Wilson administration. He was an heroic figure and yet intensely human; full of vitality, goodfellowship, and the joy of living.

I passed some four months of vacation in the State of Washington, where I still held my legal residence. As the close of my leave of absence approached there appeared in the press an announcement of a general redistribution of our diplomatic service. In view of what the President had said to me I had good reason to anticipate that my name would be included in any general changes. My residence in Chile was altogether agreeable but my children were beginning to reach an age when it was imperative that they should have better educational advantages. On their account a move to Europe was very desirable and my failure to be named in the transfers was disappointing.

[89]

I went to Washington with the purpose of seeing the President and found that he was confined to his bed as the result of an injury received in an automobile accident while touring in Massachusetts. Secretary Cortelyou received me in the most friendly way, but said that the President could not see me at that time as he was engaged, although in bed, in an important conference with Senator Penrose relative to the Pennsylvania coal strike which was then in full swing. He said, however, that he personally knew that the President had me in mind and that he thought that it would be advantageous to leave a memorandum covering the matter of my transfer or promotion to a new post. I made such a memorandum and in it quoted precisely the language which the President had used with reference to my services, calling attention to the failure to include me in the recent changes in our diplomatic service.

After handing in this memorandum I went to New York with Mrs. Wilson and sailed for Chile via Panama.

CHAPTER XV

O N OUR arrival at Colon I found a mass of telegrams relating to a transfer to Greece, to which post, it appeared, the President had appointed me the day after I sailed from the port of New York. There were telegrams from the Department of State advising me of my transfer to Greece and granting me permission either to return to the United States or to proceed to Chile and go from there to Greece. There was also a copy of a personal telegram from Secretary Hay to my brother, John Lockwood Wilson, former senator from Washington, advising my declination of the transfer. Mr. Hay's telegram confirmed my own impression that the President had unwittingly given me a transfer which could hardly be considered a promotion. I sent a telegram to the Department of State declining the appointment, adding that I was proceeding to my post in Chile. I was not aware at this time that John B. Jackson, then counsellor of the American embassy in Berlin, had been appointed as my successor in Chile. As it happened, he declined the transfer; had he accepted, considerable confusion would have ensued. President Roosevelt thought my refusal to accept the transfer unappreciative and discourteous, and was greatly provoked with John B. Jackson for declining the appointment to Chile; in fact, he never forgave Jackson and persistently refused to promote him to a post commensurate with his services and ability.

The further history of this incident is interesting. Soon after my departure from Panama our minister to Japan, Mr. Buck, died suddenly and the President was called upon to appoint his successor. At that time there was quite a movement in the State of Washington for the development of trade between Washington ports and Japan, and it was believed that a citizen of the State of Washington, if appointed to the post of minister, might contribute to the strengthening of trade relations. Accordingly, the Washington delegation, understanding that there was more probability of securing my appointment than that of another person, went to the President with a request for my transfer to Japan. They met with an abrupt refusal; the President was very free in his expressions of dissatisfaction with my course in connection with the appointment to Greece and delivered himself of some positive, even rude, criticisms in the presence of a number of representatives of the press. What he had to say was, as usual, amusing and forceful, and the correspondents lost no time in retailing it to the public.

The publication brought on an unexpected dénouement. Walter H. Clark, who was at that time the correspondent of the New York *Sun* in Washington, perhaps enjoyed more confidential relations with Roosevelt than any other press representative. Clark and I were warm friends and I had written him fully my reasons for declining the post to Greece. He felt that I was being treated unjustly and without delay went to the White House. The President, who was engaged at that time in the useful but not especially interesting process of being shaved, sputtered through soap and brushes that I had been promoted to Greece and had treated him with discourtesy. Clark said, "On the contrary, Mr. President, he has been demoted and you have treated him with discourtesy." The President said: "By George, Clark, if that is so, I will make it all right." Later, after having made the proper investigation, he notified Clark that he was in the wrong and that he would take the earliest possible opportunity of repairing the injury he had done me; his promise was not confirmed until my appointment to Belgium.

Another incident worthy of note occurred during this stay at Panama.

At the time of my arrival at Colon an American fleet under command of my friend, Admiral Casey, was stationed on the Pacific side in the bay of Panama. In some way Admiral Casey knew of my arrival and telegraphed me an invitation to visit him on board his flagship the following day. As this day was the anniversary of our marriage and Mrs. Wilson expected me to pass it with her, I telegraphed my regrets, with explanations. The Admiral immediately replied inviting us both to come aboard the flagship, adding that he desired to talk with me about some official matters. This request it was not possible to decline and we crossed the isthmus and were taken on board the Admiral's flagship.

Soon after going aboard the Admiral took me into his cabin for the purpose, as he said, of having a consultation relative to the Panama situation. He explained that he had been sent to this port with sealed instructions to protect the Panama railway, but since his arrival he had not succeeded in eliciting further orders or explanations from Washington; that he had not been able fully to comply with the letter of his instructions and was doubtful how far he might interpret their spirit in connection with the frequent interruptions by Colombian soldiers of transit across the isthmus. It seemed to him, he said, that Washington wanted him to act on his own responsibility, a course sometimes adopted when the Washington executive cannot clearly vision the situation. The Admiral was prepared to accept the responsibility but wanted advice as to methods and limitations. It seemed to me it was our clear duty to maintain an uninterrupted transit across the isthmus and that inferentially the Admiral would be justified in taking steps to accomplish this end. I advised him to place marines in sufficient numbers on all the passenger trains to protect traffic and to punish summarily acts of violence. The Admiral declared his intention of following my advice and I heard after my departure that he had taken very stringent and effective measures which preserved uninterrupted communication between the two shores of the isthmus and that in the final event his course had been approved by the Washington government.

I met Admiral Casey frequently in after years at Seattle, Washington, New York, and in Brussels. He was a splendid type of the American naval officer.

When we stopped at Guayaquil on our way down the coast, I found there the American cartoonist, Tom Nast, whom President Roosevelt had recently appointed consul at this remote post. What unhappy fate had induced the government to separate this homesick genius from

his family and assign him to a post where his predecessors had been cut down like weeds by the relentless
scourge of yellow fever? Poor Nast! I found him lone-
some and unhappy. He came aboard the ship immediately on our arrival and sent in to me an illustrated
card, which, I believe, was the last cartoon drawn by him
during life. It depicted Nast bowing with cartoonistic
exaggeration before the American minister to Chile. He
remained on board the ship with us all day and late into
the evening, returning on shore just before we left, to
take immediately to his bed from which he never rose.
Before I reached my post in Chile I learned of his death.

Our last year in Chile was very largely repetition of the
pleasant years which had preceded it. We were obliged to
take a new house and furnish it, but as I did not expect a
long stay in the country we continued the arrangement of
keeping the legation offices separate from the residence,
a manner of living and working not at all satisfactory.

After our long stay at home we found many changes
in the diplomatic circle of Santiago. A new British minister, Sir Gerald Lowther, had succeeded my good friend,
Sir Audley Gosling, and was busily occupied with the
Chilo-Argentine differences.

Sir Gerald was a large, fine-looking man, a little inclined to grossness. He kept in condition by strenuous
exercise in the way of shooting, riding, polo, and tennis.
He played an excellent game of bridge and was fond of
giving and attending dinners. He was a man of solid
rather than brilliant attainments and I think understood
better how to do a thing than how not to do it. He was
not very highly educated but was resourceful, alert, and
vigilant. His bachelor habits and establishment made

possible an independent life and augmented his popularity with the diplomatic corps and the Chilean people. During the last years of our residence in Chile, Lowther belonged, with us, to a little circle of friends who met at one another's houses almost every night and before our final departure we grew to know and to like him very much. After I left Santiago he married Miss Alice Blythe of Philadelphia and was transferred to Morocco. He was very fortunate in being sent to Morocco, as complications began almost simultaneously with his arrival, giving him the opportunity to make the record which eventually led to his promotion to the embassy at Constantinople. He died about 1914, I think.

A new Italian colleague, Count A———, had arrived from Japan; Count A——— was a person of never-failing courtesy and kindness but altogether one of the oddest specimens I have met in diplomatic life. The ravages of many years had left him with but a scanty growth of hair on the top of his head, which he arranged with mathematical precision, in such a way as to cover a multitude of desert places. This, with a face made ghastly by the use of powder, gave him a startling appearance which was greatly heightened by his invariable habit of carrying and using lorgnettes. He was affected by a peculiar disease which sometimes manifested itself in a disturbing way. While engaged in conversation he would suddenly forget who he was and where he was and begin to ejaculate incoherently in some Italian dialect. These scenes occurred frequently, and sometimes at crowded assemblages produced considerable confusion.

A new Mexican colleague, Mr. R———, with an American wife, had presented his letters and was making the round of the diplomatic circle. This American alliance had not been born of the affinities, and the differences between the couple afforded a great deal of diversion to the diplomatic corps and Santiago society. If one called and saw only Madame, one was entertained by highly pungent observations on the character of her absent lord and master. If, on the other hand, one found His Excellency, the minister, in, one learned without reserve of Madame's shiftless habits and generally reprehensible conduct. R—— was a most excellent cook and he frequently prepared below stairs the dinners with which he regaled his colleagues to a certain stage of the menu and then, divesting himself of his culinary attire, would rush frantically upstairs and enjoy their appreciation of his gastronomic creations. It frequently happened that while he was engaged in frying below his wife was engaged in roasting him above.

Mr. R—— was also quite a poultry fancier and gave a great deal of his time to the study of the physical, mental, and moral culture of fowls. At one time he invented some sort of a mechanical arrangement for accelerating the production of chickens and eggs, but the practical application of the invention led to a revolt in the chicken world, and I was gravely informed by Madame R—— that all of the hens had declined to lay for the purpose of expressing their disapproval of the tyrannical perversion of the laws of nature by the mephistophelean R——.

Upon another occasion I called and found the minister absent and was informed by Madame that he had taken out the family carriage and, after filling it inside and outside with poultry of all descriptions, had taken them out for an airing through the public thoroughfares; her comment on this performance was that her husband was a rank lunatic.

The Austrian government had just established a legation at Santiago and had sent over as its first representative Count Leonardo Starzenski, accompanied by a Secretary of Legation, Count Otto Trauttmansdorff, who then began a subsequently brilliant diplomatic career. There was nothing unusual about either minister or secretary. Both were quiet and reasonably intelligent persons, greatly bored with the life in Santiago but not openly expressing their opinions. The astonishing feature of their *ménage* and indeed the most curious personality I have met in diplomatic life was the Countess Starzenska, otherwise called Princess Gorgias. She was extremely eccentric and peculiar and, in spite of the physical disadvantage of extreme corpulency, a most attractive woman. She commenced her career in Santiago by immediately making visits on people who were supposed to constitute the first society, without having previously submitted to the form of an introduction. She then began giving a series of dinners—and very good dinners they were—to which she invited in succession all the people on whom she had called. Many of those invited, of course, declined but some accepted and Madame la Comtesse frequently sat down to table surrounded by guests of whose names and origin she knew nothing; this circumstance, however, did not interfere with her enjoyment of the affair or interrupt the steady flow of her exhaustless wit. She enlivened these occasions with good-natured but caustic comments upon the life, character, and habits of distinguished Santiago people. Her witticisms soon found circulation among those who had not participated in her hospitality, with the result that among those whose lives would not endure close inspection her dinners were awaited with about the same feeling of apprehension that one awaits an explosion of dynamite. Before she had been six months in Santiago she knew all the scandals of its society and the habits and history of everyone who was supposed to be worth knowing. She gave remarkable entertainments following her dinners, and I have frequently seen supposedly dignified diplomats performing all sorts of antics in incongruous costumes or occupying positions on the floor neither graceful nor engaging. The principal leaders in this pleasantry were Lowther and Van der Heyde, the Belgian minister. Lowther especially was an accomplished mimic and clown, and he usually took a leading part in these affairs. The Countess, however, was a tyrannical stage manager, and on one occasion, not being entirely pleased with the histrionic delineations of the versatile Van der Heyde, she applied, by way of correction and admonition, a sound kick upon that part of the anatomy which is more honoured in the breech than in the observance. This led to a *froideur* in the relations between Austria and Belgium, but apologies and explanations brought about a *rapprochement*.

The Countess was given not only to doing but to saying unconventional and embarrassing things—things that no one else could have said or done without losing the last remnant of prestige. It may be remembered by some of his erstwhile colleagues that, while her husband was serving as secretary of the Austrian embassy at Rome, she was the chief actor in a scene which scandalized the sensibilities of the ultra-mondaine elements of Roman society. This was upon the occasion of a religious festival celebrated in the presence of the Pope and to which only chiefs of diplomatic missions were invited. Madame la Comtesse announced her intention, *nolens volens*, of being present. At the appointed hour she stationed herself at the door through which the diplomats were to enter and, at a moment when the crowd was very great, cried out in strident tones: "*Je suis la maîtresse du Pape, je demands l'entrée.*" The horrified attendants tried to quiet her but she continued to repeat the phrase without intermission and eventually, to quiet her, she was admitted. Just such escapades as this she repeated at frequent intervals in Santiago, until she became the chief topic of conversation and the principal source of diversion. The Starzenskis left Santiago before us, with the hope of being transferred to a European post, but their hopes were never realized and they both finally perished at the hands of the Bolsheviki in Transylvania.

Another peculiar diplomatic character was Van der Heyde, the Belgian minister, a person of a certain amount of harmless self-conceit and over-sensitive about any apparent lack of consideration or deference which he deemed to be his due. I recall an absurd incident in this connection.

Van der Heyde lived, as is frequently the case, in the same house where the British chancellery was located, the chancellery being just above his apartments and opening into the same court. The private secretary of the British minister, Mr. Alan Kerr, lived in the chancellery but had not neighbourly relations with Van der Heyde. Upon one occasion, when they were attending dinner at the same house, some difficulty occurred between them, and Kerr, breathing vengeance, left the entertainment some time in advance of Van der Heyde's departure. Going to the chancellery he secured a large orange, attached a string to it, and opening his window laid in wait for the unsuspecting Van der Heyde, who finally arrived enlivened with wine and other intoxications of the evening.

After giving him ample time to undress and get into bed the wily Kerr lowered the orange until it was opposite Van der Heyde's window in the court and began swinging it backward and forward, producing, at regular intervals, with the impact of the orange against the window, a most unusual and lugubrious noise. After this had continued for some time Van der Heyde rose, in scanty attire, and went into the court, but of course found nothing. This performance was repeated three times and finally Van der Heyde, in a great state of fright, rose with his revolver in his hand and made such an outcry that he wakened some of the servants, who made a zealous search. Van der Heyde's nerves were entirely upset by this time and he left the house to seek refuge in a hotel.

Early the next morning, anticipating a later visit to me from Van der Heyde, Kerr turned up and gleefully recited a picturesque account of the affair, swearing me to secrecy. About an hour afterward Van der Heyde, evidently very much wrought up, put in an appearance and told me of his blood-curdling experience of the night before. Not unwilling to contribute something to the gaiety of the hour, I asked him if he attributed the noise to a supernatural agency. He said, "Not at all"; but from his appearance it was quite evident that he did, and to carry the joke a little farther I then reminded him that Fauconvalt, his predecessor, had died in the same rooms

[101]

and that a former British chargé d'affaires had also died there, and that once a man had been murdered for 40,000 pesos in the house. Before night he was telling his troubles all over the city and announcing his intentions of leaving the house.

By this time I thought that the joke had been carried far enough and I accordingly sent another member of the diplomatic corps to tell him the truth. He was, of course, greatly outraged and mortified and came to me to take my opinion as to what kind of punishment should be meted out to Kerr. His inclinations ran in the direction of a duel or a personal castigation. I reminded him that it was beneath his dignity to challenge Kerr, a mere private secretary, and that in a physical encounter he would probably get the worst of it, as Kerr was more than six feet tall and in every way his physical superior. Following my advice he finally went to Lowther, the British minister, who, after hearing his story, told him that in his opinion it was bad policy to advertise the fact that Kerr had made an "ass" of him but that he would see to it that Kerr made the *amende honorable*. This was done and a state of armed neutrality was maintained thereafter.

Our South American colleagues were changed so frequently and were so often of the same stamp—usually courteous, punctilious, and pleasantly indolent—that they have left very few lasting impressions on my mind. The Argentine Republic and Brazil usually were represented by men of experience and character.

CHAPTER XVI

The Alsop case and diplomatic pressure—Final return to the United States—Observations on Chile—National University bestows degrees of Philosophy, Humanities, and Fine Arts—Complimentary accompanying letter of Chilean Minister of Foreign Affairs.

THE relations between the government of Chile and the government of the United States at this time were all that could be desired; there was not a cloud upon the political horizon. One diplomatic incident may be worthy of note. During the time of my predecessors, Mr. Egan and Mr. Strobel, the famous Alsop case, which related to the seizure of American property in Bolivia during the war of the Pacific, for which the Chilean government had assumed responsibility under the treaty of peace, had been persistently pressed for settlement.

In the earlier days of my charge in Chile the correspondence relative to this case was desultory and perfunctory; evidently it was the desire of the government at Washington to keep the case alive but not to become unduly excited about it. Without any warning and apparently without being moved by any new facts, the State Department all at once began to send me very urgent instructions relative to the case. Notes in the sense of these instructions were duly transmitted to the Chilean foreign office but apparently produced no great amount of commotion there.

While the debate was proceeding with more or less activity, Mr. Irving B. Dudley, our minister to Peru, came to Chile, ostensibly for the purpose of visiting me, but really in the hope that he might contribute in some way to a lessening of the friction which then existed between Chile and Peru. At the time of Mr. Dudley's visit, Mr. X———, a very young but unusually able man, was Minister of Foreign Relations. He was extremely cordial to Mr. Dudley and among other courtesies he invited us to spend the week-end with him at his country estate. On Sunday, while I was walking in the garden, and my American colleague and Mr. X——— were engaged in discussion, I received a cablegram, forwarded from the legation, which placed me in an embarrassing position. The cablegram contained instructions relative to the Alsop case, very direct and unnecessarily severe. There was nothing for me to do but to carry out the instructions and I called Mr. X——— aside and read a paraphrase of the cablegram to him.

As I anticipated, he became excited and indignant and said: "But, Mr. Minister, your government does not understand this question."

I replied: "That may be true, Your Excellency, but it cannot be because of lack of opportunity to study it, as it has been under consideration since before Your Excellency was born."

The appeal to his young excellency's sense of humour was not in vain and an unpleasant incident was avoided. Very soon after, the government of Chile made through me a definite offer in settlement of the case, which our government did not consider adequate and declined to accept. The discussion of this case covered several volumes and involved some nice questions of international law; it finally reached a satisfactory adjustment.

In the spring of 1904, Mrs. Wilson returned home for the purpose of placing our sons in school. At that time Spanish was their usual language and they rarely conversed in English, speaking it with a strong Spanish accent. We were gratified with their fluency in Spanish but thought it time for them to get rid of their foreign accent in English.

In the middle of June I left for home with the definite purpose of not returning again to Chile. It was with the profoundest regret that I left this pleasant and hospitable country in which we had spent so many happy years. I carried away with me a great affection and respect for the Chilean people and retain the deepest interest in their affairs to this hour. That these sentiments were in some measure reciprocated is evidenced by the circumstance that eight years after my departure the National University of Chile bestowed upon me the degree of Doctor of Philosophy, Humanities, and Fine Arts, and that in transmitting the diploma to me the Chilean Minister of Foreign Relations expressed the following sentiment:

Chilean Legation,
Mexico, September 20, 1911.

MR. AMBASSADOR:

I have the honour to advise Your Excellency that the Faculty of Philosophy, Humanities, and Fine Arts of the University of Chile, and its session of the 12th of July last, in just recognition of the merits and intellectual gifts of

Your Excellency and your erudite labours, which have contributed to the study of American history, voted unanimously to bestow upon you the title of Honorary Member of said body.

On its part the Department of Public Instruction of Chile, taking note of the honour conferred upon you, passed a resolution to send Your Excellency the diploma of the degree conferred upon you which I have the honour to remit to you, together with the note which accompanied it.

The government of Chile, in remitting these documents to me and in advising me of the resolution adopted by the Faculty of Philosophy, Humanities, and Fine Arts of the University, in a note dated August 18th last, makes the following official statement:

"In transmitting the resolution adopted by the said institution to His Excellency, Mr. Wilson, you will have the goodness to make known to the distinguished American diplomat the great satisfaction with which the Government of Chile approves of this designation, which it considers not only a just recognition of his intellectual gifts but a cordial testimonial of appreciation of the constant proofs of affection with which His Excellency, Mr. Wilson, has earned the gratitude of our country."

In remitting to Your Excellency the documents alluded to and in complying with the special instructions which my Government has given me, it is particularly pleasing to me to send you my cordial congratulations for the distinguished and merited honour which the Government of Chile has bestowed upon you, and to renew the expression of my high consideration.

ANSELMO HEVIA R.

To His Excellency,
  Mr. Henry Lane Wilson,
    Ambassador of the United States of America.

The future of Chile cannot be uncertain. With the virile patriotism at the foundation of the national character, nourished and invigorated by a temperate climate and the free atmosphere of the seas, she must move onward—she must expand—she must grow in power, wealth, and, perhaps, sharing in the experience of all strong nations, in territory.

The disturbed condition of South American politics makes Chile a strong military power; but I am sure that the formidable front which she presents is more in the way of a defense of that which she has taken in the past and holds to-day than an indication of future aggression. Perhaps—very probably—obedient to that immutable law which compels all vigorous nations to grow without pause, she may at some remote period, as the result of a war not of her own seeking, make further addition to her territories; but, at the present time, the policy of her best statesmen is not in the direction of further aggression and absorption; the real problems to-day are of internal development and improvement, education and uplifting of the masses.

She needs to connect by railways and roads the vast mineral deposits of the north with the great central valley in which is situated her population and wealth; she needs to bind to herself closely by iron bands the great stretch of country from the river Bio Bio to the Straits of Magellan; she needs more schools, more hospitals, better harbours, a comprehensive system for the enlightenment and moral elevation of the masses of the people. To this great task the best statesmanship of Chile is addressing itself with patriotic energy, and for its accomplishment needs peace and rest from the alarums of war.

In this little republic rests the best aspirations and possibilities of the Latin race in America, and I am sure that time will prove her equal to the task which is set before her. She is moving out of the shadows of the conditions bequeathed to her by long years of Spanish régime, with her vision fixed upon the best standards of modern civilization.

CHAPTER XVII

Arrival at Washington and interview with Roosevelt—Assignment to political work and report—Frank talk with the President—Unofficial press notice of my appointment and protest of Washington senators—The President's fine attitude.

ON MY arrival in Washington I went to see President Roosevelt who, after talking with me at some length in the recess of his office, asked me to return again at 9:30 in the evening. At our evening session the President resumed the discussion of the Chilo-Argentine situation, evidently wishing to master all its details. After we had finished with this he asked me how I expected to pass my vacation, and I replied that if he desired me to take part in the campaign I was willing and prepared. He answered: "By George, I would like to have your services as well as those of some other diplomats who are good campaigners, but I am afraid it would not be a proper thing." Supposing the matter to be closed I was about to say that I would take advantage of my leave of absence to go to the State of Washington, when he interrupted me, saying: "There is something you might do. In the first place, I would like to know precisely how Jim Hill stands in this contest. Can you find out?" I replied in the affirmative and was congratulating myself on my simple assignment when he said that he also wanted me to make a thorough analysis of political conditions and requirements

[109]

in the states of Indiana, Wisconsin, Minnesota, North Dakota, Montana, Idaho, and Washington and to give him, personally, a full report with recommendations. My vacation had vanished but, endeavouring to save something from the wreckage, I intimated that I would like to have an additional sixty days at the conclusion of my work. He very affably concurred in this suggestion, adding that after this time had expired I might look forward to a transfer to another post.

Without delay I began the work assigned to me, visiting in the order named Indiana, Wisconsin, Minnesota, North Dakota, Montana, Washington, and Idaho, and at the end of six weeks returned to Washington and laid before the President a written report covering the political conditions in these states, an analysis of the trend of public opinion among labouring men, business men, and farmers, an estimate of majorities and recommendations concerning the kind of literature and speakers needed for the campaign.

The President was evidently pleased with this report, though he questioned my estimates of majorities. I remember that my estimate of the Republican majority in Indiana was forty thousand. This he thought was much too high, but in the election the state gave ninety thousand; all the other states doubled the majorities given in my estimate. The President read the report in my presence, said it was the best thing that he had had so far, and that he would make it the basis for the campaign in those states. Then turning from political matters without any ceremony he said: "I have been expecting to send you to Mexico, but Mr. Hitt [then chairman of the Committee on Foreign Affairs of the House] thinks he would like to go and, while I think he should remain where he is, his services have been of such a character that a simple request from him amounts to a command. In any event, I intend that you shall have a promotion." As matters turned out Mr. Hitt remained in Congress and I went to a European post, to be assigned five years later to Mexico, which as a diplomatic post had greatly advanced in rank in the meantime.

After this interview with the President I returned to the State of Washington, hoping to be of some service in a quiet way to my brother, John L. Wilson, who was then a candidate for the United States Senate. After this contest had resulted in the election of Mr. Samuel Piles, I wrote Mr. Francis B. Loomis, Assistant Secretary of State, to ascertain the intentions of the President with reference to my transfer, and received a reply indicating that it might be necessary for me to return temporarily to Chile and go from there to a European post. As I had left Chile with a definite intention of not resuming my residence there, the prospect of returning to set up another establishment was extremely distasteful. I telegraphed Mr. Loomis to this effect, adding that if it were necessary for me to return to Chile in order to remain in the diplomatic service, I would tender my resignation. I had an immediate reply cautioning me against tendering my resignation and indicating that my transfer to Europe would be satisfactorily arranged. Soon after it was unofficially announced in the press, in discussing changes in the diplomatic service, that I might be sent to Belgium. This brought about an amusing incident.

Senators Foster and Ankeny then represented the State of Washington in the upper House of Congress. Neither of them was, on account of political differences, friendly with me and they carried their opposition to the extent of going to the White House to protest against my appointment. Senator Foster afterward told me that the President received their protest very coldly and said very vehemently: "I am not appointing Mr. Wilson from the State of Washington but from one post in the diplomatic service to another. Candidly, I think you gentlemen, instead of coming here to protest against the appointment of Mr. Wilson, ought to be here for the purpose of thanking me for the promotion, for honourable and useful services rendered to the government, by a citizen of the State of Washington. In any event I shall promote him." Senator Foster informed me that he and his colleague left the presidential presence in anything but a state of elation. Foster said: "He is a real man and though I was opposed to your appointment, I am proud of him for his loyalty."

On my arrival in Washington, without asking for an appointment, I went immediately to see the President. When he came into the audience room, after speaking with one or two persons, he discovered me and without ceremony ejaculated loudly, "Well, Mr. Wilson, I am very glad to see you and I expect soon to congratulate you on your appointment to Belgium. Let me express the hope that the next time you are under consideration for promotion you may have some political support." It might be added here that not long afterward the newly elected Senator Piles, whom I had opposed in the election, went to the White House and thanked the President for my appointment and assured him that it met with universal approval in the State of Washington. I record here with some pardonable satisfaction that a few days afterward, when the actual appointment was made, the President announced it to the press in these words: "This appointment is made for meritorious services performed and not for political considerations."

CHAPTER XVIII

Departure for Belgium—Incidents of voyage—Arrival at Brussels and delicate situation—Compiègne—Official presentation to King Leopold and other ceremonies—Luncheon given by the King—Early estimates of Leopold—The Brussels golf links.

A S OUR children were still in school I determined to start alone for Belgium, leaving Mrs. Wilson to follow later. I accordingly embarked in the month of April on the Red Star Line Steamer *Vaterland*, carrying a large and quite distinguished list of passengers.

Among others there were two American consuls-general whose conception of the dignity of the service to which they were attached was not appreciable. A generous affection for alcohol at all hours of the day and night and great activity in the pursuit of sundry ubiquitous and unclassified females afforded a good deal of entertainment and gossip to the ship.

One night after I had retired the room steward aroused me with an invitation from these two American officials to come below and participate in some gaieties which were being celebrated in their staterooms. The prospect of any sort of entertainment aboard ship is usually welcome, and a little later I went below and found a very motley assemblage in my hosts' staterooms and in the passageways approaching them. The occasion was strictly bibulous and wholly convivial; it was entertaining, too, for on a pedestal in the corner of the farther stateroom one of the consuls was busy making a speech, interspersed with quotations from Shakespeare and extracts from personal letters of Theodore Roosevelt. As the inebriated speaker made quotations from President Roosevelt's letters, he tossed them over to the audience to be read. Some of these letters would have been politically damaging had they become public, so I quietly gathered them all together and returned them on the morrow to their indiscreet owner. This incident was reported to Washington by someone who was present and later, when the consul was a candidate for another appointment, Secretary Knox called upon me for its confirmation. I declined to confirm the story, as it seemed to me my official obligations could not be stretched to that extent. The appointment, however, was not made and this person afterward lost all standing in the service.

The most interesting part of this voyage was at its finish, the trip up what Goldsmith calls the "sluggish Scheldt." The sensation of riding on the water above roofs and steeples is a novel one; far away to the east and north stretched the fields of Flanders, dotted here and there with quaint villages and medieval churches, the battle ground of centuries—the garden of the poppies.

Arriving at Brussels, I took up my temporary residence at the Hotel Flandre and on the next day, in response to a telephone message, the minister, Mr. Lawrence Townsend, called. He informed me that he was not expecting to surrender the post for some two weeks and intimated that my presence in Brussels prior to his retirement might prove embarrassing. Though fully authorized to take charge of the legation on my arrival, it was not possible to be ungracious to such kind and charming people as the Townsends and I decided to make a two weeks' visit to Paris. Paris is always interesting to me for the first few days but soon palls. Visits to the art galleries, churches, theatres, and the promenades on the boulevard are endurable, and even enjoyable for a while, but fatigue soon ensues.

There was a diversion—one night I arranged with a Swiss guide "who had personally conducted John Hay" to make the rounds of "Paris by gaslight." One does this part of the tourist programme not because it is interesting, but because it is the custom. After a rather hectic experience in visiting wild and woolly places (a very expensive operation even in pre-war days) I finally hoisted the white flag and my accomplished Swiss guide conducted me to Maxim's for relaxation and refreshment. The gaieties at that hour were in full sway, but my sole purpose was to obtain refreshment and I proceeded to this end without delay, relying confidently on my incognito. Having dined well I was idly watching the throng when quite a hubbub arose in the rear of the place. Out of this confusion there emerged a number of young men in military formation who paraded through the place shouting "*viva el Señor Ministro*" and finally, to my horror, stopped immediately in front of me. They were Chilean youths who had recognized a familiar figure and were just sufficiently exhilarated to publish the fact to the world. My incognito was lost and I beat a hasty retreat.

I gladly left Paris to visit friends at Compiègne, the ancient seat of the Dukes of Orleans, occasionally the home of royalty and recently marking the advance point of the German drive on Paris. Here amid delightful surroundings and pleasant French and American friends, I passed some days, then returning to Brussels to be the guest of the Townsends, who soon after took their departure, much to my regret and to that of a large circle of friends. The Townsends were deservedly popular in court and society circles of Brussels and they were kindly remembered always.

Soon after the Townsends' departure King Leopold returned to Belgium and I was notified by the grand marshal of the court, Count D'Oultremont, that His Majesty would be pleased to receive me in audience. The official receptions of diplomatic officers in Belgium, which adheres with tenacity to the traditions and forms established by centuries of practice, are markedly in contrast with the simpler military ceremonial employed in the Latin-American republics. In the afternoon of May 6th, the royal coach, a magnificent affair of gilt, gold, and velvet, followed by another gorgeous coach, intended for my "suite," preceded and followed by outriders in red and gold trappings, drew up and the grand marshal of the court made formal entry into the legation, announcing that he had come to escort me into the presence of His Majesty. I descended the legation stairway, clad in the customary suit of solemn black, and expressed a willingness to be led into the presence of His Majesty. We thereupon entered the Barnum-Van Hamburg coach, followed by the enthusiastic expressions of approval of chambermaids and small street urchins, and proceeded to the royal palace.

Our entry into the royal palace was rather bewildering, but I restrained unguarded impulses to salute the footmen and gorgeous flunkies who decorated the royal stairway like a blush of the Milky Way. Ushered into the royal antechamber, I was given the right hand of fellowship by numerous gentlemen of the court to whose greetings, expressed in courteous French, I replied in excellent English. Very soon the signal of the King's readiness to receive me was made and the bodies of all the dukes, counts, and princes assumed a peculiar angle, their eyes cast downward in presumed reverence for His Majesty. Entering the royal presence I found His Majesty standing about the centre of the room. I bowed once upon entering, once halfway, and a third time when I was "up against it." His Majesty, however, was the least ceremonious of all his court. He immediately offered me his hand and began talking. We discussed President Roosevelt, American politics, American commerce, the navy, educational systems, and the Kongo question. The interview lasted fully an hour and the King's wide information, charming manners, and almost American sense of humour made it extremely interesting.

After this ceremony I began to make my official calls, spending the greater part of a week in discharging these and in keeping various dinner and luncheon engagements.

On the day following my reception the King gave what is called the annual Garden Party at his Palace of Laeken. This affair is unique in character as it is given in what is perhaps the greatest conservatory in the world; it is of vast extent, the roof exceedingly high, permitting the cultivation and growth not only of plants and flowers but of tropical trees. An impressive effect was produced by the variegated tropical growth, the magnificent toilets of the ladies, and the picturesque uniform of the Belgian military and the diplomatic corps. Only the most distinguished Belgians are invited to this function and foreigners receive invitations only upon the request of their diplomatic representative. After forming into two lines, ladies of the diplomatic corps on one side and gentlemen on the other, the King's presence was announced and with an all-embracing bow His Majesty went down the line "à la Virginia Reel," speaking to each lady as he passed, but, as I noted, longer to the good-looking than to the homely ones. This process was repeated down the other line, the King conversing for a greater or less time with each of the diplomatic representatives. Following the King, the Countess of Flanders—first lady of the court—passed down both lines and after her Prince Albert, the heir apparent to the throne, and the Princess Elizabeth.

Soon after this, His Majesty, obedient to court etiquette, became hungry, and passed into the buffet room, whither he was promptly pursued by the diplomatic corps and the Belgian nobility. After this function the official world gradually faded away.

Two days after this ceremony I was officially advised that the Count and Countess of Flanders, brother and sister-in-law of the King, and parents of Prince Albert, would be pleased to receive me in audience. The interview had some rather amusing features; His Royal Highness was very deaf and her Royal Highness had to shriek my courteous expressions into his ear. He replied in English but apparently without having understood a word. Triangular conversations are not always unmixed pleasures, but the infirmities of the great are not permitted to bar them from official duties, and not infrequently the performance of duty affords entertainment to a gaping

[119]

world. The Countess of Flanders, an exceedingly dignified person, was withal an excellent mother and wife and a model of virtue.

Following the order prescribed by etiquette I paid my official visit to His Royal Highness, Prince Albert and the Princess Elizabeth, thus beginning an acquaintance with these charming people which was to constitute one of the pleasant features of our life in Belgium.

On the following Thursday, when I had concluded my official visits, King Leopold gave me a luncheon of twenty-five covers served in the royal banquet hall. Upon this occasion I sat at the right of the King, and as he devoted himself exclusively to me, I had a further opportunity of studying the measure of his information and the character of his mind. He was undoubtedly more of a master of the art of conversation than any royal personage to whom I was subsequently presented. He impressed me as being mentally alert and tremendously acquisitive, but through all his conversation there ran a thread of cynical pessimism; his range of information was extensive and his intimate knowledge of remote things was remarkable. In the course of our conversation His Majesty asked me how I liked Brussels; of course I made the usual and proper response, and he then asked me what there was I did not like; I replied that I did not like "the climate nor the absence of golf links." He said: "I am afraid I cannot do anything about the climate but golf links are not impossible if you really are interested in the matter." I replied: "I think Your Majesty owes me something for having deprived me of the pleasure of your acquaintance for more than thirty days." He had kept me waiting for this period and enjoyed the application, saying that he would take me in his automobile to see the site which he proposed to set aside. This promise was fully carried out; the King very soon after made a gift of his Château Ravenstein to the club, and when it was formally opened I was given precedence in leading off at the first tee. The links afterward were frequented from all over Europe.

CHAPTER XIX

Personnel of the legation—Robert Woods Bliss—Snyers—Diplomatic colleagues

THE official preliminaries of my new post having been complied with, the work of the legation demanded my attention.

The secretary of the legation, Mr. X———, was the son of a distinguished American general of the Civil War through a union with a European lady of unknown antecedents. How it had been possible to secure the appointment of this young man to the diplomatic service was a mystery. He was unfitted for any chancellery work, lacking in real Americanism, and during his brief career, after my arrival, became involved in a scandalous controversy with his wife, a most excellent person, who afterward secured legal separation from him. The peculiar antics of this person became such a source of annoyance that I eventually had to secure his removal to another post. His successor, Mr. Robert Woods Bliss, who came to the legation from the embassy at St. Petersburg, was a distinct improvement and displayed then and in his later career qualities of a high order. Mr. Bliss remained in Brussels for about four years and, with an attractive wife, furnished a real asset in the official work and social life of the legation. He was afterward secretary of our legation at Buenos Aires, first secretary of our embassy in Paris, chargé d'affaires in Netherlands, third Assistant Secretary of State, and is at present American minister to Sweden.

Although the legation was supposed to have a secretary, the work of the chancellery was almost entirely in the hands of the clerk, a Belgian, Mr. Adolph Snyers, who was my competent, loyal, and efficient assistant for nearly five years.

Snyers had been the confidential clerk of the American legation at Brussels since the Grant administration. His long connection had imbued him with a sense of ownership which became especially assertive in matters affecting the prestige of the government of the United States or of any of the legation personnel. In many things he was more American than the Americans; his American patriotism burning fiercely all afternoon, while his Belgian patriotism had full sway during the morning hours when he was employed in the office of the Belgian National Railway. The hours of his employment with the railway administration, however, were hours of toil, devoid of gaiety or interesting incident; his life as a man of the world, of the literati and of mentor and adviser began with his arrival at the legation about 11:30. Then he became a new being and, after he had disposed of the dry routine of the legation's daily grind, accompanying me to luncheon either in the residence or at a convenient restaurant, he was quickly metamorphosed into a bird of gorgeous plumage; reminiscences of my predecessors, of famous Americans who had passed through Brussels, scholarly excursions into the realm of French and Belgian literature, recital of thrilling episodes in Belgian history, accurate descriptions of Belgian antiquities, wise but partisan impressions of Belgian politics, antagonism to

[123]

and apprehension of Germany, warm affection for France, suggestions and gossip, slipped trippingly from his lips.

Sometimes, Snyers, a gay companion, went along with me to Bruges or Antwerp or Ghent. He knew the history and romance of all the old monuments and palaces; with loving hand he painted Bruges with its melancholy canals, its palaces, hoary with the stain of ages, its ancient religious edifices over which the touch of medievalism still lingered and told the story of the great families which in other days had made Belgian history. Gaily he joined with me in the picturesque throngs which crowded the beautiful river Meuse from Liège by Namur on up to the quaint little town of Dinant which, clustered on the steep cliffs of the river, looked much like the gingerbread towns in children's play books.

Snyers remained with me to the end of my term, always useful, always entertaining, and always full of life and spirit. His strong emotional nature overcame him at the moment I went away and the last object I saw upon the docks of Antwerp was Snyers weeping convulsively. His subsequent career with a new minister and secretary was not altogether a happy one, as there was moderate sympathy for his whimsies and peculiarities. Two or three years later he died suddenly and I heard afterward that one of his sons was killed in the invasion of Belgium by the Germans. He was a faithful official, a good friend, and a real American in spirit, if not in the flesh.

Brussels, at the time of my residence there, was looked upon as a post where ministers were graduated out of the ministerial drab into the ambassadorial purple. One usually found there men who had been marked by their governments for promotion to other posts and possibly for distinguished diplomatic careers. Often, however, the hopes of distinguished advancement were broken upon the wheel of fortune. Political changes at home frequently place the dispensing power in the hands of officials not keenly appreciative of the services and prestige of diplomatic representatives adhering to different political tenets. In spite of political changes at home the larger part of the diplomatic representatives in Brussels are promoted to embassies.

Sir Constantine Phipps represented the British government at the time of our arrival; a man of brilliant attainments and distinguished services, who had put the brakes on his headlong career by marrying a Russian lady whom King Edward VII, it was said, had declined to receive at the Annual Drawing-room Reception. I never knew the reason for the royal austerity, but soon after we came to Brussels Sir Constantine's official life was terminated. Sir Constantine was a likeable person, entertaining, witty, and abounding with anecdotal reminiscences. He had served as a secretary of the British embassy in Washington during the time of Lincoln, and he diverted many a tedious hour by interesting stories of American public characters. These stories he illustrated by imitating, with more or less fidelity, the supposed twang, whang, or bang of American idiomatic vagaries. He told Negro minstrel stories with great gusto and in a supposed darky vernacular. One of the amusing features of the Phipps's dinners was the Phipps impersonation of King Leopold making the royal circuit at a court ball of the diplomatic corps and court functionaries. He imitated with admirable accuracy the King's strong German accent in French, accompanying his imitation of

[125]

confidential conversations with diplomats by a clever mimicry of the King's physical peculiarities. Of course, these innocent entertainments were confidential, as otherwise Sir Constantine's position in Brussels might have become uncomfortable. Soon after his retirement from the service Sir Constantine died, but what became of the Russian Lady Phipps, I never knew.

Sir Arthur Hardinge, who was generally spoken of as the coming man in the British diplomatic service, succeeded Sir Constantine Phipps. He had taken first honours at Oxford over Lord Cronemore and the Earl of Curzon, and his scholarly attainments were naturally of high order; as a philologist he was believed to be the most accomplished man in the British diplomatic service; he spoke a number of oriental dialects, including Persian, Turkish, and Hindustani; he also spoke with ease and fluency Spanish, German, Italian, and during his residence in Belgium mastered Flemish. He possessed that rare gift among the English of brilliant and forceful oratory, and in an oratorical effort he was just as much at home in the French language as in English. These useful qualities, made the more remarkable by a kind heart and a sincere and frank disposition, were somewhat marred by eccentricities which diverted attention from his real merits.

In conjunction with Sir Arthur I conducted the Kongo discussion with the Belgian Government and the King's special Kongo representative. In this discussion I found him, as I did at other times, very able and convincing in presentation of the case, but not at all resourceful in bringing forward new material. His conception of diplomacy was that it was an intrigue, a view which might have been advantageous in oriental countries but was a handicap in Europe.

Late in life Sir Arthur had married an excellent lady of about his own age, who, though a good and admirable woman, was nevertheless as absent-minded and casual as the minister himself. Her peculiarities sometimes led her into rather amusing *contretemps*, affording decided entertainment to the youthful and not too assiduously employed secretaries. Upon one occasion, being about to give a formal dinner, she unfortunately dated her invitations one month later than the date upon which the dinner was to be given. Upon having the mistake called to her attention she corrected some of the invitations but not all, a circumstance which led to the arrival of part of the guests upon one date and would have led to the arrival of the others upon the date fixed but for timely intervention and explanation. Upon another occasion, when it was intended to give a very formal official dinner, she invited part of her guests by card and part verbally, intending to confirm the verbal invitations by formal written ones. The dinner which followed had some rather startling features not anticipated in the original programme, for it appeared that the d'Arenbergs and the de Lignes, who, as the Capulets and Montagues of Brussels, were never invited at the same time, arrived simultaneously, and during the evening contributed a good deal of electricity to the occasion. In the midst of these awful moments it was discovered that the cook, an importation from Albion, had imbibed, not wisely but too well, of the vintage of sunny Champagne, and while the guests were gathering, became uproariously drunk on the front doorstep, claiming diplomatic exemption. Hurried arrangements and substitutes were improvised, but the dinner did not materialize, for it was discovered that the burgomaster of Brussels, M. Jean de Mot, had not arrived. The first secretary of the legation, Percy Windham, being appealed to, put himself in communication by telephone with the burgomaster, who said that he had received a verbal invitation from Lady Hardinge which she had said would be confirmed by a formal invitation. As no such formal inviation had reached him he was at that moment engaged in eating his dinner at his own table and declined to participate in more formal affairs. When I arrived, a heavy gloom, accentuated by the d'Arenberg-de Ligne incident, had settled down upon the guests, but I was amply repaid for my attendance by having the story recounted to me by the immensely entertained secretaries. Lady Hardinge was frequently given to such lapses but she compensated much by her charming, if naïve, manners and real kindness of heart.

The Russian minister, Count de Giers, a son of Russia's famous Minister of Foreign Affairs De Giers, was dean of the diplomatic corps. He had been some twelve years minister at Brussels and it was supposed he was kept there as sort of an official observer of conditions in Germany, France, and Great Britain, and he was *au courant* of the social and political affairs of western Europe. He had recently married a lovely Russian woman of distinguished family and unusual intelligence, who made the legation a very delightful place and who was universally popular with the diplomatic corps and Belgian society. De Giers was afterward made ambassador to Vienna and was there, I believe, at the outbreak of the World War.

During our entire stay in Brussels the German government was represented by Count Von Walwitz, a Saxon nobleman, who had married the daughter of Von Bülow. Von Walwitz was a person of military training and tastes and evidently intended that his colleagues should so understand. His dinners were given with a military precision that gave one the impression of being on the parade ground. He expected each course to be served within a specified period, and in order that there might be no failure in this respect, he guarded the serving with his watch in his hand, timing each course; the mere circumstance that some of his guests might, out of deference to the laws of proper mastication, proceed leisurely with the course, interfered not the slightest with this rigid régime, for when the number of minutes allotted to each course expired, the dishes were removed willy nilly. At the conclusion of these festive affairs the trembling guests were led into the drawing room and saturated with huge mugs of Saxon beer which they were expected not only to drink but to like. Von Walwitz had a supreme contempt for the Belgians as a military nation. These views he frequently expressed to me, and it is quite likely that he advised his government that no serious obstacle would be found in Belgium in the event of war with France.

Count Bonine, a diplomat of great culture, intelligence, and dignity, represented the Italian government and was still serving at the post when I left. The Countess Bonine, a beautiful woman, and socially very popular, belonged to an old Venetian family, some of whose representatives were in the innermost circles of the Italian court. Count Bonine, after my departure from Brussels, was made an ambassador to Madrid and I believe finally transferred to Paris.

Count Clary, a quiet and unassuming nobleman, had been representing Austria many years. His daughter had married one of the Belgian aristocracy, and both he and his distinguished wife, Countess Clary, were intimately connected with many families in Belgium. The Countess Clary was of a noble Polish family and rather disposed to take her lineage seriously, but she never forgot the good manners and courtesies which are the traditional appendages of birth and position.

Count X——, the first secretary of the Austrian legation, was appointed to that post and came there with his lovely wife during our stay. Though an able and accomplished diplomat, he was distrait and frequently became oblivious of his surroundings. Upon one occasion, during his wife's absence, he was invited to dinner at the Italian legation. Not being well posted as to localities, he mistook the Mexican legation for the residence of the Italian minister. It happened that on this night the Mexican minister, Francisco de la Barra, was also giving a dinner to which the Austrian secretary unfortunately had not been invited. Count X—— was acquainted neither with the Italian nor Mexican ministers and it was not until he was seated at table, where arrangements for his seat had been hastily and intelligently made, that he discovered the hostess was not the Countess Bonine. Greatly embarrassed, he interrogated the Mexican minister, who told him the truth but very courteously expressed the pleasure they were experiencing in having him as an unbidden guest. Without further ado the Count arose hastily and grabbing his hat disappeared from this as-

semblage, arriving tardily at the Italian legation somewhat dishevelled but cheerfully anxious to meet all the
courtesies of his Italian host.

Francisco de la Barra, the Mexican minister, I knew before his arrival in Belgium, and we were received in audience on the same day. We maintained very cordial relations in Brussels which were continued after he became
ambassador at Washington, while he was Minister of
Foreign Affairs in Mexico, after he became provisional
president, and are still maintained though he is an exile
from his own country and in the service of the French
government.

De la Barra was the son of a Chilean officer who came to
Mexico in the time of Maximilian and was naturalized
there. Francisco de la Barra was born in Mexico but of
pure Spanish blood. He had polished manners, great
learning, and real patriotism—a not too common thing
in Mexico.

There were, of course, many members of the diplomatic
corps of distinguished services and long experience; the
Dutch minister and his distinguished and popular wife,
Madame Van der Stahl; the Argentines and Chileans;
and there were many serving as secretaries who have since
had notable careers. The diplomatic corps in every capital impinges very intimately and instructively upon any
story of diplomatic experiences; in a greater or less degree
the story of their daily doings reveals more or less the life,
trend of opinion, and current events of the capital where
they are accredited. For this reason they must always
figure largely in a diplomatic reminiscence.

CHAPTER XX

THE growth of population has obliterated most of the medieval colour in Brussels; miles of splendid boulevards lined with costly modern palaces cover the ground once occupied by the lord and his henchmen. The old Porte de Hal, which, with its quaint battlements, has guarded the southern approach to the city for four hundred years, has been converted into a museum of war, and seems not to have suffered much by the buffeting which time has given it. The Hôtel de Ville, the most original and beautiful edifice of its kind in Europe, which was standing when Columbus discovered America, still survives surrounded by the old homes of the Guilds and the building of the ancient royal palace. From the windows of this ancient building one may envisage great historical pictures. Here in the presence of the estates of the realm, with pomp and splendour, Charles V laid down the sceptre of the greatest kingdom then in existence, transferring his vast possessions to a capricious, superstitious, and nearly imbecile son; here, the tumultuous Beggars of the Sea defied despotism and the creatures of despotism; here, Egmont and Horn were led out to execution, martyrs to a great cause, but prophets of a new era; from here the edicts were read which sent thousands of the most industrious classes in exile to England and America.

[132]

The social side of life in Brussels was the *pièce de résistance* of its diplomatic life. The amount of serious work in the chancelleries was not great nor was there that fatiguing drain that demands social life, with its brilliancy and colour, as relaxation; there was no seamy side to the social life unless it were the lassitude born of excess.

There were many good theatres, and in the season, excellent grand opera could be heard at reasonable prices; on certain nights, when the *haut ton* and the diplomatic corps attended, the sight was a very brilliant one. After the opera there were suppers or other entertainments which were frequently participated in by the younger members of the diplomatic corps, but the steadier and more practical seniors usually gave no more time to social events than etiquette and regard for public opinion required. The musical and literary life of Brussels was full of opportunities; both in the literary and musical world the countersign to the favour and applause of Europe was given there. Throngs of students from all over the world were constantly in Brussels under instruction of her noted music masters; on summer nights the Vokes Hall concerts in the garden theatre of the park furnished one of the really great outdoor musical treats of Europe.

The boulevard and bridle paths, parks and long stretches of public land reserves made of Brussels a veritable playground. Riding was almost universal among the devotees of society and on early summer mornings one was almost certain to meet some of one's acquaintances in the course of a ride. The driveways were especially magnificent, stretching in unbroken perfection from the centre of the city through the parks on for miles out into the open country.

Belgian culture is very strongly gallicized. The temper and tone of French philosophy, wit, and humour are woven strongly into the tissue of Belgian culture. Addresses before learned and scientific societies, public lectures, and municipal entertainments were delivered in the French language, and the larger portion of the visiting savants, statesmen, and generals, who feed the thought of the rising generation, were French or closely related to the French school. In the Middle Ages, Belgian literature occupied a foremost place, but to-day conspicuous examples are not numerous. The intensely vivid romance of Bruges La Mort, the world-wide read dramas and essays of Maeterlinck are comparable with the best of current literature. Many of the universities and private schools of Belgium maintained regular courses of lectures for the benefit of their students and their patrons and friends; this practice gave us an opportunity to hear many of the most eminent Frenchmen and a considerable sprinkling of English, Hungarian, Austrian, and Italian authors, publicists, and artists.

The stage of Belgian society was always occupied by interesting personages who had their entrances and exits, some too soon, and some too remotely. Of course the leaders were the mediatized royalty such as the Chimays, the Henri and Charles de Lignes, the ducal family of d'Arenbergs, and d'Ursels. The de Lignes were a family of Belgian origin with an Austrian title and rank, probably created at the time Belgium was a part of the Empire of Austria; there were two prominent branches of the family, with numerous cadets, all of whom carried the title. The heads of the two families, Prince Charles de Ligne and Prince Henri de Ligne, were conspicuous in different ways, Prince Charles by always being present, florid and genial, and Prince Henri by nearly always being absent and appearing perfectly bored when present. The Princess Charles de Ligne was a person of a physically imposing presence and of extremely masculine tendencies and habits. When attending festal occasions she usually joined the gentlemen on retiring for coffee, always helping herself to the biggest and strongest cigar available, which she puffed with complacent energy and persistence. The Henri de Lignes were quiet people, who entertained at long intervals, and disappeared into an outer world which may have been spelled Paris or otherwise. The Princess Henri de Ligne was a cultured, refined, and delightful woman, and their only son Henri was a youth of distinguished appearance, high attainments, and pleasing manners. He was in quite pleasant contrast with the demonstrative and noisy manners of his cousins of the other branch. This fine young man, I am told, lost his life in defense of his country during the World War.

The d'Arenbergs occupied a very unique place in Belgian society. The Duke d'Arenberg had semi-royal rank in Germany, Austria, and Belgium. This nobleman of distributed nationality married a daughter of the Prince and Princess Charles de Ligne and subsequently the even tenor of Belgian society was enlivened by the contest for precedence between the enterprising and flaxen-haired young princess and her formidable mamma, who refused to be dislodged from her position as social primate. The d'Arenbergs had a wonderful old mansion in the centre of the business section of Brussels which had resisted the encroachments of commerce and stood steadfastly with its gates and tower as it had in medieval days.

[135]

In the World War the d'Arenbergs threw their fortunes with Germany and lost. Just what fate befell them I am not quite sure, but I believe their old palace in Brussels, with its priceless collection of works of art, and their country estates were confiscated. I imagine that their German and Austrian properties have not prospered and possibly they may have fallen upon evil days.

The Chimays were a Belgian family of Burgundian origin but also holding rank and title under the Austrian Empire. The Chimay family had been variously married through several generations all over the world, and during the last two generations there have been some American marriages which have imparted a lurid character to the family history.

The d'Ursels were quiet, unpretentious people of refinement and real worth. They inhabited, as their ancestors had for generations, an ancient palace in the centre of the business section of the city and lived there as real Belgians, hemmed in by the current and noise of the city and taking an active part in public affairs.

Such a thing as an American colony can hardly be said to have existed in Brussels; there were some nice Americans whom it was a pleasure to know, but our relations with the British colony, which was large and quite worth while, were more extensive. We enjoyed participating in the services of the Anglican Church and in the social events of the British colony, and during our residence formed some English friendships which still endure.

I frequented the Belgian Cercle du Parc very seldom. It was almost wholly a card-playing club, though everything was conducted with perfect propriety and rigid etiquette. There was a small but well-situated Anglo-

American club, appropriately named the Union, which I enjoyed attending and where I went usually about five o'clock in the afternoon for cards, conversation, and news.

Our summer vacations, while in Belgium, were usually spent in England, where the time always passed happily and profitably. Pleasant days about Bournemouth, the Isle of Wight, and excursions through the New Forest, through Wiltshire by Salisbury and the Salisbury plains; trips in and about London, rides through Yorkshire and Durham, with long stops at Harrogate and York, sent us back to our Belgian duties refreshed physically and mentally. In England, we had many delightful acquaintances, with beautiful country estates, which were hospitably thrown open to us and we learned to appreciate the simplicity, informality, and true hospitality of the English home. For me one month of England were well worth a thousand spent in any other part of Europe. I am never there that I do not fall into the mood and spirit of Emerson's "Our Old Home."

The spirit of kinship with the British race ought to be reverently cherished by all Americans in whose veins its blood courses. Why not? Is Magna Charta more the inheritance of the British than of their brothers across the sea? In the gloomy greatness of Oliver Cromwell, the singing souls of Pym and Hampden, am I not as much to the manner born as those who live under the shadow of Trafalgar monument or linger on the shady side of Pall Mall?

This England—for she is the moving and abiding force of Britain—has carried her civilization and her laws to every clime, and rude mounds and pathetic crosses all around the globe testify to the valour of her sons and the titanic work she has undertaken. She has thrown great and historic pictures upon the canvas of the world with a dash of colour here for law and another there for orderly progress. The rich stream of English thought and philosophy has flowed to all nations; the restless fingers of English commerce have rested upon all the islands and the seas. With her drums beating all around the world, she has carried a message of liberty, peace, and progress.

CHAPTER XXI

Some observations about Belgium and the Belgian people—Bruges and Ghent—Cardinal Mercier—Some words about emigration to America

BELGIUM is a unique country; time has dealt gently with her traditions, her antiquities, her hoary romances, and her battle-stained castles, and the Belgium of to-day is, as in the time of Cæsar, a unique land; unique in its history which tells of battles between royal power and the stubborn independence of a democratic people; unique in its religious ideals which, while accepting the mandate of the Roman hierarchy and remaining, after centuries of religious war, a Roman Catholic country; unique in its art which yesterday revealed to the world the masterly canvases of Van Dyck, Rubens, and Memling, and to-day takes the foremost place in the domain of plastic creations; unique in that splendid system of domestic economy and adjustment which provides to seven millions of people, inhabiting a territory no larger than the State of Massachusetts, an opportunity to live and prosper. One soon realizes that the religious and political upheavals, which from century to century have shaken Europe to its depths, have left Belgium almost unscathed. Surrounded by Protestant Germany, England, the Netherlands, and skeptic France, she faithfully maintains the old religion and keeps her lamps burning and her altars fresh, while France derides the eternal truths and England falters and turns aside from the path blazed by thousands of martyrs and saints. Nor is her political history less unique. Placed alongside republican France, where five revolutions have risen and spent their force, leaving in their train some real privileges to human liberty, but others of doubtful value in the concept of an orderly state, she remains a democratic kingdom, preserving with stolid and persistent pride an ancient aristocracy and monarchical form of government.

Climate and geography play a very important part in the character building of a nation. The southern Latin, transplanted to a soil where life is sustained by constant battling with untoward climatic conditions, becomes, through gradual evolution, an alert, self-reliant, and thrifty person. The hardy Teuton set down among tropical surroundings, with the vine and the fig close at hand, slowly relapses into the sluggish habits of his primitive forbears. The people of Belgium, inhabiting the country north of a line drawn through the centre of the city of Brussels, are of Teutonic origin. Over these vast plains, now stretching in billowy waves to the sea and bedecked with the richest harvests, in remote antiquity the rude progenitors of the present race battled against the march of the constantly invading sea, against the advance of Roman legionaries and the attacks of savage barbarians, and resisted and defeated them. The sea was checked and shackled; the savage German barbarians were either absorbed or driven back; the Roman legions marched over the land but never conquered it, and Roman law, custom, or language obtained no foothold in the country of the Flemings. By infinite labour the ungenerous soil was made to bring forth bounteous harvests, and in the midst of the sterile plains sprang up the great cities of Ghent, Bruges,

Antwerp, and Brussels, rivalling in richness and beauty the cities of Italy and Greece.

To the south of the line which runs through the city of Brussels lives another race of Celtic origin, the Walloons. Supporting the same monarchy, ruled by the same laws, but differing in language, customs, blood, and traditions, the three million Walloons who live south of the line look upon the four million Flemings who live north of it as aliens and foreigners and, except upon the arbitrary divisional line, there is no racial fusion.

The Celtic Walloon is of a poetic and romantic temperament; eloquent in speech and skilled in political intrigue, but impatient of political or priestly control, having little regard for political or religious tradition but a ready disposition to absorb new faiths and modern politics. His ancestors fiercely combatted the Roman invasion, but the Roman prevailed, implanting his language and customs. Race had much to do with this; the Celt is everywhere a more adjustable and more adaptable creature than the Teuton. The natural beauty of the country and the mildness of its climate were also potent factors. It is the harsh climate and stubborn soil which develops the resistant and self-reliant qualities of races.

The Walloon country is a land blessed by nature, yielding bountiful harvests with slight effort; abounding in scenic beauty, with healthful climatic conditions. It presents a marked contrast to flat and prosaic Flanders. Rivers like the Meuse and the Sambre whirl their waters through deep gorges to the sea; the hills rise dome-like, dressed in the greenest of verdure and diversified with richly coloured foliage; valleys, peaceful and picturesque, stretch away in sinewy curves, running races with the

[141]

rivers to the sea. Glimmering in the sunshine above, one sees the graceful outlines of medieval castles, smothered in vines and embowered in roses, while below the shepherd tends his flocks on the inclines of peaceful valleys, and pleasant villages dot the landscape in the receding vista.

The characteristics of these two races, the Walloon and the Fleming, widely differ; the Walloon is volatile, passionate, eloquent, and politically liberal if not radical; the Fleming is stolid, practical, and conservative. These two elements constitute the Belgian nation as it exists to-day; whatever their legendary, romantic, or political history in the past has been, their integrity as a nation in the future depends upon their political union. Differing in race, custom, and tradition, they are yet by the force of circumstances and common danger bound together by an inseparable tie.

During periods of inactivity in the legation, I visited in a leisurely way some of the interesting historical places of Belgium. Bruges and Ghent possess a peculiar fascination for me and I never tired of their atmosphere and colour. Quaint and historically interesting, they are aside from the paths of European travel these days, yielding place to gaudy rivals in newly bedecked splendour.

Around these cities the Fleming fought his battles, established his powerful Guilds, waged his fierce feuds, created his priceless works of art, and reared the churches and public edifices which, after a thousand years of destroying time, battle, and siege, look down upon the pushing, active descendants of the same thrifty race.

Ghent has discarded much of her medieval garments and her ancient monuments are crumbling under the hand of this material and iconoclastic age. The monastery of

St. Bavon, whose origin is lost in legendary mists, is in partial preservation; within its roofless walls, standing upright in their stone coffins, are more than a hundred warriors and crusaders; the rains of centuries have fallen upon their heads but they stand there in the dumb stone, silent witnesses of a more exalted, if not purer, faith. The Palace of the Counts, stern and picturesque, has survived the storms and revolutions of a thousand years; within its walls the Emperor Charles V was born, and thence he went forth to become the monarch of more lands than Charlemagne ruled; its gloomy dungeons and keeps could, if they had tongues, whisper many a tale of priestly and kingly cruelty.

In modern days, when the sceptre of commercial supremacy shifts so variously, one forgets that Ghent was once the commercial queen of Europe; that her merchants vied with princes in splendour and played an important part in the European drama. Fierce and determined battles for civil and religious liberty were waged around her walls, and heroisms and sacrifices, such as are scattered along the path of history from Troy to Lucknow, illuminate the picture.

Bruges is not only a survival but a complete survival in her architecture and atmosphere of the best period of medievalism in Europe. Henry V of England, the Emperor Charles IV of Germany, the Prince of Orange, Louis XIV, Marlborough, and Bonaparte have waged battle within sight of her spires; the tide of religious controversy has eddied about her walls; America has been discovered and peopled with more than a hundred millions of people; the steamboat, railroad, telegraph, telephone, motor car, airplane, and radio have revolutionized and centralized

[143]

the world, but Bruges sleeps on, preserving in her mystic shrines, her sleeping palaces, her echoing streets, the legend and romance of those rude days when every man's house was his castle and the strength of his arm his shield against oppression. Here the very stones, like those of Venice, are mute chapters in history, and the musty rust of ages covers written and unwritten tragedies. Bruges, too, was a great mart of commerce, rivalling Ghent in power and wealth, but the sands of the sea dammed up her ports, leaving her isolated from the currents of the world's commerce. The modern canals which are now constructed to connect her with the sea may possibly restore her to life but never to her former greatness.

In my rambles about Malines, Ghent, and Bruges, I frequently came in contact, either by correspondence or personally, with the distinguished cardinal prince of the Roman Catholic Church, Desiré Mercier, who was destined subsequently to take such a heroic and courageous part in defense of his country against the invading German armies. Cardinal Mercier was a tall, angular man, with pronounced Roman features, expressive gray eyes, and a mouth sometimes sweet and humorous and at other times severe and determined—I have sometimes thought that the former aspect was for the deeply religious present lovely Queen of Belgium and the latter for the then Majesty, King Leopold.

Cardinal Mercier was a profound student of the history of the Low Countries, of the romance of its old castles, of the story of the religious sacrifice and passion of its great cathedrals and churches. Socially he was a delightful companion, with an immense fund of humour and wit and deep reservoirs of learning accumulated from every source.

Hardly an author or a book could be mentioned that he did not immediately display his knowledge. He believed that "Ben Hur" was the greatest novel ever written, and his quaint comments on French translations of Mark Twain's works were almost as humorous as the best passages from Twain. His heroic challenge of the German Empire, during the World War, called forth the admiration of all the world, and his recent death has as profoundly moved the Protestant world as the Roman Catholic.

Arriving and departing friends and social engagements carried us frequently to Antwerp, a wholly modern city and one of the great ports of the world. Antwerp is one of the principal ports of emigrant embarkation for the United States. Through this port flows to American shores a steady current of the flotsam and jetsam of Europe. This army of marching Poles, Russians, Italians, Slavs of all kinds, Greeks, Asiatics, and Jews attracted and absorbed my attention during my entire stay in Belgium, and long before agitation on this question began at home, I had reached the conclusion that our policy with reference to immigration—if we had any—if it served the interest of other countries, must be condemned if the best interests of the American people were to be considered.

We were then admitting into our midst vast elements of alien races, incapable of understanding our institutions and difficult of assimilation. This hodgepodge of races seeks our shores not because of a desire to share the liberties we enjoy or to yield obedience to the laws we enforce, but because they find in America a better market for the labour of their hands. It is the material and not the spiritual side of America that appeals to them. Our institutions, our language, our ideals either mean nothing to them, or are viewed with repugnance and racial antipathy. America should be primarily the home of the northwestern races, because these races only are susceptible of easy assimilation and comprehend more clearly the phrase, "Liberty with law." If we are to hold what we have, we must keep the poison of turbulence out of our veins. The question of the regulation of immigration took a very vigorous hold on me at that time, and years afterward I drew for the platform of the Republican Convention of 1920 its immigration plank. The plank which I submitted was somewhat modified in the committee, but a stand was taken which has borne fruition in legislation, legislation which I earnestly hope may be strengthened and safeguarded.

CHAPTER XXII

King Leopold—The Chinese railway—Invitations to Secretary Hay—
The Kongo question—Stories about the King—Princess Clementine

KING LEOPOLD II of Belgium was an interesting figure in the history of his period; of German ancestry and of the same royal family from which Queen Victoria was descended, and her full cousin, his blood was also blended with that of the kings and princes of France. His father, Leopold I, was a Protestant and remained so after he was elected King of the Belgians; Leopold II, however, in compliance with the terms which settled the succession to the throne of Belgium in his house, became a Roman Catholic and was brought up in that faith. Whether he was a devout believer in the tenets of any church may be doubted; religious subjects and religious persons usually afforded him a convenient target for sarcasm or invective.

Physically he was a grotesque figure, towering to almost brobdingnagian height; the impression made by his great height was marred considerably by dragging lower limbs which had been partially paralyzed. His powers of endurance were enormous, and nothing pleased him better than to keep some new diplomat standing for hours while he discussed all possible subjects relating to Belgium and to the country from which the suffering diplomat might be accredited. He had an enormous head, splendid eyes, and the prominent nose of the Orleans family, to which his mother belonged. He spoke French and English with a strong German accent, was eloquent in speech, skilled in kingcraft, and tactful in dealing with men and measures. He was by training and nature democratic and, in the private audiences which I frequently had with him, received me in the simplest possible way, endeavouring always to reach his ends by adroit personal appeals, and usually displaying thorough knowledge of American history, public men, and public questions.

The King was proud of his generally recognized qualities as a business man; reference to his accomplishments in the business world pleased him immensely, and he recounted with great glee his associations with leading business men all over the world. He was financially interested in the Canton-Hankow Railway, in which there were also large American holdings. He had camouflaged his interests under some sort of an arrangement with the banking house of J. P. Morgan & Co., of New York, intending doubtless to secure in this way the protection of his interests by the American government. He was averse to the sale and surrender of this railway property to the Chinese government and used every effort to prevent the withdrawal of the American interests. While the question of the sale was under discussion the King asked me to visit him at his private office. I found him amid simple surroundings and was received without any ceremony. His office was scantily furnished, the most prominent objects in it being busts of Theodore Roosevelt and John Hay. Parenthetically, it may be noted that whenever I visited him subsequently, the scenery and settings were always arranged to bear upon the subject under discussion.

I conveyed the King's views on the subject of the

Canton-Hankow Railway to our Department of State and as Mr. Loomis, then Acting Secretary, and President Roosevelt seemed to be in accord with the views of the King, it looked for a while as though we might save the situation. At the last moment, however, the President reversed his opinion, deciding to turn over the American interests, which included those of King Leopold, to the Chinese government. The disappointment of His Majesty was great; he felt very strongly on the subject and never failed to refer to it as an evidence of the peculiar methods of the American government.

Upon another occasion the King sent for me soon after the announcement of the visit of Secretary Hay to Europe for medical treatment. He said: "Mr. Minister, I see Mr. Secretary Hay is about to visit the continent and I would be greatly pleased to have him make me a visit." I replied: "Your Majesty, Secretary Hay is visiting the continent solely for medical treatment; he is a very sick man and I doubt whether he will accept any invitation, no matter how flattering." "But," said the King, "I have no idea of inflicting any ceremonies on Secretary Hay; I want him to come and visit me here as my friend and you may give him my pledge that he will not be disturbed or bored in any way. Secretary Hay is one of the great men of the world and I am seeking the honour of entertaining him under my own roof." Though I was quite certain what the response would be, I immediately dispatched a letter to Mr. Hay, who was then in London, conveying the King's invitation; his reply declining the invitation in the most courteous terms reached me without much delay. Much to my astonishment, when I carried Mr. Hay's letter to the King, he insisted upon my repeating the invitation

[149]

in the most urgent way; this I reluctantly did but Mr. Hay again declined. The King, however, was not to be deterred from his purpose and later, when Mr. Hay was under treatment at Bad Nauhiem, he went there, and without any ceremony or announcement, called on Mr. Hay who, of course, received him courteously.

I had a similar experience with him during one of Mr. Pierpont Morgan's visits in England; in this instance, the King, being unable to induce Mr. Morgan to come to Brussels, crossed the Channel in his private yacht and boarded Mr. Morgan's yacht in Dover harbour.

The Kongo question was a sensitive subject with the King; discussions relative to the origin and legitimacy of his title and control over Belgian Kongo were extremely distasteful to him. He regarded the Belgian Kongo as his private patrimony over which he had autocratic power and resented any intervention in its affairs by the Belgian or other foreign governments. The activities of the British and American governments in dealing with this question displeased him greatly and, while the discussion was at its height, the British minister, Sir Arthur Harding, and I, were made to feel his displeasure. At the annual court ball when the King was, according to custom, making a conversational circuit of the diplomatic corps, he pointedly overlooked the representatives of the American and British governments, passing them without so much as a sign of recognition. This seemed rather amusing to me, but our government was annoyed and President Roosevelt made some very characteristic remarks about King Leopold.

The King was absent a great deal from Brussels travelling about England, France, and Germany, always incognito.

Upon one occasion after he had returned from a visit to Spain during Lent I inquired about his trip and he said sardonically: "I always try to spend Lent in Spain; the food is so bad there that I feel I am making a full penance for my sins, which are many."

An amusing story to illustrate King Leopold's attitude in religious matters was told me a short time before his decease.

The dignitaries of the Church had long been grievously scandalized by his irregular life and upon an occasion when he fell ill it was decided he needed some special exhortations to turn aside from the paths of wickedness and repent. A priest, called Father Joseph, who had at one time performed the superfluous office of confessor to the King, was dispatched to his bedside. Aroused from slumber, His Majesty discovered Father Joseph at his bedside.

"Father Joseph," he said, "what can I do for you?"

Father Joseph replied: "Nothing, Your Majesty, but I have come here to serve you."

"Why, what service can you perform for me?" asked the King; "I am getting well and need no assistance."

"Yes, Your Majesty," replied Father Joseph, "you may be getting well in body but your soul is sick."

"What makes my soul sick?"

"Your sins, Your Majesty," replied Father Joseph.

"Who says I am a sinner?" said His Majesty.

"Oh, Your Majesty, craving Your Majesty's forgiveness, the rulers of the Holy Church say your soul is sick and needs a physician."

"What do you think about this, Father Joseph?"

"I am afraid, Your Majesty, craving Your Majesty's forgiveness, that there is some truth in what they say."

[151]

"Now, Father Joseph," said the King, "many people have spoken evil things to me about you but I have never believed them. Why, then, should you believe evil things about me? Return to those who sent you and say that the King's soul needs no physician."

The King was an autocrat in the royal circle but he was far from always having his own way. The Count and Countess of Flanders appeared very little in public and only at those court ceremonies required by etiquette. Princess Clementine was too much like the King in character to yield graciously to his wishes and their wills frequently clashed. One evening the King and the Princess arrived at a court ball both in apparent ill humour. It was soon whispered about that the cause of the trouble was the King's peremptory order to the Princess, after they had started for the ball, to return and change her gown; this she did, but arrived later at the ball in a gown which she detested and a bad temper. She soon had her revenge. The King did not permit her to dance and, while he was present, she respected his wishes; but age makes its demands on kings as on other people and His Majesty slipped away to his slumbers; thereupon the Princess descended from the dais and joined in the dancing, keeping it up as long as etiquette would permit. Human nature, especially feminine human nature, is pretty much the same in all stations of life.

The Princess Clementine lived remote from society and adhered closely in her daily life to the course prescribed by court etiquette. When she appeared in public her queenly carriage, charm of manner, and perfect equipment made a marked impression on the throng. It could hardly be said the Belgians were fond of her but they were proud of her.

There was for years a lingering love affair between the Princess and the Prince Napoleon, who resided in Brussels, which did not at all meet with the approval of King Leopold. For this reason they were not married during the life of the King. Soon after the decease of her father the Princess married Prince Napoleon and they established their residence in Italy. Prince Napoleon never appeared in public but sometimes attended small dinners. I met him once at dinner and he impressed me as being a perfectly harmless and not unusually intelligent person; perhaps my estimate was an erroneous one which a more extended acquaintance would have modified.

The King was not popular with the Belgian people, though admired for many kingly qualities. His lack of popularity was due to his personal conduct and to family incidents, which brought on social ostracism in royal circles and, in the estimation of the Belgian people, lowered the dignity of the Belgian sovereignty. Nevertheless, he was a notable figure of his time and sowed not altogether in barren soil. The Coburg blood, which flowed so evenly and respectably through the veins of Queen Victoria's spouse, played queer antics in the life of King Leopold—perhaps it was the Orleans grafting.

CHAPTER XXIII

Return to the United States—Attendance at the Chicago Republican convention—Luncheon with Mr. Taft—Trip to Italy and incidents— The Hague International Peace Conference—Story of King Leopold and Kaiser William of Germany—Intimation from Washington of transfer to an Embassy—Difficult situation in regard to posts—Appointment as Ambassador to Mexico.

IN THE summer of 1907, taking advantage of a leave of absence, I returned to the United States, and during my vacation attended the Chicago convention which eventually closed its session with the nomination of Mr. Taft. This was one of the most imposing and least sensational conventions held by the Republican party since its organization. The convention hall was thronged with some of the ablest and most brilliant men in America, but there was obviously no great contest on the stage and such oratory as was in evidence related more directly to the platform and to campaign problems than to the nomination of candidates for President and Vice-president. The nomination of Mr. Taft was assured from the moment of the opening of the convention, though there were always tendencies toward a hurrah movement for Roosevelt.

Before a nomination was made I left the convention and went to Washington. I found the atmosphere there charged with the suspicion that at some crisis in the convention a break might be made to Roosevelt. I saw Mr. Taft at luncheon during my stay and assured him that the convention was a Taft convention and that there was no

[154]

possibility of a break to any other candidate. Mr. Taft seemed to entertain this opinion himself and not to be affected by the general nervousness.

As my leave of absence was about to expire I then went to New York and after a few days sailed on the Red Star Line Steamer *Lapland* for Antwerp. Soon after Mrs. Wilson joined me and in the month of September we made a tour through Italy, visiting Milan, Florence and Venice, Naples and Rome.

At Venice we spent several pleasant days with F. Hopkinson Smith and Ridgway Knight, the American painters, dining frequently together, exploring the old churches and palaces, and passing the evenings on the mysterious canals under the spell of Venetian romance. From Venice we went to Naples for some enchanting days at Capri and Sorrento, a region made famous in poetry, song, and war, but which we found best described in Thomas Buchanan Read's "Drifting":

> "My soul to-day
> Is far away,
> Sailing the Vesuvian Bay.
>
> "My winged boat,
> A bird afloat,
> Swims round the purple peaks remote.
>
> "With dreamful eyes
> My spirit lies
> Under the walls of paradise."

At the close of our visit we spent the night—a night the early hours of which were given to witnessing national dances, given in our honour—in an old hotel which romantic history says was the former home of the poet Tasso. I was awakened at the early dawn by what sounded like a muffled orchestra, and approaching the window which gave upon a sheer descent of the rocks to the Bay of Naples, I witnessed a picturesque but probably usual incident. Over Pompeii the first rays of the morning sun were glimmering, and on the shores the fishermen were hauling in their nets, assisted by their women, accompanying their work with the musical chant, which doubtless gathered impressiveness with the distance of travel. One could imagine that in the time of Dante their ancestors chanted the same weird music as they hauled their nets from the sea.

We closed our vacation with a visit to Rome, where we were hospitably entertained by some nice Americans and by the American ambassador, Mr. Lloyd Griscom. The American colony in Rome was then very large and very distinguished, being made up of painters, poets, travellers, and the excessively devout. There is an atmosphere of cosmopolitanism always present, compensating to some extent for other uninviting aspects. We had very intimate letters of introduction to Cardinal Merry del Val, at that time the Papal Secretary, but because of the shortness of our stay or because of his absence, our letters were not presented.

Soon after our return from Italy the International Peace Conference was held at The Hague and we attended as the guests of our minister to the Netherlands, Mr. David Jayne Hill. It was a great gathering, enlivened by the intelligence, wit, and diplomatic arts of the attending celebrities. There were the American ambassadors, Porter and Choate, John W. Foster representing China, Count Apponyi for Austria-Hungary, Baron Courcel for France, Sir Henry Howard for Great Britain, and other notable personages. At the close of the conference there was an elaborate banquet followed by a reception given by the Minister and Mrs. Hill. At the banquet, General Porter made an excellent talk, displaying finished scholarship and a keen perception of the international situation. As an after-dinner speech I thought it could not be excelled, but it was followed by a spontaneous, wholly informal talk by Mr. Choate, who was in one of his best moods. Wit, sarcasm, and wisdom flowed from his eloquent tongue with an ease and a musical cadence which charmed and fascinated all who listened. In all my diplomatic experience I do not recall having met the equal of Mr. Choate in wisdom, eloquence, and unassuming dignity. If not the most successful, he was probably the ablest man this country has sent to the embassy in London.

We had formal interviews with the queen and queen mother; we were impressed not at all by the former but much by the latter.

Returning from the Peace Conference to Brussels we ran abruptly into a story which was running the rounds of the diplomatic circle, which, whether true or not, may be found of interest in connection with the subsequent World War. The tale was that King Leopold had, during a visit to Berlin where he sometimes went incognito, signed there, or in some way subscribed to, an agreement with the Kaiser, binding Belgium in the event of war between Germany and France to permit the passage of German troops over the soil of Belgium. The story went on to say that the King upon his return to Belgium had sent for one

[157]

of his advisers and revealed the transaction which had taken place in Berlin. This person, it appears, although holding official relations to the King, found it his duty to disclose the King's confidences to the Belgian cabinet. In some way this story reached the British legation, resulting in diplomatic activities in the British and Belgian foreign offices and the abrogation of the supposed understanding. About this time the Belgians began fortifying their frontiers, notably the two great strongholds, Liège and Namur, which afterward held at bay the onrush of the German army long enough to permit the French lines of defense to be reformed upon the plan which some days afterward in the Battle of the Marne culminated in the decisive German check, the salvation of Paris, and possibly changed the course of events of history.

Shortly after returning to Brussels from our trip to Italy the result of the election in the United States was announced. Somewhat later I received an intimation from Washington that it was the intention of President-elect Taft to transfer me to an embassy, and after the inaugural I was unofficially advised that the President intended to appoint me as ambassador at St. Petersburg. As the expense of properly maintaining the embassy at St. Petersburg far exceeded the salary of the ambassador and the contingent allowances, it was manifestly a post which would be difficult for me, with a limited fortune, to fill satisfactorily. I conveyed my views on the subject through the proper channels and was then asked whether an appointment to Vienna would be agreeable. To this I made the same objection I had made in the case of Russia and for the same reasons, adding that an appointment to Mexico would be gratifying. I was informed that the

Mexican post had already been disposed of but almost simultaneously was officially advised by the Secretary of State that I had been appointed as ambassador to Turkey. Realizing that I might be encroaching on the President's patience I determined to accept the post, although I believed I could render better service in Mexico. However, I received no further intimations in regard to my appointment except that my name as ambassador had been posted in the audience chamber of the Sultan.

In the month of October, 1909, nearly a year after Mr. Taft took office, I was informed by the Department of State of my appointment as ambassador to Mexico. I learned later that the person who had been originally selected for Mexico had finally declined the post and that Senators Lodge and Root, anticipating serious developments south of the Rio Grande because of the age and infirmity of President Diaz, were desirous of having a man sent to the post who was acquainted with Latin-American psychology and the Spanish language, and had jointly urged my appointment.

CHAPTER XXIV

Preparations for departure to Mexico and official visits—Prince Albert and Princess Elizabeth—Final interview with the King—His death—Appointment as special ambassador—The funeral obsequies and incidents—Enthronement of King Albert and final hospitalities— The mad Empress Carlotta.

WE IMMEDIATELY began preparations for departure; this meant not only the packing and shipping of household effects but the payment of innumerable visits of courtesy and a strict, if somewhat fatiguing, compliance with the rules covering the severance of official relations. We paid farewell visits to the Countess of Flanders, the Princess Clementine, and to Prince Albert and Princess Elizabeth, to whom we were greatly attached.

Memories of Prince Albert and Princess Elizabeth remain vivid after a long lapse of time. When we knew them they were living quietly in Brussels, discharging only those limited offices which the jealous nature of Leopold permitted them to assume. At times I sensed a latent disapproval of the old king and perhaps there was an appearance of protest against the rigid etiquette which he tyrannically prescribed for their conduct; but there was no evidence of this in their bearing toward him; always the greatest deference and respect marked their demeanour, and possibly he never deemed them lacking in obedience to him as the head of the family and as their sovereign.

Prince Albert at this time was in the full flush of youth.

His blonde hair, youthful and animated features, lively interest in all public activities, contrasted with the solemn atmosphere of the court functions, made him sometimes appear like a young college graduate. Even in those days he displayed courage of conviction, a certain reserve of power, which is the badge of kings, coupled with eminent good sense, courtesy, and kindness, qualities of which the world was to know more in later years. Through the years of his apprenticeship he prepared conscientiously for the duties of the high post, to which he was eventually to be called, by extensive travelling, study, and research. When he finally became King of the Belgians, he was amply prepared to meet the great crisis which his country was soon to confront, and displayed not only a unique courage, but great wisdom in battling against the apparently insuperable difficulties which submerged his country for a while; it is not too much to say that he emerged out of the confusion and ruin wrought by the European war in better repute than any of the allied sovereigns.

Of the grace, womanly kindness, and thoughtfulness of Princess Elizabeth, too much cannot be said. Apparently a timid and shrinking person, she possessed courage, abundant tact, and a supreme devotion to the people of Belgium which gained her esteem and love to a degree seldom enjoyed by royal personages. Of all the pleasant memories I have of Brussels those of this good woman with her active charity and benevolence, her simple and unostentatious manner, her genuine courtesy and kindness, are the best. In her home she was the loyal helpmate of her splendid husband, the devoted mother of three beautiful and intelligent children, and the kind hostess who received her guests with that absence of ceremony and reserve which is the true mark of the gentle-woman and the real sign of nobility.

For some time preceding my departure there had been a coolness between the legation and the court because of our supposed gratuitous intermeddling in the affairs of the Kongo, and I was interested in watching how His Majesty would maintain this attitude and at the same time conform to established usage in acting on my official apprisal of departure. It was mildly surprising to receive a reply from Mr. Davignon, the Minister of Foreign Affairs, saying the King would be pleased to receive me in farewell audience and that he would also be gratified to have Mrs. Wilson accompany me. The inclusion of Mrs. Wilson in the audience was a departure from the usual etiquette, indicating some special consideration. An added interest was given to the audience by the circumstance of the King's arising from a sick bed to receive us; it was his last official act in life. His Majesty's manner during the interview was extremely affable; he talked in his usual interesting way with me about international questions and about others of a different kind with Mrs. Wilson. We were really sorry to part with the old monarch; there was something original and attractive about all he said and did; while his morals might not excite one's enthusiasm, his intelligence usually did.

At this juncture I was advised that Mr. U. Grant Smith, the secretary who was being sent to take charge of the legation ad interim, would not arrive for some time. This circumstance altered our plans and Mrs. Wilson was obliged to return home alone.

Coincidentally with Mrs. Wilson's departure King Leopold passed away, and as President Taft appointed me special ambassador for the King's funeral ceremony and the enthronement of King Albert, a further delay ensued.

The funeral obsequies were rendered with great pomp and in accordance with Belgian tradition. High Mass was celebrated at the Cathedral San Gudule in the presence of the royal family, diplomatic corps, officials of the Belgian government, and army and court functionaries. The display of colour and impressive rendition of the Gregorian chant gave to the ceremony a decidedly theatrical effect. The nave of the Cathedral was occupied by military, provincial, and municipal functionaries; the transept by members of the cabinet, the diplomatic corps, the grandmaster of the court, Count Jean D'Oultremont; back of these was an elevated dais where the royal family —the just and the unjust, the goats and the sheep—was seated. King Albert and Queen Elizabeth, the Countess of Flanders and Princess Clementine were there, of course, but the royal family had been suddenly swollen out of its usual proportions by the arrival of the King's two erratic daughters, the ex-queen of Saxony, Louise, and Stephanie, for the ceremony.

In the midst of the profound solemnity of the occasion an animated altercation emanating from the reserved dais was heard, and the diplomatic corps, which was well acquainted with the history of the royal family, became ardently desirous of ascertaining the cause of the commotion. This led to a straining of necks all along until the line of projection had completely obscured the vision of the Chinese minister, who had recently arrived. Cut off from the observation of important events which his Chinese Excellency thought should be promptly reported to his government, he became very much excited and in strenuous attempts to obtain a better view of what was going on, swallowed the false teeth which evidently had been carelessly adjusted in his generous mouth, with the result that it became necessary to convey His Excellency outside the nave of the cathedral where hastily summoned surgeons sunk surgical anchors which brought to the surface the masticatory machinery of the minister and afforded him the relief necessary to permit further participation in the events of the day.

After the religious ceremony the remains of the King were solemnly escorted through the streets of Brussels, accompanied, on horseback—a traditional court custom— by the royal family and officials of the government to the Church of Laeken, where he was laid away with his father, Leopold I, his brother, the Count of Flanders, and his unfortunate son, Florien, whose tragic death had been a never-ceasing source of sorrow to him.

Thus passed to his place of history a remarkable character, who had an opportunity to do many things in this world and did some of them. The ever-recurring irony of fate found him at the last with a barren sceptre in his grasp.

> "The glories of our blood and state
> Are shadows, not substantial things,"

and the crown and the spade are mingled together in the dust. Born in the purple, undoubtedly highly endowed, he lived in contemptuous indifference of the world and its conventions and died in cynical and sybaritic pomp, with no gentle hand to touch down his eyelids in sleep. What a contrast with the life of William McKinley, born in poverty, struggling upward through penury to the highest office in the gift of a hundred million people—finally to pass from it to eternity, accompanied by the prayers and tears of a nation.

Soon after the old king's funeral ceremony King Albert was enthroned with great pomp and enthusiasm. Two special ambassadors, M. de Giers and I, were appointed for this occasion, taking precedence of all others in attendance, standing on the right and left hand of His Majesty during the act of enthronement and the protestation of the oath of fealty.

On the night following, King Albert entertained the diplomatic corps at an informal supper which, to comport with the court mourning, was made extremely simple. Unhappily this informal event terminated my official relations with their new Majesties, whose friendship and kindness had been so helpful during our stay in Brussels and for whose future I anticipated all that might bring happiness to them and the Belgian people.

During our residence in Brussels the poor mad Empress Carlotta lived there, remote from the world and immured in the palace of Laeken. There she had spun out her melancholy existence for forty years and there, having survived all earthly attachments and relations, she lived on a grim memory of the disastrous eclipse of an empire, and the sudden collapse of the romantic castles in Spain, which had lured to destruction two young and beautiful lives. She never knew of the tragic death of Maximilian and he never knew of the failure of her visit to the Emperor Napoleon or of her subsequent mental derangement in the halls of the Vatican palace, where the light which had flamed in two hemispheres went out forever. The aged

[165]

princess was tenderly looked after by King Leopold, was regarded with deepest affection by the Emperor Francis Joseph, and during the occupation of Brussels by the Germans in the recent war was treated with special consideration.

CHAPTER XXV

*Arrival at Washington and conference with the Department of State—
Our voyage from New York to Mexico—Merida—Vera Cruz—Orizaba
incident—Mexico City.*

I ARRIVED home in the early part of January and after a brief visit to my aged mother and other relatives in Indiana, returned to Washington for the purpose of making a study of the Mexican situation. I had interviews with the President, who was exceedingly kind and helpful, and many with Secretary Knox and various officials of the Department of State. In these conferences political conditions in Mexico were only lightly touched upon, the department evidently relying on a continuance of the régime which had dominated the affairs of the republic for so many years. This confidence I did not share as I had information through other channels which convinced me that there was the possibility, if not danger, of disturbed conditions.

In February of 1910, accompanied by Mrs. Wilson and my son Stewart, I embarked on the steamer *Moro Castle*, plying between New York and Vera Cruz. A large number of New York friends came to the dock to bid us farewell and we sailed for our new post amid many expressions of good will. The trip down was uneventful, the weather being ideal throughout. There were few interesting people aboard and, except for the stay of a day at Havana, where we first met Mr. Fred Morris Dearing, then first secretary of our legation in Cuba, afterward to be associated with me as first secretary at the embassy in Mexico, and now minister to Portugal, the experiences of the voyage were extremely monotonous. On our arrival at Progreso, the port of Yucatan, a number of American residents came aboard to invite us to spend the day at the neighbouring capital of Merida. Accepting the invitation, we spent the day riding through henequen fields and visiting public places.

We found Merida a scrupulously clean, modern city, largely built up and improved by the wealth flowing from the henequen district, which comprises nearly all of the southern half of the state of Yucatan; its public buildings are commodious and its benevolent and penal institutions would be a credit to any city. What impressed us most was the marvellous cleanliness of the people, a thing not usual in tropical Latin America; as a rule the women were dressed in simple but clean white garments, and the men's white shirts and trousers were as spotless and immaculate as the evening clothes of a New York devotee of fashion. Both men and women are fine types of the supposed Maya race. They are certainly racially distinct from the Aztec races of the great central plateau of Mexico.

We sailed from Progreso in the evening and arrived at Vera Cruz the morning of the 28th in the midst of a dense fog which gradually dissolved under the rays of a burning tropical sun. We were met at the port by officials of the Mexican government who came aboard to offer the usual expressions of courteous welcome and in the evening, amid the strains of the inevitable Latin-American band, left by train for Orizaba, where we had arranged to pass the night before beginning the ascent over the mountains to the City of Mexico.   Arriving at Orizaba at about eleven o'clock in the night we were obliged to walk with our belongings, no conveyance being available, more than a mile over the rocky streets to our hotel.   On our arrival at the railway station on the morrow we found no arrangements had been made by the Mexican government or by the railway officials for our trip to Mexico City.   Perhaps for this reason we found the oft-praised scenic beauties of the trip much exaggerated; the dust, confusion, and crowding occupied our entire attention to the exclusion of everything else.   At Mexico City in the evening we found waiting at the station the secretaries and clerks of the embassy and my faithful servant Clement, who, with his wife, had preceded us to Mexico.

Without delay we entered upon the task of acquiring knowledge of the Mexican capital, its places of interest, its beauties and its people.

The Mexico City of Cortez has been almost entirely swept away and the modern city, with its broad avenues, parks, and suburbs, is largely the creation of the unfortunate Empress Carlotta, who connected the business and residential parts of the city by the broad and spacious Avenue Paseo de la Reforma with the park and castle of Chapultepec and opened up various other avenues through then unpopulated districts.   The growth of population has now covered these outlying districts with pretentious homes, and the region, which twenty-five years ago was covered by the swampy lands of the ancient Mexican lakes, is now the site of palatial dwellings, intersected with streets, and resembling the best residential quarters of European and American cities.   Equestrian and heroic statues adorn the streets for miles; generous shade trees hide the homes and protect the passerby, and at night the city glows with electrical illumination. Romantic old churches exist in great numbers; public buildings conceived on a magnificent scale, benevolent institutions, colleges, and schools are everywhere. Clubs of all kinds exist in profusion; there is the famous Jockey Club, renowned for its antique tiling and its aristocratic traditions; the Country Club, actually an American institution, but nominally cosmopolitan, a beautiful edifice with extensive grounds for golf and tennis; the American, British, Spanish, German, and French clubs, devoted to colonial social interests, and the Reforma, a British club, devoted to tennis and football. There is also the small but happily constituted Paseo Club, where I spent many pleasant hours.

Outside the city to a distance of seventeen miles there are numerous beautiful suburbs connected by excellent asphalt roads; of these Tacubaya, filled with old homes and spacious gardens, is the nearest; beyond lies Mixcoac, similar in character but neither so large nor so interesting; from there on there is a straight run to San Angel, a delightful place ornamented with stately homes and possessing a French hotel called the Villa des Roses and a quaint old monastery, converted into a hotel, called the San Angel Inn. In after times we had delightful luncheon parties at both of these hostelries. Returning from San Angel one passes through the old town of Coyoacan, which contains a church built by Cortez, and the Casa de Alvarado, which is probably the oldest residence in America. It was built by Alvarado soon after the Spaniards established their control over Mexico, and remains to-day almost as it existed then, being the property of a distinguished American woman, Mrs. Zelda Nuttall, whose hospitality we frequently enjoyed and whose friendship we greatly cherish.

The population of Mexico City was then about 500,000 people, half of whom lived in either wealth or comparative comfort, the others amid surroundings of the most distressing kind. In respect to sanitation, ventilation, and space, the poorer quarters were a disgrace to civilization, and it is to be hoped that some of the numerous apostles of reform, who so frequently decorate the political checkerboard of Mexico, may address themselves to the proper housing of the poor, the supervision of food products, the maintenance of public baths, and those other concomitants of civilization which at present are lacking.

CHAPTER XXVI

Official presentation to President Diaz—A misadventure—The Mexican Cabinet—The American Embassy and its personnel—Luis d'Antin—Work of the embassy and entertainments—Death of Mirascal and appointment of Enrique Creel as Minister of Foreign Affairs—Mr. Creel and other Mexican Ministers of Foreign Affairs.

IN DUE time I was received in official audience by President Diaz. Escorted by the President's aide-de-camp, Colonel Samuel Garcia Cuellar, accompanied by the entire staff of the embassy, I arrived at the government palace, and passing through files of soldiers up the grand stairway to the entrance of the audience chamber, was greeted by the Minister of Foreign Affairs, Mr. Ignacio Mariscal, and conducted into the presence of the President who stood at the extreme end of the audience chamber, flanked on either side by the members of his cabinet. Without further ceremony, except the official bows, I took out my manuscript for the purpose of reading my address, when I found to my horror that my glasses were missing. After a moment's confusion I delivered the address as accurately as possible from memory. At the conclusion of the President's answer he invited me to be seated for a few moments' informal conversation; this, while not serious in tenor, gave an impression which confirmed in a measure the estimate which the world had already placed on the character of this remarkable man. At this time his mentality was still alert and the decadence which set in later was not evident.

On this occasion I first met José Ives Limantour, Minister of Finance, Ignacio Mariscal, Minister of Foreign Affairs, Olegarrio Molina, Minister of Fomento, and Ramon Corral, Vice-president and Minister of the Interior, all men who had rendered valuable services to Mexico but who were destined to be lost in the throes of the coming revolution.

Ramon Corral, the Vice-president and Minister of the Interior, was a man of little polish and no cosmopolitan finish; he was from the state of Sonora, where he had a successful business career, among other things dealing in a considerable way with American interests. Corral's force, courage, and severe disposition attracted the attention of Diaz and led eventually to his election as Vice-president with Diaz, when it became generally understood that he had been anointed for the succession. Before the revolution took on serious form, Corral became ill and was obliged to retire from active participation in public affairs; eventually he went to Europe for a course of treatment and died there. Had he lived, the course of the revolution might have been arrested, as he would have dealt savagely and conclusively with unruly elements. In character he more closely resembled Diaz than any other man in public life.

José Ives Limantour, Minister of Finance, was an interesting figure. He was of French extraction, polished and scholarly attainments, trained in statesmanship, urbane in manner, with all the finish and dignity of a French gentleman of the old school. He was reputed to be enormously wealthy, but I never heard any charges of irregularities in his public life. For many years Diaz leaned heavily upon the wisdom and fidelity of Limantour, but in the last days of his régime the ties which united them were considerably weakened though they never reached the breaking point.

Limantour was in a constant state of apprehension concerning the attitude of the government of the United States toward Mexico and could never banish the suspicion that our motives were only superficially friendly. With the advent of Madero he disappeared from the scene, and reappeared later on the boulevards of Paris.

Olegarrio Molina, Minister of Fomento, came from Yucatan, where he was for a long time the richest and most influential planter. He was a quiet man, of great dignity of manner, modest in deportment, able in administration, and thoroughly patriotic and honest. He, too, disappeared from the scene, but I have never learned whither his exile carried him.

The embassy was installed amid undignified and unbusinesslike surroundings; the records were incomplete, the working system out of date and wholly inadequate to deal with the amount of work which the embassy was called upon to perform. Ultimately we secured for a combined embassy and residence the building on the corner of Vera Cruz and Puebla streets, where we resided through four years of tempestuous experiences. This building later became fixed in the American public eye by the numerous pictures taken during the days of the revolution. It was of the medieval-castle type, impressive in appearance and commodious and comfortable within. There were in all some thirty rooms, the supervision and care of which required a large force of servants.

The public reception rooms were dignified and spacious. Through additions made from time to time the gardens surrounding the embassy finally became sufficiently large and cultivated to give the impression of a home atmosphere. Next, the task of reorganizing the working system and of establishing definite rules for social and official procedure was taken up and not abandoned until it reached a degree of effectiveness which enabled the embassy to meet with accuracy and dispatch the burden of work which soon fell upon it.

Mr. Fred Morris Dearing became first secretary soon after my arrival and remained there until he was attached to the Department of State and placed in charge of the division of Mexican and Central American affairs. Mr. Dearing was an able assistant; his work was thorough and conscientious and his services during the time he was attached to the embassy were of the greatest value. His subsequent transfer to the Department of State greatly facilitated the exchanges between Washington and Mexico and made possible an accurate estimate of the Mexican situation by the President and the Secretary of State. His demotion by the Wilson administration from the position of chief of the Latin-American division to secretary of the legation at Brussels deprived our government of an experienced officer at a crisis when his services were most needed. This injustice was happily remedied by the Harding administration, which made Mr. Dearing First Assistant Secretary of State and later sent him as minister to Portugal.

It is unnecessary to speak of the other secretaries as they were in a constant state of transition. Second secretary Henry F. Tennant rendered very efficient service at all times, and especially during the *Decena Trajica*. Captain Sturtevant, the military attaché, an excellent officer, was a loyal and valuable assistant. The same may be said of Captain Burnside.

To handle this work and to take care of the urgent demands made upon the embassy by Americans in Mexico, there should have been constantly at hand a large and competent clerical force. Normally, however, there were only three clerks, two of them being typists, and one, Luis d'Antin, being in charge of translations, legal questions, and routine work in the Mexican departments of government. The clerical force of the embassy rose and fell with the surgence and resurgence of important political events; at times there were in the embassy as many as six clerks and at other times the number fell to three, but whether we were supplied to the limit or reduced to normal, the work in hand always exceeded the hours of the day and sometimes extended into the middle of the night.

Luis d'Antin was born in Texas of a French father and a Mexican mother. The circumstance of his birth and education made him at home in the language, habits, and psychology of three races, but in his mental processes and traditions he was a Mexican. His Americanism, however, was very pronounced and he invariably took the American view on all questions between the two countries. He was oratorical, deferential, courteous, usually faultlessly attired, and frequently absorbed in romantic episodes which involved him in pecuniary and mental troubles; troubles which vanished with the passing day, for with him the tragedy of to-day became the comedy of to-morrow.

During the bombardment of the City of Mexico, at the time of the overthrow of Madero by Felix Diaz, the embassy was subjected to desultory firing and Luis d'Antin's nerves got the better of him—very largely, I think, because one of his latest female conquests had taken refuge in a dangerous part of the city and he was distracted between his duty to the embassy and the absent inamorata—and he continued profoundly disturbed until the change of government, when he recovered his *sang froid*, and was very useful to me in the triangular discussions which took place between the embassy, Huerta, and Felix Diaz. He remained in the embassy when I left for the United States, but afterward came to Washington and was finally employed in the Mexican embassy. During his employment there an effort was made to induce him, for a money consideration, to give false testimony against me, and I am glad to say that he stood the test and remained loyal. He was afterward ordered to Mexico by the Mexican government and was reported to have died en route between Washington and Mexico City. The accepted version of his decease, however, is that he was stabbed to death in his berth by some of the savage crew who were then in control of the government of Mexico.

D'Antin was an erratic, exotic growth, but some underlying virtue in the blood made him loyal in critical hours and redeemed his memory.

Mr. Charles B. Parker, a young man of fine character and qualities, was second clerk and remained with me to the last. He enjoyed my full confidence and was cognizant of every act performed by me, and every written word.

With this force, supplemented under pressure by special clerks from the Department of State, the work of the embassy was carried on; its correspondence, while I was in charge, exceeded that of any other embassy of the United

States, amounting, in fact, to 33 per cent. of the foreign correspondence of the Department of State.

The months of April and May were devoted to entertainments given us by officials of the Mexican government and prominent members of Mexican society, by my colleagues of the diplomatic corps, and by members of the American colony in Mexico. The Mexican entertainments were perfunctory, but those of the diplomatic corps were wholly different, being characterized by freedom from formality and by a genuine hospitality.

These affairs were interrupted by the death of Mr. Mariscal who had served as Minister of Foreign Affairs in Mexico for some twenty years and who was highly esteemed not only in his own country but in all the chancelleries of Europe. His death was a great loss to the Diaz administration, which had relied for years upon his well-known ability in dealing with international problems, and it had difficulty in finding a person with the prestige and experience necessary to meet the exacting duties of this important post.

Mr. Enrique Creel, who succeeded Mr. Mariscal as Minister of Foreign Affairs, was the son of an American, a native of Kentucky, and a relative of Henry Clay, who had gone to Chihuahua in the capacity of American consul and had there married a daughter of Terrasas, the largest landowner in the country. Mr. Creel inherited great wealth and added very rapidly to what he inherited. He was a man of large affairs, and his extensive transactions attracted the attention of General Diaz, who made him ambassador at Washington. There he made an undeniably good impression and acquired a standing which enabled him later to render useful services to his country. His selection by Diaz to be Minister of Foreign Affairs, after the death of Mariscal, was hailed generally as timely and wise. Although the son of an American, Mr. Creel had been reared in Mexican traditions; his admiration and affection for the United States was very great, but there was never any question of a divided nationality. While he was disposed to be just in treating American interests, he remained nevertheless Mexican in his viewpoint, and the interests of his native country were always paramount. He was able and adroit in the discussion of such questions as arose between the United States and Mexico, but he never uttered a word or wrote a line that might be construed as provocative. I had and retain for him the greatest respect, and I deeply regret the misfortunes which have overtaken his family, misfortunes which were not penalties for wrongs but for thrift and integrity.

One of the noticeable things in the organization of Mexican cabinets was the high character of those in charge of the portfolio of the Department of Foreign Affairs. Mr. Mariscal, Mr. Creel, Mr. De la Barra, Mr. Calero, and Mr. Lascurain, who were successively in charge of this department while I was ambassador in Mexico, were all men of excellent character and standing, honest and just in dealing with the diplomats accredited at the Mexican capital and governed in their dealings by a sincere desire not only to serve their government but to maintain good relations with all others. These ministers differed widely in character and training, but possessed in common a lively appreciation of international obligations and a profound respect for the traditions of the Mexican foreign office.

[179]

After the overthrow of Madero and the final elimination of De la Barra from Huerta's cabinet, the Mexican foreign office ceased to be an agency for the maintenance of healthy relations with foreign governments and became a mere channel for political propaganda.

CHAPTER XXVII

*Diplomatic colleagues in Mexico—Mexican "Herald"—American news-
paper correspondents—The American colony*

I FOUND in Mexico, as elsewhere, some interesting
and some peculiar diplomats.

Sir Reginald Tower was the British representative.
He had been in Mexico for some time and was well
acquainted with conditions and people. Tower was a tall,
slender person with a smiling countenance and an agreeable manner. He was correct and precise in the performance of his diplomatic duties, able and alert in dealing
with diplomatic questions, and a general favourite with
everyone. I was closely associated with him in defending
some common interests before the Mexican government
and was pleased with his intelligent coöperation. Tower
went from Mexico City to the Argentine Republic, and
with the close of the World War was made High Com-
missioner at Danzig, attaining some publicity in the tense
situation which developed there. He was succeeded in
Mexico City by Sir Francis Stronge, a Belfast Irishman,
who though of sufficiently sedate years had recently married an Irish lady of respectable maturity. Both Sir
Francis and Lady Stronge were amiable people, anxious
to be on good terms with all the world and to meet the
exigencies of the diplomatic protocol. Sir Francis had a
consuming passion for parrots, and one gathered somehow
the suspicion that they participated in his councils.

[181]

Whether in drawing room, at table, or in the chancellery, one of them was always present, perched upon His Excellency's shoulder and mingling affably but insistently in the conversation. During the critical hours of the revolution against Madero the British colony grew impatient of this eccentric side of Sir Francis's character, as well as what they esteemed his lack of initiative, and sent me a numerously signed resolution tendering their support and asking for enrollment under the American embassy. I thought this an undeserved rebuke, for although Sir Francis may have been better suited to the quieter walks of diplomacy he was not at all unmindful of his duties and was really desirous of performing them so far as his natural antipathy to noise and violence would permit.

Our first German colleague was Karl von Buentz, who left very soon after my arrival. He remained long enough, however, to give us an elaborate official dinner, remembered afterward in connection with the death of Mariscal, Minister of Foreign Affairs, who on this occasion contracted a fatal cold. Von Buentz, during the World War, figured in the German conspiracies and propaganda in the United States and was tried and found guilty for violation of our espionage laws.

Admiral Paul von Hintze succeeded Von Buentz as our German colleague. Admiral Von Hintze had begun life as a soldier, achieving some distinction in the profession. Later in his career he entered the imperial navy and through the favour of the Emperor, whose attention was attracted by his fine qualities, rose to the rank of admiral. Prior to coming to Mexico he had been naval and military attaché of the Imperial Embassy in St. Petersburg, a position always filled by one in the most intimate confidence of the Emperor. I formed a high opinion of Admiral Von Hintze from the first moment of our acquaintance and this opinion I had no occasion to modify subsequently. Through all the trying hours of the revolutions against Diaz and Madero, culminating in the bombardment of the City of Mexico, his sympathy and advice were of infinite value. While the bombardment was in progress he was especially active and supported me in every crisis with unswerving courage and absolute disregard of every consideration except the faithful performance of the duties pertaining to his high office. Although of unfaltering courage, in the midst of dangerous situations, Von Hintze was not of the sabre-rattling German military type. He was passionately patriotic in the service of the Empire; he would willingly have sacrificed himself in its behalf, but he would have committed no crime in the name of patriotism. He loved music and art and was full of quick human sympathies. Admiral Von Hintze later became the chancellor of the German Empire, figured prominently in the dramatic fall of the Kaiser, and saw the imperial standards of militant aristocracy levelled in the dust before the advancing hosts of democracy.

Italy was represented by Count Masiglia, a diplomat of training and experience. He was on leave of absence during the most critical period, and immediately after the overthrow of Madero was succeeded by Baron Carlo de Aliotti, who, in the earlier days of the provisional government of Huerta, was most active in his efforts to bring about a united action of the powers in according it recognition. In these efforts he was ably seconded by Mr. Paul May, the Belgian minister, who remained in Mexico long after my departure, but finally fell a victim to the lawless and godless government of Carranza, which had no time to deal with protesting diplomats and promptly expelled him.[1] Carranza was a Mexican of the provincial type and phrases about international obligations and courtesies had no place in his vocabulary. Without resources or military forces he vociferously and successfully challenged empires.

The French minister, Mr. Paul Le Faivre, and his accomplished wife, Madame Le Faivre, were distinct contributions to the life of the diplomatic corps; they were excellent examples of the old French school, combining rare courtesy with great culture. Mr. Le Faivre remained in Mexico until my final departure; he was at all times a loyal and intelligent colleague, anxious to coöperate in all ways in matters that were of common interest.

The Spanish minister, Börnardo de Cologan y Cologan, belonged to the old Spanish school of diplomacy and had had varied experience in the representation of his country throughout the world. He had been His Catholic Majesty's minister in China during the siege of Pekin and came to Mexico from the Chinese post. He was actively associated with me through the various revolutions and rendered valuable services in critical moments; he possessed personal courage and undeviating honesty of opinion, useful qualities in great emergencies.

The American newspaper world was well represented in Mexico City. The *Mexican Herald*, printed in English, was, in point of excellence, comparable with the newspapers of any average American city. The *Herald* was a

---

[1]When Carranza made his formal entrance into Mexico City the horses of many of the diplomatic corps were stolen and handed over to Carranza's generals, for use in the parade. May protested against the outrage and was expelled from Mexico for having made protest.

power for good not only for Mexico but for American interests during the administration of Diaz. When anti-Americanism began to take hold in Mexico, the *Herald* took the courageous and possibly impracticable stand of staunchly defending in every instance Americans and American interests. During the high tides of radicalism, the editor, Mr. Paul Hudson, was obliged to leave Mexico and abandon his property. There were American correspondents in abundance and these at critical moments kept the embassy busy, but with a single exception they were discreet and fair. I had had little contact and no differences with American correspondents in Chile or Belgium, but in Mexico where I was confronted with difficult problems and needed the support and sympathy of all American elements, some of my greatest embarrassments grew out of the malicious attitude of one single correspondent. Throughout the difficult days in Mexico I had the cordial coöperation of all American news-distributing agencies and of the American correspondents with one exception; this exception caused me some personal discomfort by his incomprehensible malice and mendacity, and his inventions and perversions of truth cast suspicion upon the character of our diplomacy in Mexico. He had unusual cleverness in the invention of sensational stories which he ingeniously linked together in complete disregard of injury done to man, woman, or government. In a dangerous crisis I expelled this correspondent from the embassy for conduct unbecoming an American and a gentleman and asked him to confine his future visits there to purely official matters. Thereafter he was a tireless enemy and upon three occasions at least fabricated, out of whole cloth, without even circumstantial basis, stories,

[185]

to which, in the interest of the good name of our diplomacy in Mexico and for the protection of my own reputation in the United States, I was obliged to enter official and substantial denial in the newspapers which had published them. Even to this day the legend which this correspondent invented of my being partly responsible for the overthrow of Madero persists in Mexico; it has been persistently repeated there, though its author was effectively silenced by a decision of the courts in this country.[1]

The matter of dealing with correspondents of American newspapers is a serious one for our diplomatic representatives, since through the influence of unscrupulous correspondents newspapers of high standing may be led to adopt a policy injurious to the interests of our government. If the attitude of an irresponsible correspondent toward a diplomatic representative had no other result than personal injury to that individual, it might be tolerated, but it must be remembered that misinterpretation of the purposes or acts of an ambassador or minister lowers his prestige with the government to which he is accredited and to that extent impairs his usefulness in rendering good service; moreover, adverse criticism by influential home journals may modify the activities of a diplomatic officer even when acting in strict accordance with official instructions. There should be complete liberty of criticism, of course, but it should be used sparingly and never abused. In moments of great stress in foreign capitals American newspapers should, unless already provided with a high standard of representation, consider it a patriotic as well as

---

[1] One of the purposes of this person's attack was to discredit me with Republican leaders. That it failed to do so is shown by the fact that in 1921, on the return of the party to power, President Harding offered me the ambassadorship to Turkey contingent on the negotiation of a treaty with that country, which I tentatively accepted.

a professional duty to dispatch correspondents of unquestioned character and experience to the scene.

The American colony at this time was large and prosperous. There were about ten thousand Americans in the City of Mexico and, though engaged in all occupations and drawn from all classes of society, they were, on the whole, creditable examples of American manhood and womanhood, displaying in trying emergencies the stronger and better qualities of our race. In the earlier days of my residence I had differences with some of the colony concerning the proposal to erect a monument to peace dedicated to President Diaz. I regarded the proposed action as unethical and impolitic and finally prevailed upon the colony to express their appreciation of the Diaz government through the presentation of a George Washington monument. This monument was dedicated with appropriate ceremonies and I believe still stands in one of the *gloriettas* of Mexico City. I am glad to say that this adjustment was satisfactory to everyone. When I left Mexico there was ample evidence that I possessed the confidence of all Americans and other nationals and I carried away with me a genuine respect for the colony and a deep sense of gratitude for its unswerving loyalty to me.

CHAPTER XXVIII

Life in Mexico City—The Mexican Centennial—Anti-American demonstration

AFTER five years of life in the humid and depressing climate of Belgium our first impressions of Mexico were delightful. The beautiful city, parked with long avenues of trees, broken by gardens and gloriettas, crowned by the vast heights of the twin mountains Popocatepetl and Ixtaccihuatl, and bathed in a wealth of sunlight or gorgeous moonlight, moves profoundly the imagination of the newcomer; these first impressions seem not to pass away but rather to grow with familiarity.

Life is essentially—for climatic reasons—a day life and an out-of-door one. The nights are cold and the open air is supposed to be unhealthful after five o'clock; but in the daytime there is a riot of sunlight. The drives are picturesque; trees and flowers are full of bloom and beauty and the outskirts are dotted with numerous villages, clubs, inns, and resorts which afford a solace to those denied the intellectual atmosphere or night gaieties of other capitals. Through four years of residence we enjoyed these phases of life to their full and when I could snatch a moment from the labours of the embassy it was spent in the open air, riding, driving, or in field sports. Until the month of October, 1910, we found Mexico City a pleasant place of residence and were well satisfied with our experiences.

After the revolution had endured for more than a year I was obliged to give up all outside distractions and devote myself to the difficult and dangerous situation which demanded a watchful eye and often instantaneous action. After the first outbreak of the revolution in October, 1910, I made it a rule to be constantly in the embassy; if absent, to have my whereabouts known. I have reason to know that the strict adherence to this rule in several instances saved American lives.

In the month of September the Mexican government celebrated with great pomp and magnificence the Centennial of Independence. Preparations for this event were made upon an elaborate scale and the energies of the federal and state governments were given up to it. Large sums of money were expended in publicity and in securing the presence of notable and distinguished people at this supposed crowning event in the career of President Diaz. Almost every government in the world was represented by delegates with sonorous titles who came thither with trains and suites and participated in the festivities for the better part of a month. There were banquets and celebrations and balls and ceremonies in fatiguing succession; monuments to Mexican, French, Spanish, and British celebrities were dedicated with formal ceremonies. The American colony upon this occasion dedicated a monument to George Washington which, on their behalf, I presented to the Mexican government in the presence of the president of the republic, his cabinet, the diplomatic corps, and foreign dignitaries. Our government had concurred in these celebrations with a large and distinguished delegation; there were two or three Senators, a number of Representatives, delegates from the bench, the bar, and the press in generous

[189]

numbers. The delegation, headed by Curtis Guild of Massachusetts, was housed and fed by the Mexican government, which carried hospitality and courtesy to the extreme limit. There followed days of fiestas, dedications, memorials, and diplomatic oratroy which, if they served no other purpose, at least marked the distinct impression which Mexico had made upon the world under the Diaz administration.

The celebration closed with the impressive ceremony of the apotheosis, followed by a magnificent ball, over which the President and Mrs. Diaz presided with true monarchical dignity and ceremony. Diaz was crowned the saviour and ruler of Mexico, but even while the acclamations of vast throngs were reverberating through the palaces and streets of Mexico City, the hour of disaster was drawing nigh; the great structure which had been built up by the wisdom, sobriety, and patriotism of one man had not been built strong enough to withstand the storms which presently broke forth; from the pinnacle which he had reached, Diaz fell to an abyss and with him fell his country.

Diaz quickly passed from the scene to spend his last days in dignified penury, but the Mexican deluge followed and endured. Parenthetically, one is impressed with the identic fate of the historic characters of Latin America—San Martín, O'Higgins, Bolivar, Miranda, and finally Diaz passed from power into exile. All achieved successful revolutions; all were elevated to supreme functions; all renounced power and all died in exile. It was not easy to make stern conditions agree with accepted theories of free government; and yet, according to their times and opportunities, these men were sincere and disinterested patriots, achieving the best results which could be achieved with the materials at hand. Ideal republics or governments do not often find birth in the storm of conflict and revolution; the practice of real liberty comes only with prosaic and sober peace, when the iron of the sword is turned into pruning hooks and the cannon rusts in the open. All these heroes, leaders, and builders were overturned and driven out in the name of liberty, but those who followed them added misgovernment, tyranny, and confusion to autocracy.

In the early part of October, after the close of the Centennial Celebration, the anti-American riots occurred in Mexico City. The riots were ostensibly provoked by the lynching of a Mexican by the name of Antonio Rodriguez in the State of Texas, but I believed at the time, and still believe, that they were fomented by certain officials of the government for the purpose of diverting public attention from the growing discontent with the régime of General Diaz. I use the word "fomented" advisedly, because there was no evidence at this time of any real differences between Mexicans and Americans resident in Mexico. Indeed, I believe the Americans were everywhere esteemed as employers of labour and as managers of the enterprises which were developing the country. For three days Mexico City was in the possession of anti-American mobs which destroyed considerable property, tore down and burned the American flag, and insulted and abused Americans whenever they were found upon the streets. The American clubs, hotels, and known business houses were attacked, and in some instances children of the American schools were assaulted. The American clubs put up an effective resistance and the Americans generally developed belligerent tendencies.

Confident that this hostile movement was artificial and designed to cloak certain political conditions from public scrutiny, I took prompt and severe methods to arrest its activities. I felt genuinely grieved that Americans who were peaceably living in Mexico should be obliged to suffer for a crime committed against a Mexican in Texas while I was constantly having to complain to the Mexican government of outrages of the worst kind against American citizens. In this frame of mind I addressed a note to the Mexican Minister of Foreign Affairs calling his attention to the disgraceful rioting which had occurred in the city, the burning of the American flag in the presence of the police, the stoning of the office of the *Mexican Herald*, and various outrages and assaults perpetrated against Americans on the streets. Reciting these events, I demanded in the most urgent way that the government should speedily suppress mob violence and asked for the punishment of those who had committed offensive acts. I also made a statement to the press, severely criticizing the Mexican local authorities and advising all Americans to remain off the streets until they could be certain of protection, and by emphatic expressions to government officials sought to abate the excitement before the occurrence of events which would certainly arouse deep feeling in the United States.

The attitude of the embassy and the indignation expressed by the American press had the desired effect; and although the movement had its echoes, as I anticipated it would, in various provincial cities, serious clashes were prevented and those who attacked Americans were usually dealt with severely by the authorities or were restrained by the bold front shown by their apparently helpless enemies.

The only persons killed were Mexicans and these met their deaths either at the hands of the authorities or of Americans acting in self-defense. One American in Guadelajara successfully resisted an attack on his home by a mob of some hundreds of Mexicans, killing three of them during the assault.

CHAPTER XXIX

First signals of the revolution—Causes of the revolution

THIS same month, reading the significance of these events in their true light, as was subsequently shown, I sent a confidential dispatch to Mr. Knox predicting the early outbreak of an armed revolution against the government. I insert here a brief quotation from this dispatch:

". . . it seems to me from my observation of the situation that we are rapidly approaching a crisis in the affairs of this nation, the result of which must be of vital importance to American commerce and to American capital invested here. . . ."

Before this dispatch reached Washington the first outbreak of the revolution had occurred in the city of Pueblo. The causes which precipitated the movement were substantially as follows:

1st: *The system of government.* This was constitutional in form but autocratic in practice, thus offering a constant invitation to political upheaval, the difference between form and substance, between profession and practice, offering ready loopholes to protest and agitation. Theoretically, Mexico is a federal republic similar in form to ours, certain specified rights being reserved to the states and certain others being exercised by the central government.

Like ours the central government is divided into three branches, viz., the legislative, executive, and judicial, but this is a nominal division only as the legislative and judicial branches are subordinate to and, in a measure, creatures of the executive. To carry on government smoothly the members of both branches of the legislature must be in political accord with the executive, and it is not in the leastwise controverted that in order to be elected either a deputy or a senator executive approval is essential; the law-making power is thus virtually in the hands of the executive. The control of the executive over the judiciary is even more absolute than that exercised over the legislative branch. Though a form of election is observed, the President actually names and removes at pleasure all of the eleven judges of the Supreme Court and the judges of the minor federal courts. Having control of the enactment of the laws of the republic through representatives of his own choosing, and of the interpretation of the laws and the administration of justice through an attached and subservient judiciary, it is not difficult to understand that the President of the republic was really an autocrat ruling and governing through republican forms but maintaining his rule by the use of the instrumentalities inherently belonging to the executive—the army and the police.

The same system which obtains in the central government extends to the state governments, whose chief executives are virtually named by the President, but whose powers and ambitions are guarded and circumscribed by a retinue of personal agents of the chief executive called *Jefes Politicos*. The power of these officials sometimes exceeds that of the governor. In other respects the state governments are exact copies of the central government, the governors exercising the power over the state legislatures and courts exercised by the President over the federal legislature and courts.

The instrumentalities through which the executive maintains his power and the enforcement of his policies are the army and the police (or rurales). The military force of the republic is never sufficiently large to combat a powerful neighbour, but in the hands of a determined and sagacious autocrat is ample for policing the country and for the maintenance of order and the permanence of a dynasty.

2d: *The growing unpopularity of the Diaz régime.* This resulted from its control by a circle of so-called "Cientificos"—the name originally applied to a small group of intellectuals and reformers whose views were obnoxious to Diaz, but gradually extended by popular misconception so as to embrace all of the principal supporters of the Diaz régime—and from the probability that this régime would be continued under Vice-president Corral, whom Diaz and his friends had selected for the presidency after the refusal of Limantour to assume the responsibilities of the office. Diaz had great confidence in Limantour and great admiration for his moral and intellectual qualities and would cheerfully have entrusted power in his hands. If Limantour had been selected as the successor to Diaz, the Madero revolution would probably not have occurred, as the Madero family had close business and personal relations with him. Limantour never faltered in his allegiance of loyalty to Diaz, but he mistakenly advocated negotiations with Madero and these negotiations fatally involved the Diaz administration.

The crisis brought about in Mexican affairs and the imperilling of the nation's life, as well as its republican institutions, by the intervention of Europe under the leadership of France; the overthrow and death of Maximilian, under circumstances which shocked the sensibilities of the civilized world; the vacillation and impotence of Juarez brought a new character into the field—one whose name was destined to be more illustrious than that of any other Mexican, and whose rule, autocratic in character but republican in form, was to endure for thirty years. Sprung from the masses, trained in the army, quick in decision, firm in purpose, Porfirio Diaz governed Mexico for thirty years, autocratically and sometimes ruthlessly, but he possessed withal undeviating personal honesty, loyalty to obligations, a real patriotism, and a lofty conception of Mexico's needs and future. His foreign policy was clear and consistent from the first days of his power; its corner stone was the cultivation of the friendliest relations with the government of the United States, coupled with an encouragement to American capital and energy to go thither and develop the marvellous richness of the country, affording them generous profits but reaping in return far greater ones for Mexico.

Diaz had two outstanding domestic policies: (1) The development of the material resources of the country; (2) the quickening of the moral life of the nation. The first of these policies he accomplished with a high measure of success, and the second he probably would have accomplished but for the undermining influences of advancing years. He covered Mexico with a network of railways; developed her resources by encouragement to foreign capital, in the form of compensation in public lands or exemption from taxation for the construction of public utilities; fostered her manufacturing and commercial interests; built hospitals and innumerable public institutions; established Mexican credit at home and abroad; and, with his army and rural police, made life as safe on a Mexican highway as on one of the public thoroughfares of the State of Massachusetts. With the materials which he had at hand he tried to establish justice, and no man with an honest cause ever suffered at his hand, and those who observed the law and kept the peace were secure in their lives and possessions; it was understood that those who broke the law must pay the penalty and this made peace. If Diaz had awakened the moral sense of the nation, if he had carried the torch of enlightenment into the dark places, the story of Mexico might have been differently written. With the lapse of years a disposition to lean upon tradition and prestige became evident and the sense of security, born of unbroken power, dulled decision and caution. Vigour and watchfulness gave way to indolent confidence; the public service became corrupt or incompetent; the army—the vital part of an autocratic machine—lost in numbers and discipline. The Diaz cabinet for the last ten years of his continuance in power was almost entirely made up of very old men past their years of usefulness. Mr. Fernandez, the Minister of Justice, was over eighty years of age; General Cosio, the Minister of War, was over eighty years of age; and Mr. Fernandez, Minister of Communications and Highways, Mr. Molina, Minister of Fomento, and Mr. Corral, Minister of the Interior, were close to seventy; the youngest members of the cabinet, Mr. Limantour and Mr. Creel, were in the neighbourhood of sixty. The régime of General

Diaz was really directed and sustained by three men—Limantour, Molina, and Corral, who with their "Cientifico" aides administered the government generally for the good of the nation, but not always so. Their relations with great American and European corporations, perhaps unavoidable, created an atmosphere of suspicion which blinded the nation to the generous scope of many of the enterprises with which they were associated. The intrigues of an army of supporters brought into evil repute a great work which might otherwise have been useful and, with the evils resulting from the "cankers of a long peace," the demoralization of the army and the courts, laid the foundation for popular discontent.

3d: *The agrarian question.* When the Spaniards completed their conquest of Mexico, they divided the country into large estates and apportioned them to Spaniards. Some of these estates were as large as Indiana or Illinois and, though the process of disintegration through sale and inheritance was very great, the soil never reached its indigenous owner, but passed to Americans, Europeans, and white Mexicans. Even now vast estates, mounting to millions of acres, are in the hands of single owners, while the indigenous population is without ownership in the soil. Perhaps 80 per cent. of the population of Mexico were without an abiding place except by sufferance and took no more than a nominal part in the affairs of the country, were unable to read or write and, while preserving the traditions and vices of their ancestors, were made infinitely worse by the engrafting of the vices of the white man. This element of the population can never be brought to the practice of democratic self-government by revolution. Their elevation to the level of self-government can be accomplished only by evolution, and the slow processes of evolution can only be worked out through control by a strong central government working to definite ends through the medium of universal education, the establishment of order and justice, and the development of the material resources of the country.

4th: *The judiciary*. The most difficult problem the embassy had to deal with while I was in Mexico, and the greatest cause of general complaint in the republic, was the lame, incompetent, and corrupt judiciary. Naturally a weak and debauched judiciary falls as an especial burden upon the people of the country in which it exists, but having in mind our investments in the country, the constant inflow of American capital, and the steady increase of American immigration, it is of prime importance for us to know in just what manner the courts are constituted, the influences which surround them, their methods of procedure, and the character of their personnel. It is important to know, 1st: that all Mexican courts are the creatures of the executive, dependent upon the will of the executive and responsible only to the executive; 2d, that judicial opinion is not the expression of law and precedent but the transmitted voice of the executive; 3d, that the Mexican legal structure, though built upon the Napoleonic code, varies from it sufficiently to clothe the executive with direct power over the life or property of any citizen; 4th, judicial decisions are not final as to the law or even as to the facts. All decisions must be reaffirmed before becoming final as to the law and the facts. This is the *crevasse* through which pours a constantly widening current of corruption and intrigue; 5th, there may be many honest judges in Mexico but there are no independent ones. While I was in charge of the embassy I was obliged, in protecting American interests, to be constantly in contact with the judiciary of the federal district, the Supreme Court, and the different states. Only by the exercise of the utmost vigilance and by pressure upon the President, upon the foreign office, by unofficial communications to governors, and by visits of representatives of the embassy to the courts, was it possible to prevent the grossest injustice to American citizens. Many of these cases were pure attempts at robbery under the form of law and in some of them, involving millions of dollars, the coterie of politicians, who surrounded the President and worked under the influence of his name but without his approval, were interested. In defending these cases with the President, the foreign office, the governors, and the judges, I sometimes exceeded the limits of usual diplomatic procedure and assumed dangerous personal risks, but I thought then, and still think, that in a country where such peculiar conditions exist there is no refuge for an American citizen whose clear and just rights are invaded save in the power and influence of his government asserted through its diplomatic representative.

CHAPTER XXX

Something about Mexico and the Mexican people—The Madero revolution—Taft mobilizes troops on the Mexican border for the protection of American citizens and to prevent violations of neutrality from American soil.

THE vice-royal colony, empire, and republic, which has flourished for three hundred years amidst intermittent, feverish disorder south of the Rio Grande, has been, in whatsoever form it has existed, a mystery, politically, ethnologically, psychologically, to the American people. Two thousand miles long and eleven hundred miles wide, washed by the waters of two oceans and watered by innumerable streams flowing from its towering mountains, it remained until the Diaz epoch a *terra incognita*, a romantic empire where millions of people were living, and where the products of all other lands were found teeming in richness and super-abundant plenty. There grew rubber, rice, hemp, coffee, sugar, and tobacco sufficient to supply the markets of the world; gold, silver, and copper dug from the soil, from the time of the Spaniard, had furnished the sinews of historic wars and marked the fall of dynasties and the rise of republics. No more healthful climate existed in the world; it is a country blessed by nature and God but for which man has done very little.

In the dim and remote centuries there came into Mexico a flood of races of unknown and mysterious origin who built vast cities rivalling Tyre and Sidon in magnificence and wealth, and established a civilization which was either the parent source of the Asiatic civilizations or the inheritor of them. Whence the Maya, the Toltec, and the Aztec came is a mystery of the ages. Whether their civilization was indigenous or traced its origin back to Syrian, Egyptian, or Hebraic sources is an unsolved problem. Legend and symbolic inscription exist, but science has not yet unravelled the mystery, nor established any determinate hypothesis assigning these peoples to their ancient racial class. Nor can they reasonably all be assigned to the same parent stem; the Maya of the south, sometimes called the White Indian, is in mental, moral, and physical character distinct from and superior to the Aztec and the Toltec of the Mexican tableland. The Indian of the northern and border Mexican states has little, if any, affinity with the other two races, being historically a descendant of the Indian tribes of North America and inheriting their good and bad qualities.

These differing races of Indians inhabited Mexico when that picturesque figure of romance, Hernando Cortes, came in quest of gold and empire. The story of the heroism and the cruelty of this man and his following of soldiers and priests has been told by Prescott and Wallace; how he overran Mexico and terrorized its population with a band insignificant in numbers when harassed by conspiracies and rebellion; how he finally triumphed over the native races in the name and by the authority of the gloomy autocrat of the Palace of the Escorial; and how, with the sword, the religion of Christ was implanted and the dominion of the Church established. But the religion of the Spaniard was only superficially accepted by the native races, and in all essentials, except superficial ones, they remain to-day in habits and character no better, if not worse, than they were when Cortes landed at Vera Cruz.

Among the Indian races the spread of intemperance, and consequent debasement of the masses, is breeding and nursing poverty, ignorance, and superstition with alarming rapidity. As this element constitutes two thirds of the population it may be readily understood what a menace these evil conditions are to the development of an orderly state. Herein lies the root of existing evil conditions which will be an ever-present menace unless righted by a strong and vigorous government moving on definite lines of policy and which, instead of attempting to set up an altruistic republic among a people unfitted by education and tradition, shall adopt a practical policy leading to a system of universal education, the implanting of sound political ideas, and a patriotism which shall be something higher and nobler than hatred of the thrifty foreigner.

The truth of this view is borne out by the history of Mexico from the time of the revolution against Spain until the present hour. Where else in the world has there been more turbulence, more violent overturnings of government, more hallelujahs of triumph, more anathemas of death and defeat? The patriot and hero of to-day becomes the fugitive with a price on his head of to-morrow, and the victor marches through slaughter to fleeting glory. Power is seized by ambitious hands, but its possessor ends his career either in exile, in prison, or by the sword. From the time of the revolution against Spain until the firm establishment of the government of General Diaz, the rulers of Mexico pass across the stage like the ghosts of Banquo—the empire of Iturbide, the tyrant Santa Anna, and the unhappy and unfortunate Maximilian, along with a multitude of vulgar and bloody tyrants, held sway over the destinies of this unfortunate country, despoiling it of its wealth, impoverishing its people, and leaving in their wake only the echoes of disappointed ambitions and sad tragedies.

The revolution of Madero sprang unarmed and motley from the national discontent with the system and administration of the Diaz régime. This discontent it neither represented nor organized. Madero was a comparatively unknown person who appeared at a psychological moment and reaped a harvest which might have gone to stronger and abler men had any such been then prominent in the public eye. His previous history had been that of a dreamer of dreams, but he was more of a mountebank than a messiah; an honest enthusiast with a disorganized brain. Madero managed, by the dissemination of literature of extremely ordinary but inflammable character, to increase discontent in the northern part of the republic and, with the aid of American and European capital—enlisted in the cause by promises of concessions or preferential favours—and finally with the assistance of the Madero fortune, equipped a force on the border which, though inconsiderable in numbers, constituted a rallying point for dissatisfied spirits and a nucleus of a certain substance for offensive action against the government. Nevertheless, the character of the revolution inaugurated by him was from its inception formidable neither in numbers nor organization. The movement gained its strength from the weakness of the government; from the well-meant but damaging overtures of Limantour who, having at one time held certain relations with the Madero family, was supposed by the government to be a proper intermediary through which to influence their actions.

The revolutionary forces under Madero, Orozco, and other border chieftains were conglomerate border bandits, roving cattlemen, and American adventurers, falstaffian in numbers and equipment. In the earlier stages of the movement it was regarded by Mexicans and foreigners as a fanatical and impotent affair destined soon to failure because of lack of support among the really solid elements of the population and of the improbability of financial assistance. But as time went on the government remained inert and repressive measures were either delayed or lacking in energy. At this juncture Gustavo Madero and probably other members of the family who had remained aloof from the revolution joined the movement, and the considerable family fortunes of the Maderos were enlisted in the cause. Financial assistance was obtained from certain sources in the United States and Europe, notably from Paris and Frankfort-on-the-Main. The records of the Department of Justice of the United States carry revelations connecting Gustavo Madero with an oil company doing business in Mexico and with the active agents of an arms company in Washington. Many events during the Madero régime abundantly confirmed the rumours that were in general circulation in the early stages of the revolution. With this aid efforts at organization and discipline were made and victories of an unimportant character, largely exaggerated by the press, were gained.

As the army of Madero remained in the field gaining recruits and support, intrigue and discontent spread throughout the republic, and the poorly organized machinery of government fell rapidly into chaos.

American interests in the revolution-infested states along the border were extensive and alarm and apprehension became prevalent through that section of Mexico. I had kept the government at Washington fully informed of the progress of events and had recommended an active observance of developments and some preparation for contingencies which might eventuate. As the situation became more complex I went north for a consultation with President Taft and gave him in detail the story of the events which were occurring and the probable tendencies. The President manifested the deepest interest, and reviewed all the phases of the revolution fully and intelligently. Taft was a firm believer in Diaz, and I think it is not misstating history to say that the action he subsequently took was inspired not only by a desire to afford protection to Americans living along the border by the actual presence of our troops and those in the interior by the wholesome warning conveyed, but to sustain, as far as our obsolete neutrality laws would permit, the government of Diaz against attacks directed from across the border. I went away from my interview with Mr. Taft confident that the government could be relied upon to take the active steps for the protection of the lives and property of its nationals in Mexico. Action came sooner than I anticipated, for in the afternoon of the day of my interview with the President, as I was on my way to the railway station, I read in the *Evening Star* the story of the mobilization of 20,000 troops for concentration at San Antonio, Texas. Rarely in the history of our government has prompt and adequate action so quickly followed decision.

CHAPTER XXXI

William H. Taft—Purpose in concentrating troops on the border—The legend about Americans being ordered from Mexico

MY EXPERIENCE with Mr. Taft during the long and difficult period covering the Mexican disturbances constantly increased my confidence in his accurate and thorough grasp of situations, in the safety of his judgment, and loyalty of his purpose.

Here was a great man, a good man, and a just man, set down by fate and fortune among politicians to play the game of politics; a rare administrator, an unequalled executive, called upon to measure swords with petty men of pygmy intellects. In playing the political game he perhaps made mistakes which, if he had been less honest and less candid, would not have been made. Intellectually, he was fully the equal of Roosevelt but he lacked the spontaneity, initiative, and headlong energy of that great leader. He viewed all public matters with a judicial eye and weighed all questions before deciding them. This quality of mind sometimes brought him to a halting decision between two courses, but when his judgment was fully formed or when he had faith in the judgment of another, he moved in a given course with astonishing rapidity and usually with marvellous effectiveness. An old correspondent who was intimately associated with Roosevelt, Taft, and Wilson once said to me: "In the details

of his official work Roosevelt moved rapidly and trans-
acted more business than either of the men who followed
him; he made mistakes, however; Taft followed Roosevelt very closely in the volume of work dispatched but
made no mistakes; Wilson never did any work except on
his own typewriter."

No man ever sat in the presidential chair with a kinder
heart, a more forgiving disposition, or a tenderer consideration for the misfortune or shortcomings of others than
William H. Taft, and no greater intellect has ever been
called to the administration of our public affairs. While
in office he was misunderstood and thus misjudged by
the American people, a judgment which has been revised
by history, revealing to minds unclouded by passion and
prejudice the true lineaments of a really great character.
In private life his charm of manner and kindness of heart
made him easily the most popular American. To the
gratification of a vast majority of the American people he
will, during the rest of his life, occupy a position as elevated and as dignified, if not as powerful, as the great
office from which he was driven by political jealousies and
intrigues.

The purpose of this military demonstration was primarily to protect our border against marauding rebels and
to enforce compliance with our neutrality laws. These
laws—since reformed—then appeared to be framed in
such a way as to encourage rebellion in neighbouring
states, and under the cover of their weakness revolutions
were constantly being fomented on Latin-American soil
to the constant profit of adventurers and unscrupulous
dealers in arms and ammunition. It was also intended
that the demonstration should impress upon not only

those in authority, but upon those in rebellion against authority, the realization that this government would not tolerate the further taking of American life or the destruction of American property. The resultant effect was useful in arousing the Mexican government to a sense of its responsibilities, and in serving as a timely warning to the revolutionary leaders that Americans in localities under their control must not be molested. No intrusion into the domestic affairs of Mexico, with which the Taft administration rightly conceived it had no concern, was intended; border conditions and the American colony in Mexico were the moving considerations. President Taft had the highest opinion of General Diaz and believed with me that the downfall of his government would result in a long period of disorder and anarchy, but he saw no just ground for peaceable or armed intervention to sustain Diaz. My understanding of the Taft policy was that if intervention for the protection of our own people or other foreigners became a matter of solemn and sacred duty, there would be no hesitation, but that intervention for other reasons would not be justified by public opinion either in this country or elsewhere.

At this point it may be useful to correct an impression made by the dissemination, for political reasons, of the story that the Taft administration had, in critical moments of the Madero administration, ordered all Americans out of Mexico.

Under the Madero régime the situation of Americans in Mexico became increasingly precarious; murders, lootings, and outrages occurred and the embassy was in constant receipt of telegrams telling of crimes committed against Americans or requesting protection against anticipated wrongs. In most cases the government of Madero could not meet the demands made upon it; in many instances it failed to afford protection and, in some, it frankly acknowledged its inability to guarantee safety. Americans in isolated places were especially endangered as they could rely on neither the federal nor state governments. To meet this emergency a telegraphic consultation was held between the Department of State and the embassy; the matter of ordering Americans out of Mexico was discussed but the orders issued by the embassy applied only to certain localities where danger was very apparent. The danger zones were clearly marked out, and within those zones Americans were, in certain emergencies, ordered to go to the nearest safe and central place. Some consuls on the border ordered Americans to take refuge on the American side and thus the legend was established that the Taft administration had ordered Americans out of Mexico. Americans were neither ordered nor officially advised to go out of Mexico during the Taft régime; under the Wilson administration they were twice and perhaps thrice ordered out.

CHAPTER XXXII

*Interview with Mr. Limantour in New York—Progress of the revo-
lution—Retirement of Diaz—Final scenes—Letter to General Diaz—The
government of De la Barra—The Catholic Church in Mexico—Memorandum of interview with De la Barra.*

BEFORE I returned to my official duties in Mexico, I went to New York to see Mr. Limantour,
who had been called home from Europe by unsettled conditions prevailing in Mexico. I saw
Limantour, with the approval of President Taft, for the
purpose of impressing upon him the wholly benign character of our military activities. He was very skeptical
about the strength of the revolutionary movement but
believed, or pretended to believe, that the concentration
of troops on the border would strengthen it and add to
the embarrassment of the Diaz government. He was
obviously suspicious of our motives and as resentful as
courtesy and the rules of propriety would permit. The
suspicions of Mr. Limantour were not shared by President Diaz nor by other members of the Diaz cabinet.

Coincidentally with my return to Mexico the battles
of Casas Grandes and Agua Prieta, in which the rebels
were victorious, weakened the federal government and
led to negotiations between Limantour and Madero, and
between De la Barra, who was then Minister of Foreign
Affairs, and Vasques Gomez, an ambitious and discon-
tented political leader. These military engagements revealed something already known to the embassy and

[212]

communicated to Washington, viz., that the federal army was in a state of hopeless disorganization and that in *effectif* it numbered only about fourteen thousand men mostly commanded by incompetent generals. An autocratic government unsupported by military forces is an anomaly which cannot long exist, and the negotiations which were entabled led to the creation of a federal cabinet designed to meet popular approval and a declaration from the President that he would retire from office whenever he could do so without imperilling public order.

The declaration of the President seemed for a time to meet the emergency, and sanguine people believed that the government to be forced on the retirement of Diaz would either embrace all elements under the form of a compromise, or else the transition from the old régime to the new would be so gradual and so prudently controlled that no great interruption in business or governmental affairs would ensue. Those who so read the signs of the times did so without knowledge of the irresponsible elements which dominated the councils of Madero; elements which were not seeking the overthrow of the old régime for the good of Mexico, but for their own profit and advancement. These elements insisted upon the immediate retirement of President Diaz and, while Madero hesitated to accept their views, he finally yielded after the battle of Juarez, as at that time it became evident that he must either act in obedience to the wishes of the aspiring chieftains about him or yield precedence to some one among them. So it was announced to the peace envoys of the federal government that nothing but the immediate retirement of the aged president with the succession of the Minister of Foreign Affairs, Mr. De la Barra, as provisional

[213]

president, would be considered. President Diaz, deserted by many of his oldest friends and reluctant to spill more Mexican blood, yielded to what seemed to be the inevitable but really was the culmination of a national hysteria which would have subsided if vigorously and unitedly opposed. Overwhelmed by a sea of disasters and suffering in body and mind, Diaz tendered his immediate resignation.

The final scenes were dramatic. Except for the ugly and aggressive mobs which infested the streets, the city was completely deserted, the houses closed, and a feeling of desolation and apprehension existed everywhere. In Cadenas Street near the house of Diaz great mobs had collected, filling the air with imprecations and threats against the aged soldier-president who had done such great and useful work in the regeneration of Mexico and who had established her credit and prestige throughout the world. Deserted by all but his family and a few faithful friends, the old hero lay upon a bed of sickness, with few to alleviate his sorrows, and protected from violence only by the troops under command of General Huerta. During all that day he was conspicuously neglected by many of those in official life. Feeling that he was being deserted, and remembering his many kindnesses to Americans and to me, I went, in spite of the protests of the embassy staff, in my automobile at three o'clock in the afternoon to pay him a visit.

Deadly and ominous quiet prevailed on the streets through which I passed until I reached the President's house. There the mobs appeared to be in control but it was only in appearance, as the soldiers stood at their guns quietly, but firmly holding in check the disorderly elements. With some difficulty I passed through the file and finally into the house, being ushered through lines of sad and weeping people to the drawing room, where I met Mrs. Diaz. Of this lovely and dignified gentlewoman too much cannot be said in praise. All through her wedded life she had been one of the chief moving forces of the Diaz administration, and her influence was always exerted wisely and beneficently. Like all others, I had known her to admire her, and my meeting with her was affecting to an unusual degree. In a state of profound agitation she told me that the President was lying in bed in great pain and that the tortures of his body were infinitely increased by the street demonstrations and cries which were then taking place. Unable to see the President, I paid Mrs. Diaz a sad adieu, passing out into the streets with the feeling that I had been the unhappy witness of the humiliation of a great and distinguished man and of a good and gracious gentlewoman.

My departure was not as easily accomplished as my arrival, as I was compelled to pass for seven blocks through a seething mob which might at any moment have been induced to commit acts of violence against the representative of the American government; but I was treated with the greatest consideration and beyond a few acts of playful familiarity had nothing to complain of. Admiral Von Hintze, the German minister, also attempted a visit to Diaz during the same hours, but I believe his experiences were not so pleasant as mine on his return trip.

On the night following these tragic scenes, in a special train which had been prepared for him by President Edward N. Brown of the Mexican National Railway, Diaz left Mexico City under the protection of a military escort commanded by General Huerta. The fallen president went that night to the station on foot, accompanied only by Mr. Brown. What memories of the past must have been awakened by their reverberating steps through the silent city, and how poignant must have been the grief of the wise old statesman who could not but have foreseen the stormy days which the future had in store for his country. The revolution was accomplished. The king was dead and therefore long live the king!

Gathering the sentiment of the diplomatic corps, I expressed it in a final note to General Diaz after he had gone aboard the ship which was to convey him to Europe. I believe the last act of General Diaz before leaving Mexico was to reply to this note in a most touching and affectionate way. I insert my letter here, because it seems to me to mark clearly the attitude of the diplomatic corps toward the administration of General Diaz:

GENERAL DIAZ:

The members of the diplomatic corps resident in Mexico desire, notwithstanding your retirement from the office of President of this Republic and the consequent severance of their official relations with you, to express in an unofficial and purely personal way their appreciation of the kindness, courtesy, and justice which has marked your intercourse with them.

My colleagues desire me to express to you their united and earnest hope that, free from the responsibilities of the great office which you have held, you may continue to enjoy in private life for many years the happiness and the peace to which you are justly entitled by your long and patriotic services to this republic.

[216]

We also beg you to be good enough to convey to the excellent lady who has so unselfishly aided you in the effectual discharge of your laborious duties our salutations of profound respect and affection and our abundant thanks for those acts of kindness which we shall ever cherish in memory.

There is not much to say of the intervening provisional government of Francisco De la Barra, except to bear testimony to its excellence. It was a government of compromise supposed to prepare the way for the government of Madero, but although De la Barra was able and patriotic, he could not, because of the constant interference with his government by the Maderos, accomplish much for the restoration of order. In every instance where he attempted the suppression of armed disorder or rebellion the Maderos interfered. This was notably so in the case of Zapata, who was encouraged to continue in rebellion as a menace to plots and plotters in Mexico City.

De la Barra laid down office with the universal plaudits of all right-thinking and patriotic Mexicans. During the period of his prominence in Mexican politics, he was generally looked upon as the leader of the so-called Catholic Party, a nebulous political organization, apparently without direction, and not wholly submissive to leadership. Very much has been said by writers on Mexico about the power and tyranny of the Roman Catholic Church in its influence with the Mexican masses. As far as my observation goes, the Catholic Church in Mexico has, since the time of Juarez, been more sinned against than sinning. Its political power from the overthrow of Maximilian down to the brief rule of Huerta was a myth. The

[217]

Roman Catholic Church as a political organization does not exist in Mexico, but it is to be doubted whether its loss of influence and the persecution of its priesthood have had a beneficial effect on the Mexican people. It is true that some four hundred years ago the Indian races then inhabiting the country were converted to the Christian religion by the sword, but nevertheless Christianity was a benevolent substitute for pagan Aztec barbarism.

After the conquest the rule of the Roman Catholic Church in Mexico was generally benevolent and uplifting. It founded and reared splendid medieval churches, established charitable organizations, places of refuge, and gave to the impoverished Indian population a primary education which it could obtain from no other source. The church was stripped of its power, property, and influence by the governments of Juarez and Diaz, but neither these presidents nor their successors had the courage—or shall we say a sufficient lack of patriotism?—to attempt to impose by military force a godless and heathen régime, having its origin in bolshevik propaganda. Not all Christians are concerned with the fate of the Roman Catholic Church in Mexico, but the matter of a complete overthrow of the Christian religion is of as much concern to any Protestant denomination as to those who pay obedience to the Pope.

During his brief administration De la Barra, I am quite sure, had no other purpose than to maintain peace and turn over the administration of Mexican affairs to the president-elect under as satisfactory conditions as possible. He was trained in the administration of public affairs and governed by well-established rules and traditions. On this account he was constantly upset and horrified by the irregular methods and constant interference in public affairs of Madero and his family. His state of mind is revealed to some extent by a memorandum of an interview which I had with him on October 25, 1911:

"I met the President by appointment to-day. He said to me that his brother, Luis De la Barra, had left for the United States with the purpose of first visiting General Reyes at San Antonio in the hope of inducing him to abandon his hostile and revolutionary attitude and for the sake of his country to return to Mexico and exercise his rights as a citizen in peaceful ways. This errand concluded, he said Don Luis would seek an interview with President Taft to explain to him, in his name and in the name of Mr. Madero, the situation in Mexico, as it related to American interests, the policy of the government in domestic questions, and the necessity of extraordinary and rigid precautions on the frontier to prevent violation of the neutrality laws by revolutionary agitators. Don Luis also was instructed to discuss with President Taft matters relating to the new Mexican ambassador to Washington, Manuel Calero, whose designation was supposed for some reason not to be agreeable to Washington. He was charged, the President informed me, to say to President Taft that because of my knowledge of existing political conditions, and the confidence the government felt in the honesty of my intentions, my full acceptability to the outgoing and incoming governments should be known. President De la Barra expressed confidentially to me his serious apprehension concerning the prospects of the Madero government, basing his opinion on the distressing state of the Mexican exchequer, which he thought would require an increase in the federal contribution—the tax contributed from the states to the central government —of from 20 to 28 per cent. He also saw serious danger in the lack of fitness of Madero for executive work and questioned his adherence to sound principles of government, qualifying his words by the statement that if the first six months of the new administration passed without trouble, the country would probably settle down to normal conditions. The President's opinion seemed to be that General Reyes in his revolutionary attitude constituted a dangerous menace to the peace of the country, an opinion which I told him was not shared by me. He said that he expected to surrender the government on November 3d or 4th, and that he would immediately go to the country and depart from there for Europe."

CHAPTER XXXIII

An interlude filled by trips to the states of Guerrero and Oaxaca—
Beauties of Oaxaca

BETWEEN the overturn of Diaz and the installation of the Madero government there was a brief interval of quiet which permitted a temporary return to normal duties and pleasures. Taking advantage of these quiet days I went, upon the suggestion of my doctor, for a two weeks' trip into the interior. An invitation from a friend who represented an American syndicate owning large tracts of timberland in the state of Guerrero opportunely came and I left Mexico, in company with others, on a special train on a typical summer morning, and after climbing over the hills which stand sentinel-like between the states of Morelos and Mexico, descended into the valley where flourish some of the largest and richest sugar estates in the world. Passing by Cuernavaca, the summer home of Maximilian and his Empress Carlotta, one of the romantic spots of Mexico, we arrived at Iguala on the banks of the Balsas River, the terminal point of the railroad. This river is the divisional line of the states of Morelos and Guerrero, a circumstance which seems to have been fully taken into account by the authorities of the latter state for Governor Damian Flores, who had come down to greet us, remained in great dignity and state on the Guerrero side, surrounded by a military escort and American and Mexican flags. Crossing over by boat we were received with great courtesy by the governor and without further delay the procession of automobiles started along the national road for Chilpancingo, the capital of the state.

Nowhere can the beauty and picturesqueness of this automobile trip be surpassed. We went for forty miles over an absolutely perfect road crossing over mountain streams and under natural bridges with the cliffs towering hundreds of feet above. But for the luxuriant and gaudy verdure which bedecked the hills on both sides, one might have imagined it a run through Switzerland, though for pure scenic beauty this bit from Iguala to Chilpancingo is far the lovelier. Dashing through tunnels and over hills in an atmosphere laden with the perfumes from the forests, we arrived at Chilpancingo, an unattractive-looking town of the old Mexican type which had not yet been subjected to the transforming processes of modern city building. The inevitable and formidable Mexican band met us on the outskirts of the city and, having lunched, we were asked to inspect one of the really successful public schools established under the Diaz régime. All the scholars were in festal attire with cleanly burnished faces and excellent company manners. We were given an opportunity to judge of their proficiency in declamation and various other exercises, concluding with a rather startling rendition of "The Star-Spangled Banner." After this ceremony and visits to the places of interest we resumed our journey toward the Pacific, expecting to reach the sea, but when almost within sight became discouraged with bad roads and turned back for a night's rest before taking up the second leg of our excursion to the state of Oaxaca which lies east of Guerrero and extends from the Atlantic to the Pacific.

On the way to Oaxaca we stopped for an hour at Puebla, the second city of Mexico. Puebla resembles both Lisbon and Montevideo. It is an attractive, well-laid-out city ornamented with handsome edifices and homes; the Yankee has been busy here as elsewhere with electricity, water, and light, and has modernized everything. It was at Puebla that Cortes received his first check in the march to Mexico City and there also the first signals of the revolution against the government of Diaz were given.

From Puebla we journeyed toward the south and that night, having been safely sidetracked, we slept under the quiet stars to the music of the gently moving forest.

With daybreak came the glories of wakening tropical life; songs of birds in the trees and the thousand articulations of an invisible insect world. Before sundown the same day we had reached the ancient city of Oaxaca, the final Mexican residence of Cortes who, as Marquis Del Valle, was sent here in pleasant banishment from Mexico City, the scene of his battles and conquests. The ingratitude of republics is proverbial but the story of the ingratitude of the Spanish monarchs toward those who carved out for them an empire in the new world, Columbus, Cortes, and Balboa, is not a pleasant one.

Oaxaca is the birthplace of Juarez, Romero, Mariscal, Diaz, and of nearly all the southern Mexicans who have been conspicuous in Mexican public life. Parenthetically, the contest for control of Mexico seems always to have been between northern and southern groups; Juarez, Diaz, Romero, and Mariscal were from the south; Madero, Carranza, and Obregon from the north. The northern

[223]

states are the least progressive and the least populous parts of Mexico; wealth, population, civilization, and traditions of order and established customs lie south of San Luis Potosi. The larger part of Diaz's cabinet, most of the members of the Supreme Court, and the leading generals of the armies came from Oaxaca. Eventually control of the destinies of Mexico must rest with the southern half of the country. The Indian races occupying the southern part of Mexico were superior in civilization, numbers, and organization to those in the north. The blended product of the union of these races with the Spaniards was in every way superior to the Mexican found on the border or in the north central states. Revolutions take quicker and firmer hold on the northern Mexicans, because the measure of civilization, racial tradition, and comfort is less there than in the south.

Oaxaca is a dream of beauty; a perfect climate and surroundings make it a delightful resting place for the tourist who never comes but whose restless spirit might be lulled to peaceful dreams if perchance he came. It is a page out of Spain; time-stained houses, narrow, curving streets, ambushed by mysterious gardens covered with peeping roses; a glint of colour here, a fountain there, and farther on a chapel, a church, and an orange grove. With night time came the serenade, the tinkle of the guitar, and the thousand mysterious sounds which fill the night in these southern cities existing without the clank, clash, and clatter of modern city life. To the west and near Oaxaca lies San Juan silver mine, an American property. This considerable mineral deposit, which had been worked by the Spaniards and possibly by the Aztecs, was now being subjected to the combing processes of modern mineral treatment. Down the chutes and through the long galleries where once the Spaniard and Aztec hacked and hammered and clawed for gold, Yankee machinery now moved with giant capacity and incredible speed. The work formerly done by thousands was now easily taken care of by hundreds.

After having been hospitably entertained by the governor, we went for an enjoyable evening on the public plaza, where we were met by the authorities and greeted by one of the best bands in America, directed by German Canseco, who wrote "Sobre las Olas," an air which was sung over the world and in recent years converted into the popular air "Three o'Clock in the Morning." Later the band discoursed a programme of American airs and led a procession about the plaza to the music of "The Star-Spangled Banner"; a delightful occasion and very kind people, from whom we parted on the morrow with regret.

CHAPTER XXXIV

Madero enters Mexico City—My prediction in dispatch to the Depart-
ment of State—Continuance of the revolution and its savage character—
Contrast with Diaz régime.

FROM this time events marched rapidly. On the
seventh day of June, 1911, Madero entered
Mexico City as a private citizen; his entrance
was greeted by vast throngs and marked by a
ceremony which resembled more a Roman triumph than a
welcome to a popular democratic hero. On the day of
this spectacular entrance I dictated a dispatch to our
government predicting a continuance of the revolution
and the probable ultimate downfall of the Madero government. This prediction was based upon the substantial
ground of the natural tendencies of the Mexican masses
to disorder and lawlessness and the inadequacy of the platform and the policies of Madero in meeting the tendencies.
The fulfilment of this prediction was not long delayed.
The revolution which began against Diaz continued
against Madero, and from the installation of his administration down to the hour of his sad and tragic death
Mexico was a seething cauldron of rebellion and violence,
with wholesale destruction of life and property.

In the midst of these unhappy conditions Madero was
elected to the presidency—Reyes having been prevented
by violence from prosecuting his campaign—by a total
of votes insignificant in a population of fifteen millions of
people.

During the progress of the election, Gustavo Madero, who was the real power in the Madero family—and unfortunately a power for evil rather than good—came to see me at the embassy, obviously for the purpose of ascertaining my views on the political situation. I called his especial attention to the attitude of the Madero family in encouraging violence toward Reyes and expressed the opinion that the assembling of mobs against Reyes under the apparent encouragement of the Madero family might be establishing a precedent which would bear an unpalatable fruit in the future. He said: "Oh, we understand these mobs and we let them go just so far and then we stop them. Reyes is about driven out of the race now and things will become quiet very soon."

Thus the President, brought into power by a revolution, had hardly clasped the emblems of authority before he was called upon to face the storms of a new revolution which blew from the four quarters of Mexico. It was a more genuine revolution than the one against Diaz; the storm raged throughout the length and breadth of the republic, pacified in some instances by homeopathic doses of supposed remedies for local troubles, but always increasing in violence and steadily aided by a falling barometer of public opinion. Entire villages and plantations were burned, their inhabitants, men, women, and children, slaughtered indiscriminately; trains were derailed and passengers murdered without mercy. Women were ravished and men mutilated with accompaniments of horror and barbarity which find no place in the chronicles of Christian warfare.

The new revolution was also marked by the ferocity of its attitude toward that class of people who were really

[227]

capable of administering scientific government; thus Limantour, De la Barra, Calero, Creel, Cuellar, Aldape, Landa, Vera Estañol, Toribio Esquivel Obregon, and others like them, were driven from Mexican soil, not because they had committed crimes against Mexico, but largely because by their superior characters, training, and education, they were able to render service to her.

Diaz's régime was not without its blemishes—blemishes which are nearly always inherent in the type of government which it appeared necessary to install in Mexico. His régime did not accomplish all for Mexico that may in time be accomplished, but it did impose order and a certain measure of justice before the courts. Its conduct of foreign affairs was dignified and patriotic; its management of national finances was thrifty and orderly. Compared with that of some of the mushroom governments which followed it, it represented more of real democracy and less of the pretended article.

CHAPTER XXXV

Weakness and vacillation of the Madero administration—Anti-American sentiment—Violation of American rights and attacks on life and property—Flight of Americans—Question of protecting American lives and property when threatened abroad—Our note of September 15, 1912—Dispatch of Mr. Lascurain to Washington—Intemperate instructions sent him by Madero—Resignation of Ambassador Calero and his statement before the Mexican Senate—Oil.

IN THE midst of this appalling revolutionary situation the federal government sat apathetic, ineffective, and either cynically indifferent or stupidly optimistic. Its councils were divided and moved in contrary directions from one day to another by the preponderance of one or another element. On this account such resolutions as were taken were incoherent, spasmodic, advancing and receding conformably with the preponderance of the conservative or radical elements or in response to the changeable gusts of public opinion. This peculiar phase of the situation was largely due to the character of the President who was one day a conservative, a reactionary, the stern avenger of society against brigandage, the tyrant who wanted an eye for an eye and a tooth for a tooth—in a word, a Diaz come again—and the next day an apostle of peace, the friend of the poor, the apologist for notorious bandits and criminals, and the enemy of monopolies, landholders, and privileged classes.

This wavering and unsettled policy finally lost the President the confidence and support of all classes, and in the last days he was sustained only by the sympathy of his numerous family, the office-holders, and the useful apprehension that the evils which existed were less than those which might be anticipated with his downfall.

In these last months the growing unpopularity of the Madero administration was marked by the severe social boycott maintained against its official functions by all elements of Mexican society. The presidential receptions were attended by only a few members of the diplomatic corps and by others of doubtful origin and peculiar appearance. Such entertainments as were given had the air of being family affairs and were conducted under the advice of persons whose presence was highly obnoxious to the diplomatic corps. These entertainments were in marked contrast with those of President Diaz, which though simple and democratic had a dignity and repose which imparted to them a definite character. Through the whole period of the Madero administration Mexican society held aloof, and the predominating influences sprang from circles of recent creation and frequently of foreign origin.

The continuance of these abnormal conditions placed upon the embassy a heavy burden of responsibility which kept me tied to my duties without intermission, recreation, or the opportunity to discharge the ordinary obligations due to society or family. At the beginning of the revolutionary movement there were in Mexico somewhere between fifty and seventy-five thousand American citizens, and American capital invested to the extent of probably a billion dollars, which is equivalent to saying that 40 per cent. of our foreign investments were at that time in Mexico. As the revolution progressed it became evi-

dent to the official representatives of the government of the
United States that there existed a strong anti-American
sentiment provoked, by agitators, among the more ignor-
ant part of the population, a sentiment which, if not
shared by the government, was at least not discounte-
nanced by it. In no single instance that can be recalled
did an official under Madero voice an appreciation of the
unselfish attitude of the American government and people
or express the smallest measure of gratitude for the material benefits which American intelligence and energy
and American capital had bestowed upon Mexico. On
numerous occasions, however, public orators, the press,
and all the organs capable of influencing public opinion
were busily engaged in inflaming the public mind and in
rendering more dangerous the lot of Americans and the
safety of their properties.

This violation of the canons of civilized policy bore its
fruit in a wide and indiscriminate attack upon everything
bearing the stamp of American origin. American interests, honestly acquired and on which vast amounts of
capital had been expended, were widely attacked on base-
less and absurd pretexts by persons in collusion with
friends of the government; were harassed by confiscatory
taxes and by the denial of that protection which the most
elemental conceptions of government would have afforded them. American citizens to a great number were
arrested on frivolous and insufficient charges and incarcerated in filthy and insanitary jails, whence neither the
protests of our own government nor the palpable and
proven injustice of their imprisonment could release them.
American citizens were foully and brutally murdered and
no diplomatic representations, entreaties, or threats served

[231]

to procure the trial or punishment of the offending criminals; the property of American citizens was destroyed, with only a deaf ear turned to their complaints and with a denial of that justice in the consideration of their claims which is incumbent upon all civilized nations. To such an extent did this persecution pass that at the time of Madero's fall probably thirty thousand of them were obliged to abandon their homes, their factories, their mines, and their haciendas and to return to the United States, sacrificing property which finally reached in value the sum of five hundred million dollars—for which the probabilities of compensation are vague and remote. During the splendid American administrations of Andrew Jackson, Abraham Lincoln, Grover Cleveland, William McKinley, William H. Taft, and Theodore Roosevelt, an American citizen rode upon the high seas with no fear in his heart save for foul weather and tempestuous waves. Then, an American citizen in any part of the world walked abroad, erect, with his head toward the stars, sure in the faith that if his cause were just, he had above him and about him the strong arm of this great government.

When the Greeks spread their commerce and civilization along the shores of the beautiful Mediterranean, the Greek phalanx and the Greek galley stood as sentinels at the gateway. Roman commerce and Roman civilization went in the wake and not in the vanguard of the Roman legions. The restless fingers of British commerce have reached out to all the seas and continents, but the drum beat of England has encircled the globe and wherever a British citizen lives and works and prays, rich or poor, he rests under the watchful eye of the British government.

The allied hands of Capital and Labour design, fashion, and offer upon the markets of the world the fruit of the American loom, the forge, the hammer, and the thousand intricate mechanisms which the ingenuity of man has contrived. To enlarge and stimulate these markets we send abroad agents; from these agents spring agencies; and from these agencies spring American colonies, centres of American trade, expansion, and culture, preserving American traditions and devotion to the American flag. Here flourish the American farmer, the American mechanic, the teacher, the preacher, the journalist, the lawyer, and all the thousand accessories of American community life—more American than the Americans; pioneers of our civilization; the men who teach the world how democracy can be made safe for the world. If these colonies happen to exist in lands where the law is supreme and where justice is undefiled, they function normally, peacefully, and without being remarked by the eye of the world. If, on the other hand, the wings of commercial adventure carry them into countries where the law is a mockery, and where justice is sold in the market place, then they have no resource in the hour of danger to their lives and their property save their own government.

The inability to secure adequate protection for American citizens, the unprovoked murder of many Americans, for which justice was not in a single instance obtained, and the failure on the part of the Mexican government to secure the arrest, detention, and punishment of the murderers, the cruel and unjust expulsion of five hundred American engineers and conductors from the national railways, the disposition to attack legally acquired American interests through trumped-up court processes, the

[233]

arbitrary arrest and imprisonment of Americans on frivolous charges and the failure of local governments actively to remedy such abuses, the savage and barbarous character of the internal warfare, finally forced our government to take a decisive stand, and on September 15, 1912, the embassy under instructions from Washington addressed a note to the Mexican government that not only evidenced the virility and alertness of the Taft administration but induced the Madero administration to dispatch the Minister of Foreign Affairs, Mr. Lascurain, to the United States with instructions to make concessions in general and vague terms to Secretary Knox and also to see President-elect Wilson for purposes unknown to me but presumably connected with the policy toward Mexico of the administration which was about to come into power. What Mr. Lascurain was directed to say to the President-elect can only be imagined but I insert here a copy of a special telegraphic instruction relating to me.[1]

(Translation)

Mexico City,
December 23, 1913.

MR. PEDRO LASCURAIN,
New York, New York.

Before returning here manage to obtain at all costs an interview with President-elect Wilson for the purpose of earnestly insisting that Ambassador Henry Lane Wilson

[1]Copies of this telegram along with others relating to me were handed to me by a minor official of the Mexican government in Mexico City soon after the establishment of the provisional government of General Huerta.

[234]

shall not further continue at this post. If it is necessary, say to him that the Mexican government some time ago advised the Washington government that he was not persona grata but suspended action in order that the new president may dismiss him without rendering necessary representations by this government. Explain the Mexican situation to him. Please answer.

FRANCISCO I. MADERO.

This telegram reveals the unstable character of Madero. He was under deep obligations to me for my sympathetic attitude in the earlier days of his administration and notwithstanding my severe attitude later he must have known it was justified by the wrongs to Americans permitted by his government. Not only was this true, but, as will be noted farther along in this book, Madero sent a note three days before his death, which is now of record in the Department of State, in which he spontaneously said that I had always been a friend of Mexico. At the time Mr. Lascurain was dispatched to the United States there was no reason for antagonism on the part of Madero toward me, except resentment for the vigorous and perhaps menacing way in which I was carrying out the instructions of the Department of State relative to the protection of American life and property. I had committed no act offensive to the Mexican government, unless the language which I was instructed to use by the government at Washington could be construed as an offence, and I had no objects to serve, except the protection of our unfortunate countrymen, their lives and property, and the maintenance of good relations between the two governments. It may be added that Madero never advised the Washington government that I was *persona non grata*. Neither diplomatic nor other agents of the government were willing to assume responsibility for such an extreme course.[1]

The Lascurain incident occurred coincidently with the sensational withdrawal of Mr. Manuel Calero, Mexican ambassador at Washington. Mr. Calero informed me at a later date that he had been instructed by Madero to inform President-elect Wilson that I was an enemy of the Mexican government, but that he had refused to do so, knowing that I had made all possible efforts to uphold the Madero government and that the hostility which existed was due solely to my vigorous and uncompromising attitude in American matters. While Mr. Calero was Mexican Minister for Foreign Affairs I had shown an earnest desire to contribute in every proper way to the strengthening of the Madero administration. This was evidenced not only by the testimony of Mr. Calero but by the records of the Mexican foreign office and those of the Department of State at Washington.

In Mexican politics Mr. Calero was in a class by himself. In the hours of monotonous peace he was likely to sound a discordant note, but in a national crisis he displayed courage and statesmanship. He was of the best Mexican type, passionate, eloquent, highly educated and able, of an exceedingly kind heart and sympathetic nature. He conducted the affairs of the Mexican foreign office with courage and ability; he was not so successful as ambassador to the United States, because of the peculiar and inconsistent instructions which were constantly being sent

[1]Precisely the same situation was developed during the administration of President Coolidge. The attitude of the press and government of Mexico were hostile to Ambassador Sheffield on account of his energetic defense of American interests, but dissatisfaction stopped short of a demand for his recall.

him by the Madero government. It is to his credit that when finally instructed to misrepresent the actual situation in Mexico and to discredit the reports emanating from the American embassy, he refused to do so, resigned his position and returned to Mexico, where he valiantly impeached the Madero administration in the Mexican senate for its insincere and undignified attitude toward the United States. Calero was so constituted that he must necessarily always be in the opposition. He was not in sympathy with the Diaz government, soon lost sympathy with the irregular methods of the Huerta government, and has ever since been in opposition to the governments which succeeded Huerta. His pamphlets and articles on the Mexican situation are as able as any that have been written, and it is to be regretted that such great abilities cannot be at the service of his country in these trying hours.

Oil began to be a disturbing factor in the Mexican situation during my time, but the oil companies were adroit and resourceful and managed to protect themselves without creating difficulties. Diaz believed that oil might be made a great factor in the development of Mexico and he dealt with the oil companies in a spirit of fairness. Madero played some favourites, but altogether his policy followed very closely that of Diaz. Huerta gave the oil companies some unhappy moments. He wanted them to pay largely and pay in an irregular way, and he was not particular about the methods employed to bring them to a show of reason.

No representative of an oil company ever approached the embassy for diplomatic intervention, but upon one occasion representatives of all the companies presented themselves for the purpose of protesting against an extraordinary tax which had been imposed. After the case had been stated, I asked these gentlemen whether they were demanding the support of the embassy as American citizens. As this was the thing which they desired to avoid, while at the same time asking the Ambassador to assume responsibility and move in some vague and undefined way in their behalf, nothing practical resulted from the discussion.

I must note here, however, that the independent oil companies, which were represented at the meeting by William F. Buckley, who afterward played such an active part in the defense of American rights, staunchly took the position that if the companies desired to receive protection, they must ask for it as American citizens.

I visited the oil regions upon the invitation of the Huasteca Petroleum Company, one of the subsidiary companies of the Mexican Petroleum Company. At that time the Huasteca was, with the exception of the Aguila Company, the heaviest producer of oil in Mexico, and its properties were supposed to be more efficiently managed than others. I saw some of the producing wells and made an effort to understand the details of the business so that in the event that oil matters should come up before the embassy, I might have some knowledge of the business. While I discovered nothing particularly enlightening about the business of producing oil, I did learn that this company was not only reaping a great harvest of wealth but that under the benevolent and generous administration of its directing spirit, Edward L. Doheny, the treatment accorded the native labourers and their families had not only been fair and just but would compare favourably in this respect with any industrial enterprise in the United States. There were hospitals, comfortable homes, and schools for the children, all maintained upon the highest level and performing a splendid work in the improvement of minds, morals, and manners of these people.

CHAPTER XXXVI

Decadence of the Madero government and its loss of popularity—Relapse to violence—Attempted revolution under Felix Diaz—Its failure

BY THE month of September, 1912, it became clearly evident that Madero could not govern his unruly people; that his government could not keep its promises, and was fast leading the country to the verge of ruin. Confronted by the intolerable conditions which existed throughout the country the administration remained impotent to remedy or offer any solution for the rapidly accumulating dangers. The cabinet was divided into warring factions of conflicting views, absorbed in petty intrigues and lilliputian politics which had little to do with the salvation of the country or the restoration of national prestige at home or abroad. On the one hand was Pino Suarez, Vice-president, Bonilla, Minister of Fomento, and Garcia Peña, Minister of War—representing anti-American prejudices, hatred of foreigners, class agitation, and the confiscation of property. This element enjoyed the powerful support of the President's family and doubtless reflected in some measure the President's ideas. The other faction headed by Ernesto Madero, Minister of Finance, an excellent man, yielded nothing to its opponents in anti-Americanism but stood for recognized governmental methods, the preservation of law and order, and a firm military policy. The energies of the government which should have been devoted to curing the ills of the country were dissipated in the intrigues and rivalries of these factions and in their efforts to secure mastery over the President who transferred his allegiance with bewildering frequency, but for no apparent reason, from one side to the other.

A specially aggravating circumstance, and one which had much to do in affecting the cordiality of my relations with the Madero régime, was the President's inexplicable course in dealing with the American employees of the Mexican Central Railway. Notwithstanding the fact that the Mexican Central Railway had been entirely built by American capital or American promotion, the Mexican government, even in the Diaz régime, adopted a hostile attitude against the American employees of the railway. Before the Madero revolution regulations were promulgated, requiring examination of employees in the Spanish language, but during the time of Diaz, these regulations were not put in force against train and equipment men, and the general management remained with the representatives of the bondholders. When the Madero people came in, flushed with victory and eager for rewards, they announced the intention of enforcing the regulations in regard to the use of the Spanish language. At that time there were some five or six hundred American employees on the railways. Some of them had lived for forty years in Mexico, and most of them had married Mexican wives. Their knowledge of Spanish was sufficient for the management of trains or whatever business they might be in charge of, but not sufficient to enable them to pass a serious examination in the language.

I regarded this proposed action of the government as very unjust and remonstrated with the President. Three different times he gave me his positive promise that the regulations would not be enforced. However, they were enforced, and these men, with wives and families in Mexico, were forced from the places they had occupied for years and at first not even given transportation to the United States. President Taft, who was deeply concerned about their situation, interested himself in securing employment for them in the United States, with what results I was never advised. American railway organizations took up the matter officially, and the Brotherhood of Railway Conductors, at their annual convention, passed resolutions condemning the Mexican government and commending my course.

It is not to be doubted that President Madero, if he had taken office unhampered by a swarm of greedy followers, might have fared better with the country; as it was, his connections were a source of continual embarrassment to the government and a scandal to the general public. Numbers of them were filling public offices—elective and appointive—and the activities of some in levying private taxation on foreign holdings could be commended on the score of enterprise but not on that of modesty.[1] The kind of government that must be evolved out of such a situation could not have been other than that which existed, namely, impotent in the face of domestic ills and dis-

---

[1] I was instructed by the Washington government to make representations to the Madero government relative to the activities of some of the Madero family where American interests were concerned, but an auspicious moment for doing so never arrived. It should not be inferred that all of the Madero family were culpable in public affairs. The President, Francisco Madero, was in no sense of the word corrupt, and his private life was a model of virtue. Ernesto Madero was a man of high character, sincerely patriotic, and imbued with a real sense of personal responsibility. I believe there were others of the family whose conduct was above reproach and some of the younger members, residing in the north, were excellent citizens, living apart from the political movements.

orders, and truculent, insolent, and insincere in its international relations.   A government which assumed power
with a reform programme and party pledges of a free
press, free elections, free education, and the division and
distribution of great estates, found itself, after a period
of little more than a year, in the position of not having
accomplished any of its high-sounding measures for the
relief of the Mexican population but responsible for the
sacrifice of thousands of human lives, the destruction of
vast material interests, aggravation of the conditions of
the poorer classes, and for desolation and ruin over a third
of the area of the republic.

The altruism so bravely heralded in the earlier and more
sanguine days gave place to a profound pessimism.   The
leader of the revolutionary protest against the despotism
of Diaz himself became a despot, practising all the forms
of tyranny against which the revolution and his election
were protests; the dreamer of Coahuila, who essayed the
rôle of a Moses, shrivelled rapidly to the dimensions of a
Castro.   Liberty of the press did not exist in fact or pre-
tense.   Of the independent metropolitan newspapers three
were purchased by the administration, two were sup-
pressed, and the editors of three were in jail.   At the close
of the Madero régime the only independent newspapers
published in the City of Mexico were the *Mexican Herald*
which, because of its American ownership, the government
hesitated to touch, and two other papers owned by deputies in Congress, and on that account immune from confiscation or violence.   In the matter of free elections,
which constituted so important a feature of the revolutionary programme, the attitude of the administration
was a travesty and a shock to those who had espoused the

revolution with enthusiasm. The presidential election was farcical and irregular in character and lacking in that numerical force which in our country would be deemed essential to constitute a free and final expression of public opinion. Hardly had the new government been seated in power when it began by intrigue in some cases and by the exercise of force in others to interfere in state elections, deposing some governors and imposing others. This policy it continued to the end.

In the matter of free education and the division and distribution of great estates which constituted an important part of the pledges of the new administration to the people, nothing was done nor did there seem to be any hope that anything would be done; not a single schoolhouse was built, and the only evidence of a purpose to distribute land was the purchase by the government of high-priced lands from a relative of the Madero family; a purchase not supplemented by any distribution. In the last days of the government the situation in Mexico was marked by an infinite number of intrigues and political deals, by intolerance of free thought and free speech, by a wide system of espionage through foreign spies and the odious Porra Society, organized by Gustavo Madero as an instrumentality through which secretly to reach the enemies of the Madero administration. In its original meaning the word signified a club or bludgeon, but through the war of violence and terrorism which it practised against society, the name finally came to be equivalent to "the rabble," an organization which marked and dogged the steps of every important public man; by deception and misrepresentation as to the actual conditions obtaining throughout the republic, and by aspersion of the motives of all those who had the independence and courage to criticize it and demand a more intelligent management of public affairs. This campaign of misrepresentation went so far as to discredit and impugn the motives of the consular and diplomatic representatives of our government who were endeavouring faithfully to portray the conditions which existed and to report the political and revolutionary events as they occurred.

In the month of October, 1912, my health gave way, and, the Department of State granting me a leave of absence, I left Mexico with Mrs. Wilson and my brother, Senator John Lockwood Wilson, for the north. I had proceeded no farther than Kansas City when a new revolution, headed by Felix Diaz, a nephew of President Diaz and a man of fine and independent character, broke out at Vera Cruz. I was called on that account to Washington and thus separated from my brother, who was in failing health and died some weeks later. The situation continued so acute that the Department of State asked me to be within easy call of Washington, and I thus remained practically on duty during my entire leave of absence.

Felix Diaz proclaimed his revolution from the city of Vera Cruz, which his supporters captured and held for a considerable time. Coincidentally with the Vera Cruz outbreak there were declarations from many places in his favour. It looked for a while as though the movement might become a very serious one for the Madero government, but it ultimately failed, partly because it was premature and partly because the Madero government paid a higher price for the loyalty of its own general than Felix Diaz was willing or able to pay. Vera Cruz fell and

Diaz was taken prisoner and placed in the military penitentiary in Mexico City, whence a few months later he escaped to accomplish the overthrow of Madero. The Madero family wished to have Diaz shot after his failure and capture, but the Supreme Court of Mexico interfered and it was impossible to execute him, except by ignoring the decision of the highest tribunal in the country.[1] Felix Diaz led two revolutionary movements, one successful and one unsuccessful; in the successful movement which overthrew Madero he came into power, but with Huerta to dispute that power. He was a man of unblemished character, of physical courage, brave in war and moderate in peace, but he was no fit antagonist for Huerta, and in the contest which followed their dual control, Huerta's stronger character asserted itself increasingly from day to day until a point was reached where it became necessary for Diaz again to precipitate a turmoil or vanish from the scene. He chose the latter course.

---

[1] This court was composed of judges appointed by President Diaz, uncle of Felix Diaz.

CHAPTER XXXVII

Discussion at Washington about note of September 15th—My insistence that all our differences with Mexico should be made part of a simultaneous settlement—Instructed to prepare a memorandum embodying my views—The gathering storm.

WHILE in Washington the matter of our reply to the Mexican government's note of November 22d, which was an answer to our note of September 15th,[1] was discussed, but no definite conclusion was reached. I was then very strongly of the opinion that all of the matters treated in our note and the reply thereto should be made part of a collective and simultaneous settlement and that we should refuse to discuss the settlement of any one question independently. The visit of Mr. Lascurain to Mr. Knox and the President modified the attitude of the Department of State and inclined it to more leniency. In harmony with this change I was advised that our government would not consider itself bound to refuse the independent discussion of any one of the matters treated in our note of September 15th. I felt that this was a mistake, and having so indicated, I was further instructed to prepare and forward to Washington a memorandum embodying my views. My dispatch and the memorandum trans-

---

[1]Our note of September 15, 1912, was peremptory, reciting our complaints fully and demanding a definite reply. The Mexican reply of November 22d was evasive and combative.

[247]

mitted with it in reply to this instruction made clear not only the difficulties we were then encountering in dealing with the Madero administration but also outlined my views as to what our policy should be. I do not believe that I can improve on the brief outline contained in that dispatch of what, in my estimation, should have been our policy toward Mexico, and as it has already officially been made public I insert it here without alteration:

". . . I wish to make my own views quite clear. I do not believe in the occupation of Mexico nor do I believe in or advocate the acquisition of a single foot of Latin-American territory. On the contrary, I am and have been, since I have had an opportunity to study Latin America and Latin-American conditions from an unusually advantageous position, more and more impressed with the circumstance that the government of these countries, alien in speech, customs, and race, is, under our form of government, a most difficult enterprise, and that each new burden which we assume and each new adventure which we essay leads to the creation of additional burdens and the invitation to more perilous adventures. At the same time my experience has taught me that these Latin-American countries should be dealt with justly and calmly but severely and undeviatingly. Any other course will forfeit to us the respect with which they have been taught to regard us and will sacrifice the genuine benefits which spring from a consistent, firm, and well-understood attitude on all international affairs.

"I am of the opinion that all of the matters treated in our note of September 15th must be made part of a direct settlement with Mexico growing out of the diplomatic correspondence based thereon, and that any other course will be tantamount to a sacrifice of national dignity and prestige. The draft of the note *verbale* or memorandum which is transmitted as enclosure No. 1 of this dispatch expresses briefly, but I think clearly, what our position is or should be in the light of the Mexican government's reply of November 22d to our note of September 15th. It may be amended, amplified, or changed to suit the department's views as to phraseology, but it expresses, in my judgment, the logical position at which we have arrived as a result of our note of September 15th. Of course, the department will understand that, unless the delivery of this proposed note should obtain satisfaction from the Mexican government, one of the several drastic courses which have been under consideration by the department, and which in my judgment, though perhaps necessarily delayed by patience, a repugnance to extreme measures, a reluctance to engage in adventurous sallies, and a natural fear of misinterpretation of our motives, must finally be adopted in the interest of peace in America and the protection of our own interests."

The memorandum[1] which was transmitted with the dispatch and which, if accepted, was to be made the basis of our policy toward Mexico, deals more fully with the situation, and is given elsewhere. (Appendix II.)

This memorandum for an instruction was not adopted by the Department of State but ultimately, convinced by the rapidly developing situation and the declarations made by Ambassador Calero, the department reversed its views

[1]Published in *Foreign Relations* for 1913.

as to the true character of the mission of Mr. Lascurain and accepted in principle the views laid down in the memorandum. This Secretary Knox informed me after he retired from office and he so stated in a public address. Had this view been earlier adopted and clearly expressed in a note to the Mexican government, it is quite probable that a change in the whole political situation might have been wrought.

It may be useful to note here that after the Wilson administration had concluded its chapter of altruistic dealings with Mexico and was confronted with the painful necessity of protesting against the barbarous cruelties practised against the Americans in Mexico, Secretary Lansing made substantially the same demands as those contained in my memorandum.

Again, in 1925-26-27, Secretary Kellogg, provoked by similar denials of justice, and by violations, or proposed violations, of international law and practice, made similar demands. The course of action suggested by Secretary Lansing's passionate note bore no fruit. The vigorous utterances of Secretary Kellogg were but a cry in the wilderness. The lesson seems never to be learned that in dealing with Mexico halfway measures are of little value. We should learn either not to commence or to go through with what we commence.

Some time in January, 1913, I reported to the Department of State that the clouds gathering over unhappy Mexico were more ominous than they had been at any time presaging the downfall of the Madero government. This pessimistic, but, as subsequently shown, accurate view of the situation was not fully shared by the Department of State, which at that time wished to avoid the assumption of responsibilities which Mr. Knox, not unreasonably, thought should be left to the consideration of the incoming administration. Events proved the department to be in error; the pessimistic views which I transmitted were to be quickly confirmed by tragic realities.

CHAPTER XXXVIII

The outbreak of the revolution under Felix Diaz and Bernardo Reyes in Mexico City—The ten days' bombardment called the Decena Trajica— The American and other colonies—Tragic and sensational incidents— Organizations for aid and protection—Visits to Madero—Efforts to protect foreign colonies—Efforts to save Madero by his withdrawal— Efforts to move the embassy—Reasons for declining.

ON SATURDAY, February 8, 1913, I made arrangements with some friends to spend the following Sunday in the country, and went to sleep that night, as indeed did the whole population of Mexico City, without a thought that upon the day following a drama of portentous character was to be ushered in. On the following morning, February 9th, I was awakened at about seven o'clock by my servant, Clement, who, in a state of breathless excitement and agitation, informed me that the prisons wherein General Reyes and Diaz, with many other political prisoners, were incarcerated, had been attacked by mutinous troops in the middle of the night and that both of these generals had been liberated. The report went on to say that various regiments, the mounted police, and part of the rurales had also revolted and that General Reyes had taken command of an attack against the National Palace, while General Felix Diaz was leading a force of unknown strength against the Citadel, the national reserve and storehouse of military arms and supplies. I immediately descended to the main floor of the embassy and found there a few straggling American tourists evidently badly frightened and badly informed, but none of the secretaries or clerks. A hasty survey of near-by deserted streets showed that people were more or less conversant with the situation and were keeping strictly within doors. I then dispatched hurried telephone messages to the secretaries and clerks, and about ten o'clock the working force was practically complete. The embassy staff at this time consisted of Mr. Montgomery Schuyler of New York, first secretary; Mr. Henry Tennant of New York, second secretary; Captain W. N. Burnside, military attaché; Mr. Louis d'Antin and Mr. Charles B. Parker, clerks. Our working force happened at this particular moment to be smaller than at any other time before or afterward but there was a willing disposition to meet the difficult and dangerous duties of the hour and I found a ready obedience and prompt response from all my subordinates, which was of infinite value.

Not until one o'clock in the afternoon could a reliable account of what had occurred be obtained though the embassy had in the meantime become thronged with anxious Americans and other foreigners. I was then able to report to Washington that the Tlalpam cadets had revolted and released General Felix Diaz and General Reyes, with other political prisoners; that these forces had been joined by the mounted police, the 20th Infantry, and the 1st Artillery; that some one thousand soldiers and noncombatants had been killed; that Reyes had fallen in an attack on the National Palace, which was still in the possession of the government troops under the command of General Huerta; that Felix Diaz had seized after a brief attack the national Citadel and was holding it with three thousand troops. In the meantime the entire diplomatic corps, headed by Mr. Bernardo Cologan, Spanish minister, Admiral von Hintze, German minister, and Sir Francis Stronge, the British minister, had assembled at the embassy and had authorized me to take steps with both the federal government and the revolutionists, to insure the protection of the foreign colonies. The second secretary of the embassy, Mr. Tennant, was dispatched with a memorandum expressing the views of the diplomatic corps, which he was directed to read to General Diaz, and at one o'clock at night I sent a note to the Minister of Foreign Affairs, Mr. Lascurain, transmitting the resolutions adopted by the diplomatic corps. Through the entire day and night the firing continued intermittently, and the embassy was overwhelmed with a mass of fugitives of all nationalities, who were cared for and reassured by Mrs. Wilson and the embassy staff.

In the meantime, we had taken in and provided for on the third floor of the embassy many persons who remained there until the restoration of order. Among them were Consul-general Arnold Shanklin; the first secretary of the embassy, Mr. Schuyler and Mrs. Schuyler; the military attaché, Captain Burnside and Mrs. Burnside; the second secretary of the embassy, Mr. Tennant; the clerks, d'Antin and Charles B. Parker, Mr. and Mrs. Harold Walker of Washington, D. C., and Mrs. Blair Flandrau of St. Paul. These people and others were accommodated on the living floor of the embassy. On the first floor every room and the hallways were occupied by Americans who were sleeping in the embassy either to be of service or because they had no other place; on the ground floor, which was large and commodious, and where nearly all of the relief work was carried on, there were numbers of people taken care of every night. Altogether, I think, one hundred and seventy-five persons must have found shelter and sustenance under the embassy roof during the ten days of trouble.

On February 10th, the second day of the *emeute*, I set about forming organizations for the rescue and aid of American and other foreign residents, a duty which seemed to be supremely important in view of the dangerous situation which was developing. With the aid of various active and intelligent Americans I organized a commissariat force, a relief force, a house-locating force, a medical aid corps, an American military guard, an embassy post and telegraph office, a bank, and a newspaper. These organizations rendered valuable and effective aid to Americans, other foreigners, and Mexicans during the bombardment. Throughout the disorders the American embassy was the centre of non-combatant activity, a shelter for hundreds and the source of advice and consolation to thousands who have placed their testimony on record.

I sent letters to the inspector-general of police and to the captains of all the precincts in the City of Mexico requesting the closing of drinking places and, with the authority of the diplomatic corps, forwarded unofficial notes to the Minister of Foreign Affairs and to General Felix Diaz, requesting that the bombardment of the city be conducted in such way as to cause as little damage as possible to the residential district. These notes were supplemented by one sent to the Minister of Foreign Affairs at his residence, informing him of the intention of the American and other foreign elements to form volunteer

[255]

guards for their protection, and I received a reply stating that a government patrol would be immediately established, a promise undoubtedly made in sincerity but never fulfilled. While the correspondence was being carried on I rented or obtained in other ways some houses in the immediate vicinity of the embassy as a refuge for Americans and other foreigners taken out of the line of fire by our automobile relief corps.

On February 11th, the third day, government troops and heavy artillery having been brought in from various places, the fighting became more strenuous. Repeated but unsuccessful attempts, during which a thousand federals were killed and some hundreds of non-combatants, were made to take the Citadel held by General Felix Diaz. The firing all day long was heavy and indiscriminate, inflicting great damage on the business and residential portions of the city; shells exploded in many of the houses, and quantities of bullets penetrated the rear of the embassy building. Diligent but futile efforts to communicate with the government were made by the embassy and members of the diplomatic corps, but no replies to our representations were received and no attention was paid to our complaints. It became increasingly apparent every hour that the civil authority had ceased to exercise its functions and that we were simply non-combatants hemmed in between two hostile armies with no protection or rights, except those which we might secure by our own courage and resourcefulness.

On February 12th, the fourth day, the situation had become so serious that some drastic action seemed imperative and, after consultation with the German and Spanish ministers, I determined to pay a visit to the President for the purpose of obtaining from him some guarantees with which we might reassure and calm the panic-stricken elements in the different colonies. At eleven o'clock Admiral von Hintze, Mr. Cologan, and I left the embassy in an automobile, followed by the cheers of the anxious thousands gathered outside. Although the federals and the revolutionists had been notified of our intention to visit the national palace, there was no cessation of firing. The trip was exciting but not amusing. A deadly pall of silence interrupted by the frequent booming of cannon reigned in the streets, and singing bullets passed overhead and about us.

Arriving at the national palace with great difficulty and some danger, due to the indiscriminate firing of soldiers on every one coming from the outside, we finally reached the President. Without ceremony I stated to him on behalf of my government and those of my colleagues that we had come to protest against a continuance of indiscriminate hostilities in the city. I informed him of the loss of American lives and damage to property and particularly of the destruction of the American consulate-general, and stated that my government was greatly concerned for the safety of its nationals. My colleagues made similar statements and were very emphatic. Madero was visibly embarrassed by our statements and endeavoured to fix the responsibility for the indiscriminate firing upon Felix Diaz. What he said carried no conviction as we were very well informed in the premises. He assured us that measures were being taken by his forces which would end the rebellion by the next evening, but his statements made little impression. We insisted that there should be a real and not nominal cessation of

[257]

hostilities until we could make representations to General Diaz at the Citadel. To this the President assented.

Returning to the embassy under the same dangerous circumstances, as the President apparently issued no orders to put a stop to the firing, we were there joined by the British minister and proceeded to visit General Felix Diaz at the Citadel for the purpose of making representations similar to those made to the President. Our approach to the Citadel was made through solid lines of soldiers, and we were finally received by General Felix Diaz with full military honours near a building which stood in the centre of the Citadel grounds. On behalf of the diplomatic corps I presented our views and General Diaz read a written reply, the substance of which was that the federals were committing the acts complained of and that the revolutionary forces would respect any territory which the federals did not occupy. My colleagues and I were pleased with the frankness as well as with the humane views expressed by General Diaz, and I must record here that during the entire bombardment the revolutionary forces paid more respect to the rights of non-combatants than did the Madero forces; the latter shot the Red Cross and the White Cross organizations to pieces and seized their automobiles and repeatedly located batteries or firing squads in the houses of foreigners without giving even the briefest notice. As we left the Citadel a rain of federal bullets fell all about us, striking in some cases and badly frightening the chauffeurs. The British minister remarked, "This is very unpleasant."

During the fifth and sixth days of the bombardment the firing continued, increasing in intensity and covering a wide area with destruction and death. The centre of the circle of the conflict approached nearer and nearer to us, and in three different directions encounters could be witnessed from the embassy windows and the dead and wounded could be seen lying exposed in the streets. All through these days the throngs about the embassy increased; tales of suffering and horror multiplied; our water and lights were cut off, producing intolerable sanitary conditions; our food supplies, reduced to the simplest and most primitive basis, would have been entirely eliminated but for the courage and enterprise of loyal Americans who went in automobiles to suburban towns and, in spite of the bullets and guards, furnished us and the some eighteen hundred American refugees whom we had installed in the vicinity of the embassy with relief. Through the nights the booming of cannon filled the air and the skies were lighted with the flames of the opposing batteries. Day and night ceased to have their usual meaning, and labour went on without respect to hours; little sleep, great work, the task of healing and helping, the atmosphere of great tragedies, and the fear of an unknown future.

On the seventh day of the bombardment, deeply concerned for the safety of many Americans remaining within the firing lines and who could not be rescued, I went to the national palace with Von Hintze for the purpose of procuring from General Huerta an armistice, during the continuation of which foreigners might be removed to places of safety. Upon our arrival at the palace, much to our regret, because we hoped for prompt action from Huerta, we were taken to see the President whom we had not asked to see, and it was only by insistence that we were permitted to have an interview with General Huerta in the presence of Mr. Lascurain. I asked (1) that the

[259]

military dispositions of the government should be made so as to avoid firing at the Citadel over the residential quarter; (2) that the American embassy should be treated as a humanitarian establishment and a free zone established around it; (3) that the government should unite with an American committee in establishing centres for the distribution of bread to the poor; (4) that federal soldiers on American buildings which had been made places of refuge should be removed; (5) that an armistice of three hours should be given to enable our rescue committee to take starving Americans and other foreigners out of the firing line; (6) that an armistice of twelve hours should be given to enable foreigners to leave the city by train. These demands were finally agreed to by General Huerta and the President. The President then showed to me a copy of a telegram relative to the revolutionary situation which he had sent to President Taft; most of it was misleading and inexact and I so informed him, quoting the information I had received from the country at large. At this interview the President also urged me to remove the embassy to a house in the suburban town of Tacubaya which he said he would place at my disposition. This offer had previously been made to me by Mr. Lascurain and it was declined in both instances, although it was supported by tentative instructions from Washington. Our government had placed me there in charge of its records, archives, and property, and there all of the system of aids for the American colony had been centred. If the firing became intolerable I was prepared to remove all women and men who so desired, but to transfer the embassy to the suburbs would have been a calamity to the entire American colony and would have spread a panic through all the foreign colonies. Nor could Americans be urged to go to safer places, because there were none; outside the firing line were bandits, and within, bullets. The rules of civilized warfare and of international precedents are of little value in urban fighting where shrapnels are used on both sides and where the location of batteries is made in hospitals.

The establishment of the armistice and the subsequent rescue work by the embassy committees were distinctly humanitarian acts. All day long a steady procession of automobiles carrying distressed families from the firing zone passed to the embassy and were distributed to the houses we had secured. Some fifteen hundred of these people, mostly Americans, some of them in a starving condition, were removed from the danger zone. There were moving and pathetic scenes, of course, but there was little time to heal wounds other than physical, and sentiment was put aside until another day.

CHAPTER XXXIX

*Meeting of the diplomatic corps and unofficial representations to Madero
—Correspondence with Madero and Lascurain*

AFTER nightfall, February 15th, acting in accordance with the views of the diplomatic corps and Mexican and foreign sentiment, I requested the British, German, and Spanish ministers, who were near, to come to the embassy to consider what course should be taken in view of the increasing horrors which surrounded us. Our military attaché, Captain Burnside, had just reported to me that the Citadel could not be taken with double the number of troops at present loyal to the government and that a prolongation of the conflict could result in nothing but additional effusion of blood and wholesale destruction of property. From the information furnished me by my colleagues and from other sources I was reasonably sure that the federal army was disloyal to Madero and that by prompt action only could a violent *coup d'état* be averted. The Spanish and German ministers, who with the Italian, British, and French ministers represented the large foreign colonies, arrived at the embassy without incident, but the automobile dispatched for the British minister was fired upon repeatedly by federal soldiers and finally held up and robbed. This experience did not tempt Sir Francis to make the return trip and he slept that night at the embassy. As all the available space in the embassy was already occupied, I could offer only very simple conveniences to Sir Francis. He slept that night on a couch in the embassy library. In the early morn I awakened him with an invitation to view the scene of the conflict from one of the embassy towers. As we came out upon the roof, we saw the marks of destruction in every direction, but the whistling of stray bullets lessened our interest and hastened our descent.

When my colleagues were assembled I asked for a spontaneous expression of their views both as to the situation and as to the course to be taken for its solution. The discussion lasted until three o'clock in the morning and developed identity of opinion on the following points: (1) that the Citadel could not be taken with the available government forces; (2) that numbers of federal officers and a large part of the federal army were disloyal to the government; (3) that a continuation of the fighting would lead to additional bloodshed, rioting, and acts of pillage and violence by the starving populace; (4) that unless Madero made amicable and peaceful arrangements for his retirement he would probably be overthrown violently, involving the lives of his family and many of his personal followers who were at that time objects of popular antipathy; (5) that in view of the abnormal situation we ought to assume the responsibility of making unofficial representations to Madero, urging him in the interests of peace and the suppression of bloodshed to resign and place his powers in the hands of Congress.

The duty of carrying these unofficial representations to the President was assigned to our highly esteemed colleague the Spanish minister, Mr. Cologan, who in the performance of his office went to the government palace

[263]

the next morning, meeting on his entrance a delegation of forty senators who had been to the President on the same mission and had been badly received. The President did not receive our good offices in the spirit in which they were offered but rebuked the Spanish minister and immediately sent telegrams, through the Mexican embassy in Washington, to our government, charging me with inciting the action of the diplomatic corps and stating that I would probably try to land American troops in Mexico. This act made a most disagreeable impression upon me, as it did upon my colleagues, and gave place to the following correspondence which, I think, reveals certain features of Madero's character better than any other evidence could:

American Embassy,
Mexico, February 17, 1913.

Mr. President: My government has transmitted to me, by telegraph, the text of a note delivered by the Mexican embassy in Washington to the Department of State. The note is as follows:

"At the instigation of Ambassador Wilson, and a part of the diplomatic corps, one of its members was commissioned to notify President Madero that he should resign his position in order to solve the present conflict in the city. The president refused to recognize the right of the diplomatic representatives to interfere in the domestic affairs of the nation and informed them that he was resolved to die at his post before permitting foreign interference. The Ambassador, in view of local circumstances, perhaps will try to disembark marines and this will produce an international conflict of terrible consequences. It is urgent, therefore, to avoid disembarkation. The president will give all possible protection to Americans and their interests."

As the statements contained in this note are untrue and as its evident purpose is to discredit me with the Chief Executive of my country, I have the honour to request that you direct the Mexican embassy in Washington to immediately withdraw it, and that such other amends be made as a proper sense of decorum and understanding of established diplomatic methods would indicate.

I have, etc.,

HENRY LANE WILSON.

It will be observed that this note, while purposely severe in tone, was kept within the limits of conventional diplomatic correspondence. The reply of Madero, which follows, not only shows a lack of sincerity but contains an obvious invitation to discredit a colleague, who had acted in perfect good faith as a representative of the diplomatic corps.

National Palace,
Mexico, February 17, 1913.

MY DEAR MR. AMBASSADOR: I have just received Your Excellency's note of this date, in which you send me the note which the Mexican embassy at Washington transmitted to the Department of State on the 15th instant.

You intimate that such note was sent for the purpose of discrediting you before your government and you ask me to address the embassy in Washington directing it to withdraw or conveniently amend said note.

Your Excellency's note has been pleasing to me and I shall be very glad to make the proper rectification. I only beg you to send a note denying Minister Cologan's authority, as he told me in your name and that of other foreign ministers, that the only solution was my resignation. When such a note is received I shall immediately make the rectification, and you may be sure, Mr. Ambassador, that the Mexican government has had no intention of placing you in a bad light before your government, as you know we esteem you and we appreciate the proofs of friendship you have given us in the name of your government.

With assurances of, etc.

Fco. I. Madero.

In the reply which I made to this note I endeavoured to hold Madero strictly to points under discussion and to prevent a misinterpretation of my attitude.

American Embassy,
Mexico, February 17, 1913.

Mr. President: I beg to acknowledge receipt of Your Excellency's note of February 17, 1913, in reply to my note of the same date. It is quite evident, from the reading of Your Excellency's note, that you misunderstood the purpose of mine, which was to deny the statement made in the note from the Mexican embassy to the Department of State at Washington that I had instigated a meeting of a portion of the diplomatic corps for the purpose of making representations to Your Excellency in an official way that in view of the existing alarming conditions you should retire from the presidency of Mexico.

I desire to say to Your Excellency that I did not instigate the meeting of the diplomatic corps but simply acted in obedience to a generally expressed wish in the corps, and that the information conveyed through Mr Cologan was not official and that Your Excellency was informed that it was not official, but simply friendly advice conveyed in a manner which clearly indicated its character. The assumption is that Mr. Cologan faithfully reflected in his conversation with Your Excellency the sentiments which moved our unofficial representations, and I know of no reason for making his action a matter of discussion.

Your Excellency's action in directing the sending of this note has caused the greatest regret not only to me but to my British, German, and Spanish colleagues, and they have informed their governments, as I have mine, of the exact circumstances in connection with our action.

With this explanation, which I trust may be satisfactory to Your Excellency, I must again request the retirement by the Mexican embassy of the note which is under discussion.

I have, etc.

HENRY LANE WILSON.

National Palace,
Mexico, February 17, 1913.

MR. AMBASSADOR: I have read Your Excellency's note of this date stating that you did not instigate the meeting of your colleagues held on the 15th instant at 1 A. M., but that you acted in obedience to the wishes of the diplomatic corps which were made known to me on that day by Mr. Cologan in an unofficial and clearly friendly manner. You have been pleased to add that Minister Cologan during the conversation he had with me faithfully indicated the above sentiments of friendship which inspired Your Excellency's and your colleagues' unofficial attitude, and that therefore the action of Minister Cologan cannot be a matter for discussion.

In view of the declarations which Your Excellency has been good enough to make, I see no inconvenience in sending a message to Washington, addressed to the embassy, which shall read as follows: "Referring to message you transmitted to the Department of State on the 15th, please say that in view of satisfactory explanations from the ambassador that he did not instigate the meeting of the diplomatic corps, which acted unofficially, the above message should be rectified in this sense."

With assurances of my consideration, etc.,

Fco. I. Madero.

It will be noted that the President not only withdrew instructions and cancelled directions to the Mexican embassy in Washington which were sent in apparent misinterpretation of the unofficial acts of the diplomatic corps, but in his note notifying me of the withdrawal of the instructions he placed upon record a statement that I was esteemed in Mexico and that the government appreciated the proofs of friendship which I had officially given it. This is in exact contradiction to the telegraphic instructions sent some two months before to Mr. Lascurain, printed on page 234. About this time I learned from our consuls that President Madero was sending telegrams to the governors of the different states announc-

[268]

ing that intervention had already taken place and that the public should be so informed. This was so obviously untrue and so calculated to endanger American lives throughout the republic that I dispatched to Mr. Lascurain a note which is here inserted:

American Embassy,
Mexico, February 17, 1913.

MY DEAR MR. LASCURAIN: My government has been informed by various American consuls in Mexico that His Excellency, the President of the Republic, has addressed communications to the governors of the different Mexican states alleging that American intervention is about to occur. My government, believing that these communications are likely to cause acts of hostility and violence against peaceful Americans residing in Mexico, deeply regrets that the President of the Republic should have been so forgetful of his obligations to foreigners dependent upon him for protection and of sentiments of humanity, as to permit himself to be misled into taking this action, and directs me to say, without further discussion of the question, that the President of the Republic and his advisers are assuming a heavy responsibility in thus contributing to the general insecurity of Americans in Mexico.

In this connection I beg to call Your Excellency's attention to the fact that several newspapers professing adhesion to the federal government are now publishing articles tending to arouse hostility to Americans in Mexico City. Among other things these papers have stated that Mr. Manuel Calero is at present in this embassy, which statement is entirely false, though I would cheerfully give asylum to him or any other Mexican citizen being

[269]

pursued for purely political offences. I earnestly request Your Excellency to bring about the immediate suppression and confiscation of these newspapers and at a future time I shall request the arrest and trial of the persons controlling and editing them.

Confidential: Information has just been brought to me, from an unquestioned source, but one which I cannot reveal, that His Excellency, Pino Suarez, Vice-president of the Republic, and Mr. Gonzales Garza, governor of the federal district, have directly instigated certain officers of the police force to seize Mr. Francisco de la Barra, who is now in the British legation, and cause him to be shot. Mr. De la Barra has been provisional president of this Republic, has served as ambassador of Mexico to the United States, and I assume the privilege of advising Your Excellency that any act of violence toward him would cause the profoundest indignation in the United States and in all civilized countries. While this circumstance is one beyond the province of my diplomatic attributes I believe it to be my duty as a friend of Mexico to urge upon you the exercise of all diligence in preventing crimes of this kind against distinguished Mexican citizens who happen not to be in accord with the government's policy but who are, nevertheless, not engaged in open rebellion against the constituted authorities.

With expressions of highest esteem, believe me, etc.,

HENRY LANE WILSON.

Mr. Lascurain's letter in reply is marked "strictly personal and confidential" and therefore cannot be used. It is no violation of confidence, however, to say that Lascurain, who was a scrupulously honest person, fully understood the abnormal character of Madero and anticipated the grave irregularities he might commit at any moment. Later Mr. Lascurain wrote me the following note:

My dear Mr. Ambassador:

Replying to your courteous letter of even date enclosing copy of a telegram sent yesterday by the Mexican embassy in Washington to the Department of State, which telegram you state is contrary to the facts and at variance with the interview you had with me on Friday the 14th, you ask me to explain my understanding of what was said during the interview. I regret very much, Mr. Ambassador, that this incident ever occurred.

In the meeting you certainly stated, in replying to a question of mine, that you did not have control of the marines and that you had not asked for their landing.

During the day, the reports from the United States relating to the imminence of disembarkation greatly concerned us and our preoccupation increased on Saturday because of the suggestion made to the President by members of the diplomatic corps that he resign to avoid an international conflict; such a step, it was thought, would put an end to the internal conflict which is worrying everybody.

Solely to avoid an international conflict this telegram was sent and to prevent disembarkation, an act which would only be authorized as a result of information sent by your embassy.

By considering the telegram in this light, you will see, Mr. Ambassador, that its scope depended upon future conditions. These anticipated future conditions are that a situation might arise in which European powers would ask the United States to give protection to their nationals. This sad possibility prompted the sending of the telegram protesting against the landing of marines.

I do not doubt, Mr. Ambassador, that these declarations will meet the purpose you had in asking me for them. Such is my desire and I trust that you are fully satisfied.

Yours very sincerely,
PEDRO LASCURAIN.

CHAPTER XL

*Preludes to the overthrow of Madero—The news brought to the embassy
—My request for the protection of the life of Madero—Correspondence
with General Huerta.*

ON THE ninth day of the bombardment, and the
17th of the month, the firing continued without
intermission and the dead and dying filled all
the streets within the firing zone. The firing,
too, became more indiscriminate and bullets were constantly entering the exposed side of the embassy. In the
afternoon it was discovered by the embassy messengers
that the troops of General Blanquet had arrived but were
taking no part in the conflict and that their heavy guns
were turned toward Chapultepec Castle—a most ominous
sign.

At this point it may be useful to relate an incident which
was—for political purposes—unduly magnified and falsely
interpreted. It was freely asserted that herein lay the
evidence identifying the embassy with a conspiracy for
the overthrow of Madero. It may be useful, therefore,
to make the following explanation: On the seventh day
of the bombardment I desired to communicate directly
and urgently with General Huerta for the purpose of having a battery, which was being established in the immediate vicinity of the embassy, removed. The matter
became urgent because the location fixed upon for the
battery would have immediately drawn fire and thus

[273]

have become a menace to the foreign residents of that part of the city. Our Consul-general, Mr. Shanklin, introduced to me a Mexican by the name of Cepeda, who said that he knew General Huerta well and would carry the message. He went away on the errand and, although in the meantime I had by threats and arguments induced the commander of the battery to remove it, Cepeda finally returned with the order in due form, saying to me at the same time that General Huerta desired a meeting with me and others of the diplomatic corps. He brought the same message to me twice afterward, stating both times that General Huerta contemplated a course which would bring about a cessation of the intolerable situation that existed. No meeting occurred, however, and prior to the arrest of Madero I saw Huerta only once and then in the presence of the President. All of the messages that Cepeda brought were received in the presence of American witnesses whose affidavits are on file in the Department of State, and I sent no messages by him, except one, when I began to take him seriously, to the effect that "violence and bloodshed ought under all circumstances to be avoided." My interviews with him were limited to not more than a dozen words, and each interview was reported to my colleagues and to the Department of State at Washington. When circumstances tended to confirm his mysterious and epigrammatic statements, I assumed that an arrangement might be under contemplation which would lead to the peaceful retirement of Madero following the surrender of his powers to Congress and an agreement for a new election, a consummation most devoutly wished for by all sane-thinking people. I did not for a moment suppose that

[274]

a violent *coup d'état* would occur or that Madero would be subjected to more than the pressure of overwhelming circumstances. Such messages as were sent to Huerta by this person were sent in behalf of the American and foreign colonies and are of record in the Department of State. I was quite prepared to make use of any instrumentalities which would subserve that purpose. I knew neither General Huerta nor Felix Diaz, nor did I know Cepeda, prior to the bombardment of the City of Mexico.[1]

On the tenth day of the bombardment, the 18th of the month, Cepeda arrived at the embassy at 2 P. M., wounded in the hand and greatly agitated. He was immediately furnished first-aid treatment by Doctor Ryan, the embassy physician, who had volunteered his services to the embassy after the destruction of the Red Cross organization by Madero's soldiers, and who not only gave first-aid treatment to hundreds of wounded but acted as embassy messenger to General Felix Diaz. As soon as Cepeda could talk clearly he informed me that the President and all of his ministers had been made prisoners by General Blanquet; that in the turmoil President Madero had killed, with his own hand, Colonels Riverol and Izquierdo and two common soldiers; that the brother of the Minister of the Interior, Rafael Hernandez, had also been killed. He said that Gustavo Madero had been made a prisoner, but knew nothing of his fate. As the presence of Cepeda in the embassy was a source of embarrassment to me I asked him to return to his own home as soon as his condition would permit.

---

[1]These explanations are made at some length, for the purpose of making clear the entire untruthfulness of statements circulated subsequently that the American embassy was involved in the overthrow of Madero.

A short time afterward Harry Berliner, one of the messengers of the embassy, arrived with a verbal message from General Huerta, who was evidently acting in conjunction with Blanquet, announcing the overthrow of the government. This message was delivered to me in the presence of Mrs. Wilson, and I immediately dispatched Berliner with a card to Huerta, on which Mrs. Wilson wrote at my dictation: "On no account permit any violence against the persons of the President and Vice-president."[1]

The overthrow of Madero was confirmed later in the afternoon by a note from General Huerta asking me, as its dean, officially to advise the diplomatic corps of what had occurred. I did this and, to prevent further conflict, unofficially advised General Diaz of what had occurred. The diplomatic corps was assembled at that moment in the embassy and on their behalf I sent a reply to Huerta merely asking that order be maintained. This note is inserted here:

American Embassy,
Mexico, February 18, 1913.

GENERAL:

I beg to acknowledge the receipt of Your Excellency's note of this date announcing that you have made prisoner the President of the Republic and also that his ministers are in your power. The resident diplomatic corps is at this moment assembled in the embassy and the information contained in Your Excellency's note has been brought to their knowledge. My colleagues instruct me to say

---

[1]Berliner subsequently made affidavit confirming this incident, but mistakenly attributed the note to Mrs. Wilson, who took my dictation on her personal card.

that they rely upon you and the Mexican army to preserve order in the City of Mexico and trust that you will use your best efforts to induce Mexicans of all elements to coöperate to the same end.

I have, etc.

HENRY LANE WILSON.

On my own responsibility I dispatched at the same time a note to General Huerta suggesting that he turn over his powers to Congress. I herewith insert a copy of this note:

American Embassy,
Mexico, February 18, 1913.

GENERAL:

I have the honour to acknowledge the receipt of Your Excellency's note of this date informing me that you have made prisoner of the President of the Republic and that his ministers are in your power. The expressions of patriotism and of duty to the country which you have been kind enough to communicate to me have been duly noted and I confidently rely upon your ability and good intentions to carry them into practical effect.

Without desiring in the least to intrude into Mexican domestic affairs, I beg to suggest the desirability, in view of the chaotic conditions which now exist, that you place yourself and the army under your command at the disposition of the Mexican Congress.

I have already communicated the facts related in Your Excellency's note to His Excellency, President Taft, and in due time I shall have the pleasure of advising you of his reply thereto.

[277]

I also have unofficially communicated the events related in your note to General Diaz and I shall immediately send him a formal note.

I have, etc.

HENRY LANE WILSON.

I also requested General Huerta, through Mr. Henry C. Tennant, Second Secretary of the embassy, to release the Minister of Foreign Affairs, Mr. Lascurain, the Minister of Finance, Mr. Ernesto Madero, and the Minister of Interior, Mr. Hernandez. Not only they but all of their colleagues were immediately liberated, and at that time I am sure it was Huerta's intention to free Madero also.

CHAPTER XLI

Reasons and decisions for calling Huerta and Felix Diaz to the embassy—Lamentable situation of the people of Mexico City and the need for peace—Deliberations at the embassy and final agreement—Rejoicing of the people.

LATER in the day I determined that I must take a decisive step on my own responsibility to bring about a restoration of order. This was the situation: Two hostile armies were in possession of the capital and all civil authority had disappeared; sinister bands of looters and robbers were beginning to appear in many of the streets of the capital; starving men, women, and children were parading in many public thoroughfares. Some 35,000 foreigners who, as developed during the bombardment, seemed to rely upon the embassy for protection, were at the mercy of the mob or exposed to indiscriminate firing which might at any moment begin between the forces of General Huerta and General Felix Diaz, thus reinvolving the lives and property of non-combatants. Without having conferred with any one, I decided to ask Generals Huerta and Diaz to come to the embassy, which, as neutral ground, would guarantee good faith and protection, for a consultation. My object was to have them enter into an agreement for the suspension of hostilities and for joint submission to the federal congress.

Near the hour fixed General Diaz, accompanied by officials of the embassy and two or three persons of his own selection, came to the embassy under the protection of the American flag. On entering he thanked me very earnestly for my attempts to exercise good offices for the procurement of peace. After introducing him to some of the ladies and other friends in the embassy, I went to the front entrance to receive General Huerta, who was just entering the embassy, officially escorted under the protection of the American flag. The scene outside and in the embassy during these official exchanges was impressive. Extra electric lights had been set up and from these the whole scene was revealed. There were probably twenty thousand people crowded in the streets adjacent to the embassy, and the embassy itself was packed to overflowing with Americans, the diplomatic corps, and the officers of Diaz and Huerta. It could hardly be described as a gay scene, as we were in the midst of tragic moments, but it was not sombre; the brilliancy of the lights, the handsome uniforms, and the presence of women brightened and relieved the picture.

I lost no time in bringing the two generals together in the embassy library whither, to my dismay, they brought a number of retainers and advisers. These so-called advisers soon engaged in wordy conflicts betokening unknown duration and infinite possibilities. This was not the purpose of the meeting, and I was finally obliged to ask all but General Huerta and General Diaz and my clerk, d'Antin, to withdraw. I then said to the two generals that I had called them together solely for the purpose of terminating the conditions which had existed in Mexico for the last ten days, conditions which had inflicted incredible suffering on the population of the city, had involved the destruction of ten thousand lives and a vast amount of public and private property; that these conditions must continue indefinitely unless the two belligerents arranged their differences and submitted to Congress, the only existing representative of the people. Three times, when the discussion was broken off, I entered the room and with appeals to their reason and patriotism induced them to continue. Finally, to force a decision, I said to them that unless they brought about peace the demand by European powers for intervention might become too strong to be resisted by the Washington government. This had the desired effect, and at one o'clock in the morning, the agreement was signed, deposited in the embassy safe, and a proclamation announcing the cessation of hostilities was issued. During this conference, exceedingly dramatic in some of its phases, a throng of anxious thousands surrounded the embassy. Within there was subdued but animated discussion, a battle of conflicting interests; without, the vast throng waited expectantly, patiently, for the announcement of a decision which so closely concerned their lives, their property, and their country. When it was finally announced that by the agreement of all parties an arrangement had been reached, and that with the authority of Congress General Huerta was to be provisional president and General Diaz was to be free to pursue his candidacy for the presidency, the news ran like wildfire through the city and was welcomed with universal rejoicing. That night thirty thousand people paraded through the streets of Mexico City giving thanks for peace and to the American government for having been instrumental in bringing it about. President Wilson considered the part played by the embassy as an intrusion in the domestic affairs of Mexico; persons who rest pleasantly by the home fires sometimes have curious conceptions of what the conduct of a public officer should be under critical and dangerous conditions. After years of mature consideration I do not hesitate to say that if I were confronted with the same situation under the same conditions I should take precisely the same course.

The consummation of this arrangement I regard as the most successful and far-reaching of the difficult work I was called upon to perform during the revolution, in that it stopped further effusion of blood, allowed the population of the city to resume its usual peaceful occupations, and led finally to the creation of a provisional government which rapidly restored peace throughout the republic. In my own experience of seventeen years in the diplomatic service I performed no act which so intimately concerned the preservation of a vast number of human lives as this. This single act is especially mentioned and commended as humanitarian and in the interest of peace by all public resolutions relating to the part played by the embassy in the revolution and by the letters of my colleagues. (See Appendices V and VI.)

CHAPTER XLII

Precautions taken to protect Madero—Death of Madero and Suarez—Notice to De la Barra and his subsequent report to me concerning the death of Madero—The problem of fixing guilt.

SOON after the overthrow of Madero the Washington government instructed me to take precautions to see that his life and that of the ex-Vice-president were preserved. Complying with these instructions I visited General Huerta with Admiral von Hintze and we jointly made representations in the sense of the department's instructions. (See Appendix II, a letter of Von Hintze.) At this interview General Huerta informed us that the ex-President would probably be sent out of the country; that a train was then ready at the station for that purpose and that some of the Madero family were already aboard it. General Huerta authorized me to say to Mrs. Madero that she need feel no apprehension about her husband's future, and he coupled this statement with assurances to us that he would not permit harm to be done to the ex-President.

On my return to the embassy with Von Hintze I found Mrs. Madero there with Mrs. Wilson and delivered Huerta's message to her. As a matter of history it may be stated that the train spoken of was gotten ready to take Madero and his family to the coast, and but for the indiscreet conduct of General Velasco, military commander of Vera Cruz, who, at the telegraphic instigation of some partisans of Madero in Mexico City, agreed to rise in his behalf, the unfortunate ex-President would probably at the present moment be in security either at home or abroad.

I went the same day to the Minister of Foreign Affairs, to the Minister of Fomento, and to the Minister of War, urging that Madero and Suarez be carefully guarded against attack, and tendered Ernesto Madero, the ex-Minister of Finance, and Pedro Lascurain, the ex-Minister of Foreign Affairs, asylum at the embassy.

On the day following the events just recited Mrs. Madero came a second time to see me. She seemed still to be apprehensive about the fate of her husband and also about his comfort. During this interview she handed me, written on an ordinary piece of paper, an unaddressed note from the mother of Madero, which I understood to be intended for me, but which, nevertheless, I transmitted to Washington without alteration. (See Appendix III for letter of Madero's mother.) *You were so cruel to Mrs Madero!*

Though I believed Mrs. Madero to be unduly apprehensive, I again went to General Huerta, in company with the German minister, who fully approved of all that was said and done, to make additional representations with reference to the safety of the ex-President. General Huerta then informed us that his original plan of sending Madero out of the country had been frustrated by the activities of the Madero family, whose telegrams had been intercepted and were of record: that as he was now provisional president he was responsible to the Mexican nation for whatever might occur and that we could accept his assurances that no violence was under contemplation. He then asked me directly whether I thought it better to have Madero impeached by Congress for violation of the constitution or to incarcerate him in a lunatic asylum. I answered, with the concurrence of the German minister, that I had no authority to speak in the premises and could only express the hope that he would do what was right and best for the peace of Mexico. As we were closing the interview I requested Huerta to transfer the ex-President to more commodious quarters and to provide him with his customary food and other things essential to his always delicate state of health. The substance of this interview was reported to Mrs. Madero, to the diplomatic corps, and to Washington. So far as I know, only one of my colleagues, Mr. Riquelme, the Chilean minister, who was on intimate terms with the Madero family, felt concern for the future of the ex-President. *You lie. How about the Cuban minister whom you don't mention*

On the morning of February 23d, I was informed at an early hour that during the preceding night the government had attempted to transfer Madero and Suarez from the national palace to the national penitentiary; that while en route the automobiles had been attacked and, in the struggle which followed, Madero and Suarez had been shot to death by their guards. Profoundly shocked by this unhappy event, I immediately requested a suspension of the diplomatic reception which Mr. De la Barra, the new Minister of Foreign Affairs, was about to give, and during that day and the day following efforts were made by the embassy to ascertain the exact truth of what had occurred. The evidence of at least twelve persons claiming to be eye witnesses was taken, but there was a plain lack of agreement in their statements and none had the semblance of reasonable and truthful accounts.

While I was endeavouring to mark my course, Francisco

de la Barra, whom I had known intimately for ten or twelve years, came to the embassy and in the most unequivocal terms informed me that neither the government nor General Huerta was in any way connected with the death of Mr. Madero; that his death had resulted from an organized conspiracy of people whose relatives had been killed during the Madero régime and who were, by reason of their close contact with the government, able to obtain information of the proposed transfer to the penitentiary. Mr. De la Barra, who had been ambassador at Washington and afterward provisional president of Mexico, was well known throughout Latin America as a high-minded and honourable gentleman, unusually humane and gentle in temperament. I knew he would not remain a single day as member of a government whose hands he believed to be stained with murder; he undoubtedly was honest, but he may have been deceived. His statement made a deep impression upon me, and as I was unable to secure reliable evidence of what had actually occurred, I adopted the only course which the unusual situation and the necessities of the moment seemed to warrant: I accepted the government's version and, pending further investigation, asked for suspension of American opinion. In this course I was supported by the entire diplomatic corps and by all foreign and American opinion in Mexico.

lie again

Profoundly as the violent death of Madero must be regretted by all right-thinking people, it should be remembered that he had resigned the office of President and at the time of his death was a simple Mexican citizen in no wise entitled through accepted international practice to the diplomatic intervention of any foreign government. (See Appendix IV for Madero's letter of resignation.) Cer-

tainly his death should not have excited greater sorrow
than the death of scores of Americans who had been sacrificed during the Madero régime, unrequited of justice,
with no idle sentimentalist to cry from the housetops the
story of their wrongs.

Madero was a person of unsound intellect, of imperfect
education and vision. He was a disciple of the French
school in politics and economics, but never gathered for the
uses of practical application its threads of philosophy or
comprehended in the least the deep common sense which
lies at the root of all French political opinion. He came
into power as an apostle of liberty but he was simply a man
of disordered intellect who happened to be in the public
eye at the psychological moment. The responsibilities of
office and the disappointments growing out of rivalries and
intrigues shattered his reason completely, and in the last
days of his government, during the bombardment of the
capital, his mental qualities, always abnormal, developed
into a homicidal, dangerous form of lunacy. Remote from
the great position where his misguided ambition carried
him he would doubtless have remained a quiet and simple
country gentleman of benevolent ideals and blameless life;
clothed with the chief power of the nation, dormant evil
qualities in the blood or in the race came to the surface
and wrought ruin to him and to thousands of the Mexican
people.

Eventually the world may learn that the death of
Madero and Suarez was brought about by a military conspiracy in revenge for the deaths of General Ruiz, who was
shot to death in the national palace without trial; for the
alleged shooting without trial of two young military
cadets; for the shooting by Madero of Colonels Riverol

and Izquierdo, and for the imprisonment and death of General Reyes.   Huerta, in my opinion, was not responsible for the death of Madero, unless he betrayed to others his intention of transfering Madero elsewhere, or was guilty of contributory negligence in furnishing such an inadequate escort to his new prison.

CHAPTER XLIII

Meeting of Society of the American Colony and resolution of approval by all American organizations—Presentation of gift to Mrs. Wilson— Organization of the Huerta Cabinet—Its high character—The legality of the Huerta succession—An estimate and history of Huerta—Interview with President Madero about Villa—Huerta's victory over Orozco— Acceptance by Secretary Knox of the legality of the procedure of installing Huerta—Reasons for delay in recognition—Philander Knox.

IMMEDIATELY after the installation of the provisional government the Society of the American Colony and other organizations in Mexico met and passed resolutions of approval of the embassy's management of the situation during the bombardment. It was also resolved at a public meeting of Americans to send a delegation to Washington recommending, on account of the critical situation, my retention as ambassador until the crisis had passed.

Parenthetically, it may be said here that sometime after the election of President Wilson, but before his inaugural, I sent a confidential communication to the Vice-president-elect, Mr. Marshall, who had been my intimate friend from childhood, detailing the difficult situation existing in Mexico, and expressed my desire to retire from the post as soon as the public interest would permit. In the memorandum I tendered some advice relative to the retention of certain officials in the Department of State and offered my gratuitous services at Washington for the period necessary for my successor to become instructed in

[289]

the duties of a new post. This letter was read by the Vice-president to the President and destroyed in his presence. No expression of the President's views as to the recommendations made in it reached me, but subsequent events demonstrated that it had no effect on the administration's Mexican policy.

The committee of the Society of the American Colony went to Washington in April and conferred with the President and Secretary of State relative to matters in Mexico. The written statement made by the committee to the President was afterward printed and copies were furnished me. The pamphlet contained the letter of the chairman of the committee to me; the telegram of the committee to the President and the argument made before the President by the delegation; the resolutions passed by the mass meeting of the American colony and by the subsequent conference of fifty leading American citizens; the resolutions of the American clergymen (Protestant and Roman Catholic) in Mexico City; the resolutions of the British colony, the Young Men's Christian Association, and the Mexican Society of New York. These, together with the commendatory letters of President Taft, Secretary Bryan, the tributary letters of my active colleagues in the diplomatic corps, and the affidavit covering the entire situation during the bombardment, voluntarily executed by the staff of the embassy, are elsewhere printed. (See Appendices V, VI, VII, and VIII.)

It is very gratifying to me to note here that leading members of the American colony, wishing to give some expression to the general sentiment of the colony, formally presented Mrs. Wilson with a beautiful solid silver tea and coffee set. Throughout the tragic scenes of the revolution, she had been a serene and helpful aid, and by her kindness and courtesy for everyone had made a deep impression.

While these events were taking place the Huerta provisional government had been installed and was addressing itself to the task of reorganizing the government and to the suppression of rebellion. The ceremony of its induction into power was simple. Congress was legally called together by its own officers and the resignations of President Madero and Vice-president Pino Suarez were placed before the extraordinary session. Under the provisions of the Mexican constitution the Minister of Foreign Affairs becomes provisional president in the event of the death or resignation of the President and Vice-president. The Minister of Foreign Affairs, Mr. Lascurain, took the oath of office as provisional president. His accession to power was approved by Congress and, after having appointed General Huerta Minister of Gobernacion, he immediately resigned. By provision of the Mexican constitution General Huerta thus became automatically provisional president of the republic and his title was approved by Congress without a dissenting vote. Probably a quorum of Congress was present, but this is not material, as it is an accepted principle of parliamentary law that the point of no quorum cannot be raised unless based upon a record of protest made at the time of the procedure. The official procedure in the succession of Huerta to the provisional presidency differed in no respects from the steps taken at the time Mr. De la Barra was made provisional president following the resignation of President Diaz.

Victoriano Huerta was of pure Indian blood, a native

[291]

of the state of Jalisco.   In early youth his intelligence and activity attracted the attention of wealthy people, who assisted in his primary education, and later became sponsors for his entrance into Chapultepec military academy, from which he graduated with honours.   He was rapidly promoted and became a full general of brigade under the presidency of General Diaz, whose full confidence he possessed and to whom he adhered until the final act of resignation and retirement.   After the triumph of Madero he passed for a time into eclipse, but his abilities were finally recognized and his influence in military circles grew apace.

After the defeat and suicide of General Salas, who had been sent north by Madero to grapple with the Orozco rebellion, the stability of the Madero government became very uncertain and, much against his inclinations, Madero was obliged to call Huerta from comparative retirement to the command of the armies in the north.   His careful preparations, both in equipment and discipline, and his sound tactics finally led to the complete overthrow of Orozco, a subsidence of military activities in the north, and the restoration of something approaching normal conditions in the border states.

During this military expedition to the north some incidents occurred which may be thought worthy of being recounted, as they bring into relief the character of Madero and introduced into official notice for the first time the celebrated Mexican bandit, Francisco Villa.

After Huerta was placed in command of Madero's army and sent north to engage Orozco, who had taken up arms against the government, a number of border chieftains were given commissions and ordered to report to Huerta.

Among these chieftains was Francisco Villa, who had been leading the life of a bandit in the mountains of Durango, a fugitive from justice in the time of Diaz but early gaining the confidence of Madero. Villa reported to Huerta but afterward led his followers on marauding expeditions against the civil population in the region through which they were passing. At that time many of the great estates in the north were owned by Americans who, suffering injury to person and property through the uniformed bandits of Villa, communicated through consuls and directly with the embassy, asking for protection. I immediately brought the complaints to the attention of the President in a personal interview. He questioned the reliability of my information, saying that Villa was a "patriot and an honourable gentleman." I then, in compliance with the President's wish, made a second investigation, which confirmed the reports that had inspired my representations in the first instance. Armed with this information I went a second time to the President and gave him full and conclusive information. To my astonishment he again impugned the character of the testimony which had been given me and seemed inclined to maintain his position. I then quietly but formally requested him to "arrest Villa and have him tried by court-martial." When he demurred to my request, I said to him that he was forcing me to the unpleasant course of asking my own government to send troops across the border to furnish the protection to American citizens which he declined to give. The President then observed that this would mean war. I said to him that "when soldiers in the uniform of a government attacked the persons and property of citizens of a friendly government and reparation was denied by the offending government, an act of war had been committed." As I announced this dictum a perceptible change took place in his manner and he said: "Very well, Mr. Ambassador, I will have the man arrested and tried." This promise was carried out. Villa was arrested and tried by a court-martial over which General Huerta presided. He was found guilty of the crimes charged and sentenced to be shot at daybreak on the following day. Madero, however, interfered and commuted his sentence to imprisonment in the military penitentiary at Mexico City. From this prison Villa finally escaped and was in arms against Madero when Madero was overthrown. After that event he continued in revolution against Huerta.

Huerta returned to Mexico City after his victory in the north expecting to be received with honour and applause; he became instead an object of jealous suspicion to the Madero family which respected his talents but feared his popularity. In the month of January, 1913, Madero revealed to me his lack of trust in Huerta and described him as being a "very bad man." At that time I had never seen or known Huerta, but I volunteered the suggestion to the President that "in troubled times men of his courage and fitness ought to be attached rather than driven away." When the Diaz rebellion broke out in Mexico City the Maderos again reluctantly made use of the military training of Huerta to meet the emergency, but during the conflict he remained in the government palace under close watch and virtually a prisoner; there can be little doubt that his life was at all times in danger, and probably this circumstance sowed the first seed of rebellion in his mind.

Huerta was a man of iron mould and courage. He had all the brevity and incisiveness of speech of the man who has lived in camps rather than in courts. He had Indian persistence, stubborn insistence, a mind and body trained to military precision and discipline; unfortunately he had no training whatsoever in civil practices or the science of government, and he had an utter contempt for both. With this character he was able, as often happens, to rise to power but, lacking the wisdom, training, and experience to retain that which had been grasped, he quickly fell. He possessed abundant vices but was not without great qualities of mind and heart. He had an unusual gift of eloquence and sufficient natural diplomacy and statesmanship to put into confusion and ridicule "the Puritan of the north," as he called President Wilson. He was a devout Roman Catholic, a believer in the Diaz régime and policies, and with all his faults I am convinced that he was a sincere patriot and in happier times might have had a career honourable to himself and useful to his country. He fell from power, the victim of narrow-visioned American diplomacy, and died a sacrifice to the same overweening jealousy and egoism which, with the power of a great people behind it, had brought about his downfall.

Perhaps no other Mexican cabinet has contained men of such exceptional ability and high character as did the cabinet of General Huerta in the initial months of his administration. The selection of this cabinet was not at all due to the intelligence or sympathetic initiative of General Huerta. Every member was selected by General Felix Diaz according to the agreement which the two chieftains had entered into when peace was made. Huerta complied formally with this agreement but proceeded as rapidly as possible to rid himself of a cabinet not in sympathy with his ambitions and which could not be expected to approve of his unlawful methods; if he had remained faithful to his agreement with Diaz and had retained at his side the able and patriotic men under whose charge his government was ushered in, the hazardous and lamentable interference of the President of the United States would have had to meet a united and ably governed Mexican nation, and the story of phantom governments by savage bandits might not have been written.

This new cabinet was solicitous for the reorganization of the domestic affairs of the country and desirous of bringing about its pacification as quickly as possible. Huerta's government went into office accompanied by the hope of thirteen million Mexicans who wanted peace and order before all else. In its earlier stages it showed great activity and an earnest desire to meet its international obligations, especially those long pending with our government and, had it received sympathetic support from the American government, it would probably have made its control effective in every part of the republic and thousands of lives and millions in property would have been saved.

After the installation of the new provisional government the administration of President Taft, which was still in power, accepted, in principle, the view that it was legally constituted and entitled to recognition, but it delayed recognition for the purpose of securing the settlement of certain long-standing differences with the Mexican government. Principal among these differences were the Chamizal case, which had been pending for many years; the Colorado River and Imperial Valley case, a recent case but of urgent importance; the Tlalhualilo case, which had been the subject of correspondence and negotiation for seventeen years; and the specific and general damage cases, claims growing out of the revolutions, the specific ones falling under a clear rule of international law and the general ones requiring an international agreement. Without violation of the secrets of the Department of State, it may be said that the government of General Huerta agreed in principle to all the demands made by our government, except that relating to general claims for damages growing out of the revolution. In this particular instance I was demanding, with the support of the entire diplomatic corps, that an international court should be established and that it should have jurisdiction over claims of all kinds, independently of the provisions of the Mexican constitution. The Huerta government was reluctant to give its agreement to this mode of procedure, and while the debate was being carried on the Taft administration went out of office.

Some years after, Mr. Knox told me, in the Waldorf Astoria Hotel in New York, that if the Huerta government had conceded our demands in full he would, even as late as ten o'clock on the morning of March 4th, have recommended to President Taft that full recognition be accorded. Whatever the faults or sins of the Huerta administration may have been it was undoubtedly, under the established practice of international law, entitled to recognition. When it came to the question of law, usage, and practice, Mr. Knox's judgment was infallible.

Philander Knox was in some respects a master mind in the management of foreign affairs. With the restraints imposed by judicial training and traditions, he clearly

[297]

understood the proper direction of our foreign relations, their scope and their limitations; his presentation of a policy or interpretation of the aspects of a foreign question was accurate, but his life-long training in the law and his profound reverence for orderly and calm procedure sometimes affected or delayed the vigour of his action in acute crises. Honest by the highest standards and saturated with our own traditions, it was not always easy for him to understand that foreign chancelleries might not be actuated by similarly high motives. He recoiled from questioning the good faith of the representatives of foreign governments and, imbued with the spirit of our own tribunals, reluctantly impugned the uprightness of the courts of other countries. He was eminently just, quick to recognize and acknowledge his own mistakes, and possessed withal a generous, kind, and loving disposition. The details of the work of the Department of State wearied him almost to the point of cynicism, and he fled from them as frequently as the executive work would permit; but, as I have reason to know, his moments of apparent leisure were given to the study and preparation of the really great state policies and papers associated with his name. He unwillingly left the Senate and was happy to return to it. Knox was a politician of a high order, caring little for small things but much for those which concerned the dignity and prosperity of the country. He was devotedly fond of Roosevelt but, in the unhappy controversy which arose between Taft and his former chief, his aid and his sympathy were all for Taft.

CHAPTER XLIV

Advent of Wilson administration—General recognition of the Huerta government—Impatience of the attitude of the government of the United States—My unsatisfactory situation—Memoranda of interviews with Huerta—Correspondence with the Department of State about recognition —The Wilson policy and its unsoundness—Secret and personal agents of the Washington administration arrive in Mexico—William Bayard Hale—Reginald del Valle.

IT WAS the belief of those identified with the government of General Huerta that the administration of President Wilson would be less severe in its attitude toward Mexican affairs than had been that of President Taft, and it was hoped that settlement of many of the differences which existed between the United States and Mexico would be made. To some extent this opinion was justified in the early stages of the Wilson administration. There were indications of its desire to lessen the military and naval demonstrations on the Mexican border and in the Mexican waters, and it definitely took a position—one which we may find exceedingly awkward if called upon under the Monroe Doctrine to protect the property of foreigners—that the American property owners in Mexico need not expect the protection of this government. This remarkable doctrine was not announced by presidential message but it was repeatedly stated by Secretary Bryan in interviews with Americans whose properties were being destroyed.

All the European governments, together with China

and Japan, recognized the Mexican provisional government. The governments of Chile and Brazil, then the only South American governments having representatives in Mexico, withheld recognition, not because the policy of our government was endorsed or approved, but because these representatives had formally agreed with me, under instructions from their governments, that in all matters pertaining to the recognition of the new government they would act in accord with me as the representative of the government of the United States and that their recognition would be given only with and at the same time as ours.

The embarrassment to the Mexican government resulting from the refusal of our government to accord recognition was very great. Its effect was to encourage rebellion against a regularly constituted authority and one upon which, at that time, were based the hopes of a vast majority of peaceable Mexicans. It lowered the government's credit abroad and made the financing of its affairs difficult and expensive; it excited the hostility and derision of the resident diplomatic corps and of all foreign colonies in Mexico, including our own; it subjected our own people to enormous burdens and great sacrifices and it neither has been nor can be justified either in sound statesmanship or good morals. The transaction of diplomatic business with Mexico from this time became extremely difficult, and the embassy lost in prestige and ability to serve our own people and interests constantly from the moment Mr. Bryan assumed charge of the Department of State.

The anomalous situation resulting from the attitude of the government at Washington I was obliged to endure in silence as there seemed to be no cure for it. The reports and recommendations which it was my duty to make I made and then waited patiently, trusting that a certain amount of experience would teach the administration the course which it ought to pursue in the interest of the welfare of the Mexican nation and for the good of our people living in Mexico. From this attitude of inactivity and expectancy I was awakened on May 7th by a message from President Huerta requesting me to pay him a visit. I made a careful memorandum of the conversation which took place at this interview which, inserted here, describes the irritation and resentment existing at that time and the disastrous effect the attitude of our government had upon important American interests.

Mexico, May 7, 1913.

"I saw the President to-day at his request. He said that he had been wanting to have a consultation with me for some time relative to the delayed recognition of this government by the government of the United States. I replied that believing the interests of our own country as well as those of Mexico were involved in the early recognition of the latter by the former, I had made repeated representations to Washington urging the resumption of full and cordial official relations, but that neither the Department of State nor the President had given expression to any views and that I was without any guidance as to our attitude, save by conjecture. I said to him that possibly immediate recognition might be brought about by the prompt and unreserved settlement of all of the questions pending between the two governments which formed the basis of my letter of February 24, 1913, to him. I added that I could only surmise that this might be the reason for withholding recognition and that my government might, in deference to a certain section of public opinion, be delaying its action so as to follow other nations in making official recognition; that perhaps the question of recognition might be influenced by the complete reëstablishment of peace in Mexico.

"The President then asked me if he might talk to me unreservedly as a friend of Mexico and as his personal friend. I consented to this with the reservations that I could have no secrets from my government concerning political matters. He then went on to say, speaking with much earnestness, eloquence, and some bitterness, 'that the Mexican nation was solvent and independent and that his administration, though not elected, had been as legally constituted as any government could possibly be and had entered upon the task of reëstablishing peace with a bankrupt treasury left by the Madero administration, which had plundered the nation, and with no army; that by careful administration and skillful direction of public funds a new army had been built up and equipped and was about to take the field for active operations against the rebels'; this recruiting he said was now going on at the rate of eight hundred soldiers a day; that peace was being rapidly established throughout the republic, except in certain districts on or near the border and in the state of Morelos; all other outbreaks he said were pure brigandage; that by the end of June he expected to have peace reëstablished throughout the republic. He stated that the loan which the government had been negotiating for some time was about to be closed and that the governments of Germany, France, and Italy would soon follow England and Spain in recognizing this republic.

"In view of these facts the President said he felt that 'the attitude of the government of the United States in refusing to accord recognition to this government was unwise, unfriendly and, in the event that it should fail to sustain itself, the opinion of the world was certain to place the responsibility for whatever disasters might follow upon the administration at Washington.' In view of this situation he said 'that his government did not feel that it would be justified, in the face of a hostile public opinion and because of the undignified position in which it would be placed by so doing, in concluding the questions at present pending between the two governments; that is to say, the Chamizal, the Colorado River case, the special claims cases, and the general claims.' He added 'that the Washington government's views in these cases, together with the Tlalhualilo case, which had been entirely concluded, had been accepted in principle by this government and that if the government of the United States would place his government in the position of discussing the questions as matters between two friendly and sovereign, if not equally powerful, states, their prompt settlement could be expected, but not before.'"

I reported this interview to Washington, as I did the recognition of the provisional government by European powers, but replies placing me in possession of the policy of the government, which I was supposed to be representing, were not forthcoming. Accordingly, on June 9th, I made a telegraphic résumé of the reasons why recognition should be accorded and the desirability of acquainting me for my own guidance with a precise definition of the administration's policy. While making clear my own views as to what our policy should be, I endeavoured in this appeal to make it equally clear that I was prepared to carry out faithfully any policy which the President might determine upon.

The reply to this telegram came on June 15th. It was substantially a statement of what was later known to be the attitude of the Washington administration toward Mexico. It is not an easy matter to interpret or define the attitude or policy of the Wilson administration toward Mexico. Whatever may have been the conception of the so-called "policy," that policy, transmitted into effect, meant simply that no government established in Mexico by a revolution would be recognized by the American government if, according to our estimate, the revolution were unjustified. We thus constituted ourselves the judges of the laws and the facts, and the dictum amounted to a subversion of the sovereignty of Mexico and a threat against all Latin-American governments established by revolution. This amounted to a complete reversal of our traditional policy of non-interference which was announced by Franklin Pierce and adhered to by every President from Pierce to Wilson. Unfortunately, this doctrine may obtain permanent lodgment in our foreign policy and, if so, may be expected to bring on unfortunate incidents in our future relations with Latin America.

The instruction was worded in such a manner as to indicate a desire on the part of the Department of State that it should be brought to the attention of the provisional president and, accordingly, on June 25th, I visited him and read him a paraphrase of the telegraphic correspondence, but gave him no copies of the department's or my own telegrams. I insert an extract from a memorandum of the interview:

[304]

". . . On the question of recognition the President said it had been a matter of vital importance at one time, because of difficulties raised by the bankers who were making the loan to Mexico; but now that these difficulties had all been overcome and Mexico has sufficient financial resources to prosecute the war vigorously, recognition, while it would of course be welcomed gladly, had ceased to be essential."

I asked him whether he was a partisan of General Diaz, and he replied, "I am a partisan of the country, but of no man. I intend to see that the election is honestly carried out and that everybody shall have an equal opportunity." He added, "I am thoroughly tired of this position and will welcome the election as the signal of my release and retirement into private life. I expect to take up my residence in the state of Chihuahua and to place my son in Harvard University, as I believe that all Mexicans should be as well posted in American history, customs, and literature as in Mexican."

The policy of the Mexican government of ignoring our government was faithfully adhered to. The usefulness of the embassy in looking after American interests was ended, and aside from being the titular American ambassador in Mexico my functions were suspended. Acting conformably with what seemed to be the policy of the Wilson administration, I ceased attending meetings of the diplomatic corps and refrained from discussing with my colleagues questions in which their governments and ours possessed a common interest.

In the meantime, Mr. William Bayard Hale came to Mexico preceded by an Associated Press announcement that his visit was in connection with some proposed magazine work but that he might possibly make an unofficial report to the President on Mexican affairs. Though I had had no previous acquaintance with Mr. Hale and his presence in Mexico was distasteful to me, I received him courteously and furnished him with all the information which I could properly place in his hands. He stated to me that he was engaged in the preparation of an article for a magazine and that he was busy accumulating material for that purpose and indicated that the universal testimony as to the excellence of my work had made a most agreeable impression upon him. In the course of our conversation I advised him to visit different members of the diplomatic corps and leading and responsible Americans of all shades of opinion. This, so far as I was able to discover, he never did, but without loss of time he began expressing opinions on political events, opinions which could not possibly have been formed in such a brief time but must have been the result of impressions or suggestions received before he arrived in Mexico City.

Unfortunately for our country and for the President and for every interest concerned in bringing about peace in Mexico, Mr. Hale fell under the control of influences which were more occupied in advancing peculiar interests than in subserving the welfare of the people of both countries. This small group of persons, perhaps half a dozen in number, were hostile to the new provisional government and to the embassy, not for reasons which would appeal to the American people but for some intimately connected with their own personal affairs. Most of them had at one time or another received the timely assistance of the embassy, but their gratitude ceased either with the termination of their difficulties or with the opportunity to take up enterprises which a conscientious diplomatic officer would regard with suspicion.   One of these persons represented an American oil company which, according to a Secret Service report on file in the Department of Justice, financed to some extent the Madero campaign against Diaz; another was the representative of a large banking firm in New York heavily interested in Mexican securities; another, the legal representative of one of the largest American land-holding interests in Mexico, the head of which was endeavouring to bring on intervention; another, an embittered newspaper correspondent.   From this coterie Mr. Hale, according to the testimony of Americans in Mexico, received his information and upon their suggestions made his reports to Washington.   What these reports were I had no means of knowing except by the results which followed.

After a certain length of time Mr. Hale's affable and courteous attitude toward the embassy altered and I frequently heard that his intimate circle of acquaintances was quoting him as hostile to me.   To make the confusion worse, another confidential representative in the person of Mr. Reginald del Valle arrived on the scene.   Mr. Del Valle was of Mexican descent but resided in the State of California and was an American citizen.   He was selected for the mission by Mr. Bryan and did not approve of Mr. Hale or of Carranza, whom he had visited in the north, or finally, after full investigation, of the Madero régime. He afterward made a report to the Department of State embodying these views and, I am told, spoke in a handsome way of the services which I had been able to render. Mr. Del Valle refused to be used by any particular faction of the colony but visited Mexicans, foreigners, and Americans generally. He was apparently serious in his efforts to ascertain the truth, and although I met him only upon two occasions, I knew that he was making up his report very carefully. I learned of its character after my arrival in the United States. It may easily be imagined how embarrassing it was to me and how much it interfered with the usefulness of my work, as the officially accredited agent of the government of the United States, to have two secret agents of my own government proclaiming up and down the highways of Mexico that they were political representatives of our government. Probably there is not another similar instance in the history of diplomacy, and it well illustrates the loose and inadequate hands into which the conduct of our foreign affairs had fallen at this time.

CHAPTER XLV

Meeting of the diplomatic corps and request to Washington government for recognition of Mexican government—My summons to Washington—New anti-American riots—My departure and lack of usual courtesies—Interview with President Wilson and Secretary Bryan—My written recommendations—Called to testify before Senate Committee on Foreign Relations—President Wilson objects—My resignation accepted—Uneasy feeling at Washington at the development of the President's new policy—Some errors made by the President.

ON THE Fourth of July it was the custom of the American colony in Mexico to stage an elaborate celebration to which the President of the Republic, his cabinet, and the diplomatic corps were invited. As Secretary Bryan desired that nothing should be done which might be interpreted as a recognition of Huerta, he instructed me not to participate in this ceremony and to be absent from the city. After unsuccessfully attempting to have the official character of the celebration changed, I arranged with Admiral Beatty, at that time in command of the American fleet at Vera Cruz, to receive me as a guest on July 4th. This procedure was wholly ridiculous and wholly unnecessary, but in diplomatic matters Mr. Bryan's mind, as I discovered, moved negatively and was occupied more with retreats than charges.

During my absence at Vera Cruz the resident diplomatic corps met and determined to make identic recommendations to their respective governments urging that representations should be made to the government at Washington relative to the expediency of an early recognition of the present provisional government or, in the event that such recognition could not be accorded, the assumption by our government of its full responsibilities under the Monroe Doctrine, i.e., Washington was to be told either to help the administration of Huerta to restore order or to accept responsibility for conditions which might result from withholding the recognition. I do not affirm that these were the exact representations made by the different governments to Washington. I can only say that my information came from Sir Francis Stronge, the British minister, who came to see me immediately upon my return from Vera Cruz. I was deeply distressed by the action which had been taken by my colleagues and immediately, as was my duty, reported the matter to Washington, in order that the department and the President might be properly prepared to deal with such representations as might be made through the embassies accredited there.

I was informed later that upon receipt of my cablegram, Mr. Hale, who was still in Mexico, was instructed to investigate the circumstances connected with the collective action of the diplomatic corps and that he reported that the meeting and action taken by my colleagues had been inspired and instigated by me. Thereupon Mr. Bryan sent me a cablegram instructing me to come to Washington for "consultation relative to the Mexican situation." I should be glad to believe that my information on this point was in error, as a more wicked falsehood could not be imagined. My colleagues in Mexico City were independent and scrupulously conscientious representatives of their governments; whatever action they took at that time or at any other time must undoubtedly have been inspired by a sense of duty and by a strict regard for the necessities of the hour. Their action was not agreeable to me, but as Washington had virtually deprived me of official standing in Mexico I had no right either to influence their course or to protest their conclusion. If our policy had been moving in accord with the views of European powers and with the recommendations of our own embassy in Mexico, no action would have been taken by my colleagues without first giving me an opportunity to express an opinion.

Although the summons to Washington was unexpected, because of the manifest importance of my presence in Mexico at that time, I made all arrangements, packed my trunks, and in a great flurry of excitement among the embassy employees and servants left for Vera Cruz twelve hours after the summons. I left all of my personal property, furniture, pictures, and library in the embassy, accepting the cablegram of the Secretary of State in good faith and supposing that I was called to Washington simply for the purpose of orally presenting my views to the President and being immediately returned thereafter to remain until a more normal situation developed.

A few days prior to my departure, anti-American riots, either spontaneous or incited, again broke out in Mexico City. These demonstrations were expressive of the resentment felt at the failure of the Washington government to accord recognition to the Huerta administration. I immediately addressed strong letters of protest to the Minister of Foreign Affairs, and my notes were couched in such severe terms that the government immediately took the matter in hand, though my notes remained un-answered. There was, however, a strong feeling of resent-ment against my vigorous action, and this feeling was evidenced by the failure to extend to me the usual cour-tesies accorded to a departing ambassador. No Mexican official was at the station to say farewell, and except for the presence of friends and colleagues my leave-taking was marked by none of the usual evidences of respect. I con-soled myself, however, with the Bismarckian philosophy that "an ambassador ought not to be too popular in the country to which he is accredited."

I arrived in New York on August 1st, and found many reporters on the dock seeking an interview. For the pur-pose of arousing public opinion I gave to the correspond-ents an outline of the true conditions which were pre-vailing in Mexico. The story I gave was faithfully reproduced by the press and, diffused through the country, it furnished the first true picture of the actual doings and conditions south of the Rio Grande.

Arriving at Washington, I immediately had a conference with Secretary Bryan, who told me that the President desired me to prepare a memorandum covering the history of events in Mexico from the time of Diaz to the time of my departure from Mexico. As the information to be contained in such a memorandum was already in the pos-session of the department and accessible to the President, the request caused me some surprise. But I dictated the memorandum to a person in Mr. Bryan's confidence and supplemented it with citations to different reports which had not been called for. Secretary Bryan informed me that I would be expected to meet the President after he had had an opportunity to study the memorandum.

On the day fixed I went to the White House and was immediately shown into the presence of the President and Secretary Bryan. The President was affable and pleasant in his demeanour, revealing that charm of manner that characterized his earlier public life. Without referring to the memorandum which I had furnished him, he asked for a brief summary of the Mexican situation, and as I proceeded, commented, as I thought, irrelevantly. I noticed a certain inflexibility of preconceived views which rendered discussion and a faithful presentation of the situation difficult. He impressed me as being under the influence of opinions other than those which I had been reporting to the department and as having perhaps a different version of the events that had occurred in Mexico. He made no comment on the recommendations contained in my memorandum, which were remedial and comprehensive, but expressed skepticism of the honesty of Huerta's expressions of readiness to meet the views of the United States in a general way and specifically to carry to conclusion our agreements for the settlement of the long-standing differences between the two countries. The President's questions suggested a lack of knowledge of the psychology and facts of the situation in Mexico, and it was quite evident that he had not availed himself of the information accessible to him at the Department of State. I learned afterward that he had only read the last serial number of my reports, a superficial method of ascertaining effects while ignoring causes. I was fully convinced after the interview that I had made no impression upon the President and that we were about to be committed to further experiments in Mexican affairs.

The remedial part of the memorandum which I submitted to the President was afterward read to the Senate Committee on Foreign Relations, when I was called to testify before it:

RECOGNITION

"Recognition under the present circumstances cannot be made with the same effect and with the same result as immediately after the assumption of power by the new administration. It would be misconstrued now as a yielding to pressure and force and would result in the loss of great prestige.

"If recognition is accorded it should be done in the following way:

"First: By a preamble, recognizing the remarkable and unprecedented situation in Mexico, the desire of the United States to contribute to the restoration of order in a neighbouring and friendly state, and the necessity, on account of the important matters daily pending between the two governments, to establish full official relations with all of the benefits and obligations resulting therefrom.

"Second: No recognition should be accorded unless the important international questions, such as the Chamizal and the Colorado River claims cases, shall be immediately closed upon the basis presented by the government of the United States, and agreed to by the government of Mexico in correspondence and verbally with the ambassador.

"Third: Recognition should not be accorded unless the proposal for an international claims commission, having jurisdiction over all kinds and classes of claims arising out of the revolutionary movements during the last three years, shall be admitted in principle by the Mexican government.

[314]

"Fourth: Recognition should not be accorded unless ample guarantee for the holding of a constitutional presidential election during the month of October shall be given and this would involve the removal of the present Minister of Gobernacion, and the substitution therefor of a Mexican of force and power—say Calero—thoroughly committed to the principle of constitutional government.

"Fifth: Recognition should not be accorded unless the federal government is able to furnish evidence of its ability to restore peace and order to the 26th parallel.

"Sixth: Recognition should not be accorded unless an arrangement can be made by which the American government, in coöperation with the Mexican government, will be permitted to cross the border and aid the federal authorities in the restoration of order down to the 25th parallel, always giving ample stipulation for the retirement of our troops whenever, in the judgment of duly appointed commissioners of United States and Mexico, order and peace have been reëstablished.

"Recognition accorded in this manner will restore our lost prestige, impress foreign and native opinion in Mexico, and undoubtedly restore peace and prevent further bloodshed.

INTERVENTION

"If recognition is not accorded in some form or other our duties as a civilized nation, pledged to the world to preserve order in this hemisphere, point directly to immediate and effective intervention.

"Intervention should be carried out in the following way:

"First: By discreetly removing the already decimated and ruined American population from Mexico.

"Second: By the transfer of the charge of our diplomatic and consular establishments to the representative of another power.

"Third: By the massing of our army fully equipped for invasion at every strategic point lying on the border states, and the calling out of the reserves in all border states.

"Fourth: By the appointment of commissioners, one of whom should be the ambassador, another the general-in-chief of the army, another the ranking officer of the investing fleet, and another a member of the Committee on Foreign Relations of the Senate. The duty of this commission would be to seek, by a preliminary action, a reconciliation of all the contending forces in Mexico, with the understanding that their work should be urgent, expeditious, and not detained by any dilatory methods, and with a further understanding that they should follow in the path of invasion, reëstablishing the rule of law and dispensing justice and order in the name of the United States.

"Any invasion should be accompanied by a public statement that our purpose is not one of aggression but that we are acting in the discharge of a duty to humanity and civilization and that when once constitutional methods and practices are reëstablished and firm government installed our troops will retire to the United States."

These recommendations, though they apparently had little weight with the President, later made a favourable impression on the Senate Committee on Foreign Relations, and their insertion is of some importance to the reader. In my interview with the President it was intimated to me that I would be permitted to take a vacation of some weeks; the intimation was unaccompanied by any suggestion as to the duration of my leave of absence.

After my visit to the President I was requested by Senator Bacon, chairman of the Senate Committee on Foreign Relations, to appear before that committee for the purpose of giving evidence on the Mexican situation. With the consent of the Department of State, rather reluctantly accorded, and armed with copies of official documents bearing on Mexico, I told the story of what had occurred and gave my recommendations for dealing with the crisis. The Department of State had furnished me with copies of all my correspondence with it and otherwise but declined to furnish me or the committee with copies of its correspondence with the embassy in Mexico City. The correspondence of the embassy was brought into the Senate Foreign Relations Committee room in charge of Mr. Jenkinson of the Department of State, who was familiar with it. The mass of evidence was very formidable and, when I stated at the outset of my examination that I had come prepared to substantiate every statement I made, if called upon to do so, seemed to have a repressive if not depressive influence on the committee. The committee listened to me courteously and attentively and the circumstance that I was not called upon to produce a single document in proof of my testimony afforded me some satisfaction. This evidence made, as I was told by Democratic and Republican senators, a strong impression upon the committee; indeed the impression created was so marked that it inspired, though foreign to my intention, criticism of the policy of the administration. The changing atmosphere did not suit the President, and when later Chairman Flood of the House Committee on Foreign

Affairs invited me to appear before that body, the President called him up by telephone and asked him to cancel the invitation as he wanted "no further exploitation of my views." He also interviewed various senators of the Senate Committee on Foreign Relations, and my testimony before that body was never concluded. The course of the President in this instance was the more reprehensible in that I had referred to him in only the most courteous way during my examination and carefully avoided anything that would appear to give a partisan character to the evidence. My testimony was a simple recital of the events which had occurred in Mexico and was concluded with a recommendation of the remedial steps which I thought ought to be taken. It did not vary materially from that given to the President, and I am confident it was well received by the Democratic members of the committee.

In the latter part of August I was called to the Department of State by Mr. Bryan who, with apparent embarrassment, informed me that the President had decided to accept my resignation. He submitted a form of statement to be given to the public which simply stated that the resignation was accepted because of lack of agreement as to policy. I said to him that I had expected this result, but was not satisfied with the form of statement, inasmuch as I had twice tendered my resignation while in Mexico and as the President had had an opportunity to accept it while I was there, it seemed only just that his announcement should express some recognition of the character of the services which I had rendered the government for seventeen years, services which had the indorsement and approval of President Wilson's three immediate predecessors. I called his attention to the circumstance that I was about to give to the press Mr. Taft's fine letter of indorsement and that it seemed fair that a substantially similar commendation should be given me by President Wilson. The Secretary's observation was that I must not expect the President to accept the views of President Taft. I replied that I was referring to facts and not to views; that I could not understand why he should not accept the version of President Taft, who had been in charge of the situation from the time I became ambassador to Mexico until the termination of the events which brought into power the present Mexican administration, and that as I had been especially commended by him, by President Roosevelt, and by President McKinley, a line of approval from President Wilson would be accepted by the public solely as a decent act of courtesy to a retiring officer. The Secretary seemed to be impressed with what I said and volunteered to submit the point immediately to the President, together with three other points relating to business matters with the department.

Meeting the Secretary an hour afterward, he informed me that the President approved of the suggestion I had made with reference to the government's responsibility in certain business matters, but declined to change the form or wording of the notice to be given to the press. Mr. Bryan explained that the President had a perfectly open mind regarding the matter but that as he was not in possession of all of the facts he was not able to go farther than he had gone in the public declaration. I observed to the Secretary that the action of the President would be interpreted by the public as partisan and petty. This he seemed to think of no consequence but immediately addressed himself to the matter of my future movements, suggesting that I should not return to Mexico for the purpose of settling my personal affairs, as my presence there might result in street demonstrations; he added that the government would assume responsibility for any damage or loss which might occur to my effects.

The interview with Mr. Bryan was not a pleasant one although he was abundantly kind and I am sure desired to do what was right; the restraint on his action evidently came from elsewhere.

On issuing from the Department of State I gave out a statement to the press which was intended to be reassuring in character and to be of service to the administration in a most difficult hour. I did this because I anticipated that the manner in which my resignation was accepted would not meet with the sanction of public opinion; in the event the condemnation of the press was general. The press résumé of the Department of State showed that public opinion was adverse to the attitude of the President, and when the announcement was made that Mr. John Lind was to be sent to Mexico as his personal representative, the criticisms became even more severe. These criticisms were specifically directed at the appointment of Mr. Lind. Mr. Lind was a very worthy gentleman, born in Sweden, and an excellent citizen of the State of Minnesota, but he had not distinguished himself in civil or diplomatic affairs to a sufficient extent to warrant any hope of brilliant diplomatic triumphs. He had left the Republican party and joined the Democratic party as a devoted follower of Bryan on the issue of the "free coinage of silver, at the ratio of 16 to 1," and was doubtless one of those "deserving Democrats" to whom Mr. Bryan sometimes referred.

Following the acceptance of my resignation and the designation of the Lind mission, the signs of dissatisfaction in the Senate Committee on Foreign Relations—which had not been consulted concerning, and which was not enamoured of, the President's policy toward Mexico—became so marked that the senators of the committee were invited individually to come to the White House for a conference. From reliable sources I learned that what occurred at the interview was about as follows:

There was unmistakable evidence that these senators, members of the Committee on Foreign Relations and the sworn advisers of the Executive, had been called together rather as a matter of form than for the purpose of ascertaining their views in a grave crisis of our relations with Mexico. In the desultory discussion which took place it became quite evident that the Secretary of State's knowledge of the Mexican situation was limited. He failed to put before the senators the substance or the nature of the instructions to Mr. Lind, furnishing them only with the information which they had already received from the press, viz., that the character of Mr. Lind's mission had been misinterpreted and exaggerated. Of course every senator present knew that its character had not been misinterpreted or exaggerated and knew that Mr. Lind had gone to Mexico for the purpose of endeavouring to subvert by negotiation and persuasion a legally constituted government; the senators knew, too, that the Lind mission was highly distasteful to the Mexican government and repugnant to the Mexican people.

The President stated during the interview that I had informed him that General Huerta had been bribed for the sum of four hundred thousand dollars to remain true

[321]

to the Madero government at the time of the first and unsuccessful uprising of Felix Diaz at Vera Cruz. The obvious error of this statement is to be found in the fact that General Huerta was not in command of any troops at the time of this uprising. The President evidently referred to another statement of mine that it had been reported that Madero had paid Huerta to remain loyal when fighting Orozco in the north. My purpose in repeating this report along with others to the President was to impress him with the true character of the Madero government in its last stages. It seemed, however, that I had only drawn his attention to the person alleged to be corrupted and not to him who was attempting to corrupt.

A number of questions were asked by senators which the Secretary of State was not able to answer, and he showed by his replies that he was badly or not fully informed; that he was acting upon representations made by irresponsible and adventurous Mexicans or Americans rather than in obedience to the reports furnished by a sworn officer of the government. The White House interview achieved no good results; it revealed no policy to the senators but left upon the minds of those participating the impression that the administration by the uncertainty of its attitude was contributing to the grave conditions which existed in Mexico.

CHAPTER XLVI

The President and Mr. Bryan express approval of a fake telegram from London criticizing my address to Huerta—I publicly resent this statement and tell the true story—The President apologizes to the British government and sends me a note of reproof.

I INTENDED, after the acceptance of my resignation, to maintain an attitude of complete silence in regard to Mexican matters, but an unpleasant event occurred which caused me to alter this attitude for the purpose of defending the correctness of my official acts.

A European news agency gave out a dispatch purporting to quote the British Foreign Office to the effect that among the considerations which had brought about its recognition of the provisional government of Mexico was the circumstance of my congratulatory speech on the occasion of the reception of the diplomatic corps by the provisional or de facto president. Years of contact had made me familiar with the methods of the British Foreign Office, and upon reading this dispatch I decided that it was a canard and unworthy of attention. A few days afterward, however, I was chagrined to learn that the administration had given out a notice to the press quoting approvingly this telegram which called into question the acts of an official of the American government as an evidence of the propitiatory attitude of the British government. Telegraphic inquiry revealed the complete

[323]

falsity of the report crediting the British government with any public statement. I then gave to the press the following statement, which was published by all the news agencies of the country:

"If this statement really emanated from the British Foreign Office, it is at variance with its traditions and with the character which it has maintained before the world for two centuries. I doubt the genuineness of the statement, as it is a pure subterfuge unworthy of the British Foreign Office. As there existed at the time of this reception only a provisional government in Mexico, the government of Great Britain could naturally recognize nothing but a provisional government, which it did in exactly the same manner and practically the same phraseology as other European governments. That Great Britain was moved to recognition of Mexico by its desire to assist in the restoration of order is most likely true, and I believe this factor was the determining one with all governments which followed the example of Great Britain, though most of them recognized the Mexican provisional government at a much later date. The action of the government of Great Britain was not in the slightest degree affected by the so-called "congratulatory speech" made by me on behalf of the diplomatic corps. This address was not written by me as I personally declined responsibility for its wording, but by the Spanish and British ministers at the request of the entire resident diplomatic corps. The resolution, as written, was expressed in French, and it was so drawn as to avoid clearly any question of recognition of more than a de facto government. In the form in which it finally appeared it was the expression of the views of the entire diplomatic corps representing governments which had none of them at that time recognized the provisional government as a de jure government. For more than a month after this diplomatic reception the British government maintained an attitude of hostility toward the government of General Huerta, and when finally recognition was accorded it came as the result of a complete reversal of policy. The governments of the other European powers recognized the Mexican provisional government as a de jure government following recognition by Great Britain and after waiting vainly for the recognition of the government of the United States, which they universally thought should be accorded.

"The truth of the statement I have made here is of record in the Department of State at Washington and doubtless also upon the records of every government accredited to Mexico at that time."

This announcement to the press was, it appears, interpreted by the President and Mr. Bryan as a veiled attack, and it occasioned their deep resentment. By what interpretation they could possibly have imagined this public statement to be offensive to the British government I was unable to understand then, nor do I now, but the fact remains that, without waiting to ascertain whether the press notice referred to had emanated from the British Foreign Office, Mr. Bryan cabled our ambassador in London to make explanations and apologies to Sir Edward Gray. This course was entirely without diplomatic precedent as there was nothing in the nature of the statement to warrant spontaneous action, even if it were offensive.

As it developed, however, the British government had not even seen more than a résumé of the statement and it was therefore obliged to obtain a copy in order to ascertain for what offence the American government was apologizing. The New York *Times* carried a press dispatch from London, which placed the whole matter in a ridiculous light, as it pictured the officials of Downing Street busily engaged in endeavouring to ascertain, through the reading of my interview, wherein lay the offence against His Majesty's government. This action revealed to the diplomatic world the spirit of reckless adventure which presided over the Department of State and cannot be said to have added anything to our reputation for cleverness in dealing with international affairs. A copy of the instructions which were sent to our ambassador in London was transmitted to me with a note from the Secretary of State, in which the hope was expressed that it would be a "sufficient reminder to me of my official obligations." At that time the situation at Mexico was so delicate on account of the resentment felt over the dispatch of the President's unofficial representative, Mr. Lind, that I thought it better not to prolong the controversy and contented myself with placing on the records of the Department of State the following memorandum:

"The Ambassador to Mexico, Mr. Wilson, requests Mr. Long to say to the Secretary of State, Mr. Bryan, that on account of the delicate situation which exists at the present moment in our relations with Mexico and for the further reason that he does not desire to embarrass or affect in any way the mission of Governor Lind by a public utterance, he has refrained from making any comment on the Secretary's note of the 14th instant or on the telegram

transmitted therewith, and that whenever he shall feel it his duty to reply thereto, he will do so in such a manner as will place the matter of present publicity entirely within the control of the Secretary.
August 18, 1913."

This I supplemented some ten days later by a letter to Mr. Bryan, which I did not give to the press until the middle of October following. (See Appendix IX.)

CHAPTER XLVII

Mr. Taft's public approval of my course in Mexico—Public addresses—
The Melville Stone incident—The Lind mission to Mexico

ON THE day of the acceptance of my resignation I gave to the press the following letter from Mr. Taft. This letter was a substitute for another and stronger one which it was not thought advisable to publish at that time. It is now published (Appendix VII) with Mr. Taft's consent.

New Haven, Conn.
June 29, 1913.

MY DEAR MR. WILSON:

You were Ambassador from the United States to Mexico during the most trying times that the people of Mexico have passed through and during a period when the relations between us and Mexico were constantly being subjected to a serious strain. I have great pleasure in expressing my high approval of your zealous and courageous efforts in the protection of American interests and indeed the interests of foreign governments generally during the critical periods of Mexican disorders. No one can understand the difficulties of your position and the exceptional excellence of the work you did who is not familiar with the constantly changing circumstances of the situation and the variety of the exigencies which you had to meet.

You have my full permission to publish this letter.

Sincerely yours,

WM. H. TAFT.

Hon. Henry Lane Wilson,
American Ambassador,
Mexico. Mexico.

The attitude of the administration was in marked contrast with Mr. Taft's letter, for not only had it declined on my retirement to grant a courteous letter of approval but in an apparent spirit of malice it interfered in the settlement of my accounts, interrupted some of my meetings, secured cancellation of others, and subsequently refused to appoint my son Warden, who had creditably passed the examinations and obtained his certificate, to be a secretary in the diplomatic service. I have always believed that these petty and malevolent acts were the work of over-zealous political underlings, and have assumed that the President had no knowledge of them. It is impossible to think otherwise. Better than anything else the following incident illustrates the undignified methods of reprisal.

Pending the acceptance of my resignation as ambassador to Mexico and while I was still in the service of the government, I went to the Pacific Coast and on the day of my separation from the service I delivered an informal speech at a banquet given me by the citizens of Spokane, Washington, in which I commented on the Mexican situation and related some personal incidents connected therewith.

Returning from the coast a little later I delivered an

address before the Union Club at Cleveland, followed by one at Washington City in the Belasco Theatre which was largely attended. In this address I attacked the Mexican policies of the administration severely but treated the President with great courtesy and consideration.

I went from Washington to New York and after my arrival there I received a telephone message from Mr. Melville Stone, director of the Associated Press, with whom I had maintained friendly relations for many years, asking me to dine with him at the Metropolitan Club. During the dinner Mr. Stone recounted the following incident: A few days prior, having been called to Washington by the President, and after some conversation relative to other matters, the President said to him that he wished it might be possible for the Associated Press to be in harmony with the administration's policy relative to Mexico. To this Mr. Stone replied that the Associated Press had no policy, except to report the news as it found it and events as they occurred. The President replied that in international emergencies the news-gathering services ought to be in harmony with the administration. Mr. Stone then said: "But, Mr. President, I am not in sympathy with the policy of your administration in Mexican matters, as I have the best of reasons for approving the course of Mr. Wilson who has just retired from the charge of the embassy." Thereupon the President in a rather heated manner said: "Mr. Stone, if you knew all the circumstances, you would think differently. Mr. Wilson, on his own evidence, was responsible in some measure for the overthrow of the Madero government."[1] Mr. Stone

[1]In justice to the President, it may be said that the telegram he had in mind and quoted probably was the garbled one published in *Harper's Weekly*. I have been so in-

replied: "Are you sure of that, Mr. President?" The President then quoted an alleged telegram and asked Mr. Stone for his opinion. Mr. Stone responded: "If you have quoted Mr. Wilson correctly, he would suffer in my estimation." The interview terminated here. "Now," said Mr. Stone to me, "I have asked you to come here for the purpose of giving you an opportunity to refute the serious charge which the President made against you." I asked Mr. Stone if he could come with me to the Waldorf Astoria Hotel where I had in my room the bound and printed dispatches of the Department of State covering the Mexican revolutionary period given to me on an order signed by Mr. Bryan. I handed Mr. Stone the dispatch in question and asked him to compare it with the one which the President had quoted, and to read all other dispatches bearing on these incidents. He did so carefully and having finished said:

"The President is in error and has, unintentionally, I think, done you a grave injustice. You should make sure that this version has not had extensive circulation."

As Mr. Taft was President during the revolution against Diaz and had closely followed the events leading up to the overthrow of Madero and the establishment of the Huerta

formed. The true telegram was of 4:00 P.M., February 17, 1913, and is printed on page 718, *Foreign Relations*–1913, as follows:

American Embassy
Mexico, February 17, 1913, 4 P.M.

Huerta notifies me to expect some action that will remove Madero from power at any moment; plans fully matured, the purpose of delay being to avoid any violence or bloodshed. I asked his messenger no questions, and made no suggestions beyond requesting that no lives be taken except by due process of law. I am unable to say whether or not these plans will materialize; I simply report to the Government the word sent to me, which I feel bound to listen to as it so intimately concerns our nationals.

WILSON.

[331]

provisional government, his estimate may be regarded as of greater value than that of one fresh from academic fields and wholly without instruction in international matters. I may add, however, that some months later Colonel Roosevelt, under whom I served for seven years, expressed to me his disapproval of the so-called "policy" of the Wilson administration and was kind enough to indicate verbally to me his sympathy and approval of my recent services. The former president expressed himself in a similar way to others.

Soon after this the announcement of the administration's future "policy" toward Mexico was made by Mr. Bryan. In substance it consisted of sending to Mexico Mr. John Lind of Minnesota as the President's personal representative, with instructions which were to constitute the basis of the representations to be made to the Mexican government. Mr. Lind's designation for this important mission without the consent of the Senate of the United States, which shares with the President the responsibility for the conduct of our foreign relations, was an irregularity and an example of the kind of personal government which has not been looked upon with favour in the United States; one which could not but be highly offensive and humiliating to the Mexican government which, as a sovereign power, could not but regard such lapses from established precedent in dealing with it as indicative of small respect. Mr. Lind's instructions in brief were as follows: first, to indicate to General Huerta that the American government would not recognize him as provisional president; second, that a constitutional presidential election must be held; and third, that General Huerta must not be a candidate to succeed himself.

The Lind mission was so entirely without precedent, and so obviously an act of gratuitous offence to a sovereign nation, that its failure was foredoomed before Mr. Lind left these shores. Not only was his presence certain to be resented by Mexican public opinion but it was bound to be regarded by Americans and all foreigners in Mexico as an evidence of blundering diplomacy and of ill-advised activity in dealing with a situation that cried urgently for the application of practical methods and for the lending of those aids in reëstablishment of peace and order which a country torn by revolution needed far more than homeopathic doses of altruistic democracy.

The Lind mission was doomed to failure for three reasons: 1st: His dispatch thither without formal diplomatic character was an act of offensive intervention in the affairs of a friendly nation; 2d: His mission was personally offensive to the provisional president of Mexico—Huerta was told that he was unfit to be President and asked to give his adherence to that opinion; 3d: The demand for a constitutional election was impossible of fulfilment, because the machinery for a constitutional election does not exist in Mexico. Let it be recalled that 80 per cent. of the population is Indian, unable to read or write, with no ideas of citizenship or notions of constitutional government. The implanting by decree of democratic institutions in soil like this is obviously a thing impossible of accomplishment. One might as well expect the Statue of Liberty to stand if built upon quicksand, as to hope for good results from an attempt to implant an altruistic republic by mere *ipse dixit* among a people having such largely preponderant elements of ignorance and unfitness. The engrafting of our ideas, institutions, and customs,

[333]

which presuppose that sense of responsibility that springs from a high degree of civilization, upon the Mexican people without having prepared them by education and training, is a task so obviously impossible of accomplishment, and its processes are so likely to be attended by a continuation of disorder, bloodshed, and crime, that those clothed with authority might well take the time to study the lesson taught for a thousand years, that in the conduct of foreign relations idealism is a dangerous element and that morals and expediency are nearly always identic. It may be said without exaggeration that the sending of the Lind mission to Mexico not only did infinite damage to our interests there but it fixed the attention and aroused the suspicion of all Latin America and excited the derision and ridicule of the European press.

As is known to all the world, President Huerta refused to receive Mr. Lind, and although the views of this government presented through him and the embassy were courteously treated, the correspondence exchanged revealed, under the attacks of the astute Mr. Federico Gamboa, Under-Secretary of Foreign Affairs, the weakness of the American position, the irregularities of the proceedings put on foot, and the false and misleading advice which had been given to the President by the amateur agents upon whose representations his "policy" had been based.

During the progress of these negotiations press reports emanating from Washington announced one day that Huerta was about to yield, the next day that he would not yield; one day that the Mexican government was conciliatory in its attitude, the next day that it defied the United States by insisting upon conducting its affairs independently of outside advice. Finally, when it was evident, even to the most optimistic, that no laurels could be gathered from the mission and Lind had departed for Vera Cruz, the administration at Washington, instead of immediately instructing him to return to the United States without submitting our government to further humiliation, formally advised all Americans to leave Mexico and to abandon their homes and their property without any guarantee of future compensation. Thousands of Americans in remote districts, believing that intervention was impending, followed this publicly given advice and at great personal sacrifice and loss returned to the United States. But none of them, either returning here or remaining there, whatever their station in life or occupation, approved of the policy of the Wilson administration in its dealings with Mexico.

Nor did the results of this disastrous and amateurish policy—a policy not initiated in response to any pressure of American public opinion—extend solely to distracted Mexico and our abandoned nationals there. The story crossed the sea and became a factor in the decision of Germany to precipitate a European war. So important a personage as Count von Reventlow, who at that time was supposed to interpret and defend the course and acts of Germany, has stated that those who were directing the destinies of the Empire in those critical moments believed and counted upon a wavering, vacillating, and retreating policy on the part of the government of the United States. This belief was justified later by the slogan, "He kept us out of war." The American public did not follow President Wilson in the World War—he reluctantly followed them.

APPENDICES

[337]

CONTENTS OF APPENDICES

APPENDIX I

For a period of more than two years now the republic of Mexico has been in a state of revolution: first against the long-established government of President Diaz and, subsequently, against that of President Madero. During all of this long period a state of anarchy, intermittent, sporadic, and rising and falling as the tides, has prevailed through a large part of the territory supposedly under the control of the Mexican government and for the administration of which it is responsible not only to its own citizens but, under accepted principles of international law, to the nations of the world which, upon the invitation of Mexico, have sent hither their nationals and their capital, relying upon the ability of this government to afford to both the usual safeguards guaranteed by civilized states.

The present revolution which began under the presidency of General Diaz and which has continued without intermission to the present hour has brought neither order, peace, prosperity, nor happiness to the Mexican people. On the contrary, there has been a vast sacrifice of human life, enormous destruction of property, a riot of barbarity and inhuman savagery throughout large parts of the republic. Government and the law have ceased to be respected and general and local administrations are helpless and impotent to deal with a situation of constantly in-

creasing gravity and which not only has become a menace
to the material interests of foreigners who have invested
their money in Mexico and contributed to the development
of the resources of the republic, but has also placed in
jeopardy and in numerous cases actually sacrificed the
lives of foreigners who must necessarily rely upon the
government for protection.

The American government, though embarrassed by
obsolete neutrality laws, honestly endeavoured during the
revolution against the government of General Diaz to
discharge its full obligations toward the recognized government of a friendly state. When the government of
General Diaz fell and was succeeded by the administration
of President Madero, the American government promptly
recognized its duties in the new order of things and, by
word and deed, gave its loyal and friendly support to the
government which it understood to be the choice of the
Mexican people. Not content with these ordinary demonstrations of good will and believing that by so doing
it would contribute in no inconsiderable measure to the
restoration of peaceful conditions in Mexico, it amended
its neutrality laws and in conformity therewith, and for
the proper execution thereof, has maintained upon the
Mexican frontier since February, 1911, a military force
varying in number from ten to forty thousand men and
has, moreover, at a great expense, and to the detriment
of other localities, kept there a not inconsiderable number
of extraordinary employees of the Departments of Justice, Labour, and the Treasury, expecting no other recom-
pense for the sacrifices incurred than the grateful appreciation of the Mexican government, the just treatment of
American citizens, and the protection of their lives and

property against the assaults of the elements of disorder, the tyranny of local administrations, and the collusive confiscatory intrigues of those who, being unable to lay up fortunes by industry, toil, and intelligence, find it both convenient and popular to prey upon the foreigner who has brought hither his thrift and his capital.

On the 15th of September, 1912, the government of the United States, after a long, prudent, and patient series of representations to the Mexican government touching individual causes of complaint, addressed a most vigorous and direct but nevertheless friendly note to it setting forth in a general way its dissatisfaction with the situation recited above and supporting its averments by the citation of many, but not nearly all, of the cases which gave ground to its complaint. The purpose of this note was to recall the government of Mexico to a realization of its unfulfilled obligations and to an appreciation of the dangerous situation which it was confronting with reference not only to the American government, but to all other governments having substantial interests in the country. The American government permitted itself to believe that the Mexican government would heed this solemn but friendly warning and bestir itself in a practical and evident way to procure a betterment of the evils complained of. The hope was indulged in, having in mind our patient attitude, that the answer of Mexico to our just and reasonable demands would be moderate, conciliatory, and specific. On the contrary, the American government has been obliged to note with the greatest regret and distress that Mexico, far from appreciating the grave and solemn warning contained in its note, delayed reply for a period suggestive of international discourtesy, and that the answer which it finally gave was evasive, disingenuous, frivolous, at variance with the facts, illogical in its conclusions, and lacking in that seriousness of tone and dignity of utterance which should characterize the diplomatic exchanges of governments seeking the support of a just cause before the world. The averments contained in the embassy's note of September 15th are each and every one of them sustained by positive and unequivocal evidence which will stand the test of revelation to the world and the judgment of history. The performance of exact justice in each and every instance is insisted upon by the government of the United States.

In addition to the specific complaints which were set forth in this note and which the government of the United States has not the least intention of abating or subtracting from and for the righting of which it demands and will expect specific performance, it must, having due regard for the responsibilities with which it is charged, call the attention of the Mexican government to the deep apprehension of the American government and people that the present administration will not be able to cope successfully with the armed revolution and the sporadic and widespread brigandage which has now for some two years been existent within its territory.

Notwithstanding repeated assurances by the Mexican government of the procurement of positive and definite results, and in spite of the optimistic appreciations of the situation which have been actively spread abroad through the world, the revolutionary movement continues, brigandage grows apace, the destruction of property increases, and the economic situation has become an immediate menace. Independently of the losses and sufferings incurred by American citizens, the government of the United States cannot for a much longer period, having due regard for the peace and order of this continent, permit a savage and desolating war to continue at its threshold. The government of the United States recognizes that within certain sound and established limitations every sovereign government has the right to put its own household in order, but it cannot commit itself to the principle that a cruel and devastating warfare, the sole object of which, as nearly as can be judged by an impartial opinion, is the gratification of the rival ambitions of aspiring chieftains, can be carried on in territories contiguous to it for an indefinite period.

Finally, and in the exercise of its great patience, preferring to secure redress and amelioration of conditions through methods and by an attitude in keeping with its constant and undeviating policy with all nations of the world, the American government solemnly and firmly, but none the less in a friendly spirit, adjures and warns the Mexican government that there must be a just and prompt adjustment of the grievances set forth in its note of September 15th, and that substantial guarantees of future protection to American life and property against armed violence, against malicious intrigue, against anti-foreign sentiment, shall be given, and that those who take American life and American property shall be swiftly pursued by justice and punished adequately and quickly by competent courts.

APPENDIX II

Peking, China,
January 8, 1916.

MY DEAR MR. AMBASSADOR:

By a lucky chance your letter, dated from the 8th of November, dropped on my desk. I was rather surprised as generally "my friend the enemy" is trying his very best to get hold of my correspondence and succeeds extremely well. I wonder whether he simply enjoys reading letters meant for me or whether he answers them as well. It's a strange world nowadays and though as you know not in the slightest sentimental, I cannot help sometimes sighing a little bit when thinking of my English friends of former days. Do they condemn such questionable proceedings as some of their countrymen are indulging in—as undoubtedly they would have done in former days—or do they yell with the mob? Well, well, I shall stop asking questions and take to sighing again, it helps digestion.

We have had a jolly good time in Mexico, my dear Mr. Ambassador, and you are mistaken in recommending me to walk the more prosaic—if less exciting—paths of diplomacy. Diplomacy, that dear old lady, does but little appeal to me and I dare say, confidentially, I take her for as old and mossy as Methusalem's donkey. We have outgrown the old-fashioned diplomacy of the teacup and the

[344]

petticoat and the backstairs and I fervently hope we shall tread upon another sort of international intercourse whose principle may be "straightforward, plain, and live and let live." I plunged here into another revolution and enjoy it. One day, they will cut my throat; the enemy is deadly set against me, and I hope I shall bear it with the accustomed satirical grin. Now, then, here, too, they are out to chase a president. I try to help him as best I can, which is not much but very little less and sometimes more than the honourable colleagues can or will do. I remember the time of poor Madero, an idealist, reformer, and a courageous man. I remember very well Wednesday, the 19th of February, 1913, when early in the morning I called on you and found you and Mrs. Wilson, after a short dialogue, enthusiastic over the necessity of saving the life of unfortunate Madero. We went together to the Palace and saw General Huerta and we got from him his word of honour as a caballero and a soldier to protect the life of his abated opponent. We got some more promises. Do you remember that I told you when we reached your Embassy, "in future days you will realize that by to-day's action you have added a laurel wreath to the Crown of the United States"? You have— and I am sure you and every American are proud of it. My warmest and kindest regards to Mrs. Wilson. How good and sweet and calm she was in all those exciting days!

Believe me, my dear Mr. Ambassador,

Yours, very sincerely,

VON HINTZE.

APPENDIX III

I beg of you to intercede so as to bring about for my son Francisco, Mr. Pino Suarez and his friends, the fulfilment of the agreement made with General Huerta to permit them to go to Europe.

Their lives are in danger and above all things, they have a right to liberty because they have been men of honour and because that was the expressed condition of his surrender according to a letter to some foreign diplomats who intervened in the affair.

I address myself to you as a mother in distress who sees in you the only person whose influence can save the life of her son and secure liberty for him and for his dearest friends.

MERCEDES G. DE MADERO.

APPENDIX IV

THE SECRETARIES OF THE CHAMBER OF DEPUTIES:

In view of the events which have occurred since yesterday in the nation and for its greater tranquillity we formally resign our posts of President and Vice President, respectively, to which we were elected. We concur in whatever may be necessary.

FRANCISCO I. MADERO.
JOSE M. PINO SUAREZ.

Mexico, February 19, 1913.

[347]

APPENDIX V (a)

Mexico, D. F., April 30, 1913.

THE HONOURABLE HENRY LANE WILSON,
  American Ambassador,
    Mexico, D. F.

DEAR SIR:

At a recent meeting of the Executive Committee of the
Society of the American Colony of Mexico City, I was directed to inform Your Excellency of certain steps which
have been 'taken by the Americans residing in this ity
and throughout the Republic, looking to your retention at
your present post of Ambassador to Mexico.

Prior to the presidential election in the United States,
the Americans domiciled in Mexico generally entertained
the hope that Your Excellency might be retained in your
present position, even though the political complexion
of the administration in Washington should be changed.
After the revolt which resulted in the overthrow of the
Madero Government, our nationals here became convinced that it was not only desirable, but essential, to
the interests of our nation and our people in Mexico, and
to the conservation of existing cordial international rela-

[348]

tions, that no change be made in the diplomatic representation of our government to this country.

Acting upon this conviction the American citizens here resolved to take action with view to the accomplishment of this end.

The first step taken was to send a cablegram to President Wilson, on the 5th of March, apprising him of the conditions obtaining here, with the suggestion that Your Excellency be retained here, together with our reasons therefor. This cable was signed by a committee of the leading American citizens in this city, as will be shown by the copy which is transmitted herewith.

Thereafter it was deemed advisable that a committee be sent to Washington to call upon the President and the Secretary of State with view to laying before them more fully than could be done by cable, the facts in regard to this situation. This committee proceeded to Washington, called upon the President and the Secretary of State, and explained to them fully the conditions prevailing in this country at the present time, and suggested that in view of Your Excellency's long experience in the diplomatic service, your ample knowledge of the Mexican situation as a result of your three years service in this country, and especially in view of your knowledge of the conditions arising out of the overthrow of the Madero Government, no change be made at this post at the present time.

At the request of the President and of the Secretary of State, the committee filed a memorandum with these gentlemen covering the salient points brought out in the interviews of the committee with them, a copy of which is transmitted herewith:

Trusting that the action taken by your nationals in the Republic will meet with your approval and assuring Your Excellency of my high respect and esteem, I am,

Very sincerely yours,

GEORGE W. COOK,

Chairman of the Executive Committee.

APPENDIX V (b)

TELEGRAM OF COMMITTEE OF THE AMERICAN COLONY TO THE PRESIDENT

Mexico, March 4, 1913.

THE PRESIDENT,

Washington, D. C.

The undersigned committee representing the American Colony of the City of Mexico and virtually all Americans throughout this Republic urgently request Your Excellency to retain the Honourable Henry Lane Wilson in his present post as Ambassador to Mexico for the following reasons:

The situation here resulting from the sudden and violent overthrow of the Madero Government continues to be exceedingly critical. The invaluable services rendered by Ambassador Wilson to all foreigners during the recent crisis by aiding them in the preservation of their lives and properties and the important personal service which he rendered Generals Huerta and Diaz after the fall of Madero, place him in a position to contribute powerfully to the prompt and proper working out of the present situation in a manner satisfactory to all interests and especially useful to the present needs and to the future welfare of American interests in this country. It is a matter of common knowledge that after Madero's fall Huerta and Diaz were not in accord and a conflict between them threatened, which, had it occurred, would have been most disastrous. It was through the personal mediation of Ambassador Wilson that their differences were adjusted and harmony between them established. In consequence of this service he gained and continues to have the implicit confidence of both parties and is daily, at their solicitation, rendering them useful aid looking to the immediate pacification of the country and the prompt reëstablishment of a permanent government.

Ambassador Wilson has been in Mexico since before the inception of the Madero Revolution of 1910 and has served our nation and our nationals here with ability and success. In view of the foregoing facts we unhesitatingly but respectfully submit the opinion that Ambassador Wilson is in a position to render a service to Mexico and all foreign interests, which a new man, however competent, could hardly be expected to accomplish.

The gravity of the present situation from the standpoint of the future of American interests in Mexico cannot be overstated. It is not too much to say that under the complicated and delicate conditions which obtain here, the announcement of a change in our diplomatic representation would be viewed by all elements of this community, both Mexican and foreign, with serious apprehension and alarm.

A committee representing this colony desires to call on you at an early date and with your permission will lay before you at greater length the facts in connection with this situation and our reasons for making this request. Confidential: C. H. M. y Agramonte, President American

Colony, G. W. Cook, Chairman Committee, E. N. Brown, George J. McCarty, W. F. Layer, J. N. Galbraith, C. F. de Ganahl, Burton W. Wilson, J. E. Long, T. J. Ryder, H. Walker, L. R. Wilfley, Paul Hudson, Fred Tackaberry.

APPENDIX V (c)

MEMORANDUM FOR THE PRESIDENT FROM THE CHAIRMAN OF COMMITTEE OF THE AMERICAN COLONY

MR. SECRETARY: The delegation which has the honour to address you for the purpose of requesting the retention of the Honourable Henry Lane Wilson in the post which he now occupies as American Ambassador to Mexico, is composed of professional and business men who have been sent here for this specific purpose by the American citizens of the City of Mexico, as per our credentials which have already been laid before you. The mere fact that these gentlemen have been willing to undertake a journey of over 3,000 miles, occupying seven days and seven nights, and have sacrificed their business interests and time to undertake this mission, is a substantial evidence of the sincerity of purpose and depth of conviction which has induced them to come on this errand.

If we request at your hands the retention of Ambassador Wilson, notwithstanding the recent change in the political administration at Washington, we realize that we must present to you sufficient and convincing reasons for our request, and must explain to you why we believe that no other American, be he ever so able and patriotic, can hope to exercise the same beneficent influence in connection with the existing critical state of affairs in Mexico, as can our present Ambassador, Mr. Wilson. That sufficient and convincing reasons exist, no American citizen who passed through the horrors of the recent bombardment and who was cognizant of the events which were transpiring and the frightful possibilities of their tragic issue, will deny.

For the nine days prior to the last day of the bombardment the Ambassador dedicated and limited his activities to efforts to ameliorate the horrible conditions prevailing in the Mexican capital; to rescuing Americans and other foreigners whose homes were within the zone of the heaviest firing; to providing succour and refuge for such American citizens as found themselves in want of food or shelter, owing to the sudden and unexpected outbreak of hostilities; to organizing a guard to patrol the district inhabited by Americans, and to be ready to offer assistance and protection in case of attack; to providing a suitable hospital with the requisite medical and nursing facilities for any who might be wounded; to establishing banking facilities in the Embassy for such Americans as might find themselves in need of funds; to organizing a corps of intrepid messengers for the carrying of cablegrams and letters from the Embassy to the cable and post-offices in the heart of the city, which service was open to all Americans and foreigners; and for the transmission of messages from the diplomatic corps to the Mexican Government authorities and the leaders of the two hostile camps; to allaying the fears and anxieties of his countrymen and giving them wise counsel as they gathered in large numbers day after day at the Embassy; and the keeping in constant touch and communication with the other members of the diplomatic corps in the Mexican capital, who naturally looked to him as their dean for leadership.

[353]

The last day of the "bloody ten days," as the period of the bombardment is now designated by the Mexicans, was the critical day which saw the arrest and imprisonment of President Madero and his cabinet, an event which created a situation giving rise to intense anxiety and well-grounded fear for its results. The Mexican nation suddenly found itself practically without a Government. A part of the Federal army under the control of General Huerta was in possession of the Palace and the greater part of the Mexican capital. Another part of the Federal army, headed by General Felix Diaz, was still in possession of the Arsenal, with its guns and large reserve stores of ammunition. The residents of Mexico with direst forebodings breathlessly awaited the outcome. Would General Huerta and General Diaz come to a clash, continue their bombardment and fight out the battle to its bitter end, thus accentuating the dangers and prolonging the horrible situation already existing in the capital? Or could these two contending generals, up to this time embroiled in a fierce and bloody fight, be induced to come together to compose their differences and to arrive at an agreement which would put an end to the wretched spectacle of a battle in the heart of a capital city, begun without notice to non-combatants and continued without giving them a definite opportunity to withdraw from the city to points of safety? Conditions in the city were becoming unbearable. The dead were unburied, and in some instances were burned in the streets. Provisions had soared skyward in price, and in many places could not be obtained at any price. Milk for the children, medical attention for the sick, religious consolation for the dying, all were difficult to be obtained. The city was absolutely without police protection; water had been cut off in certain parts of the city; the sewers were blocked for lack of flushing; the streets at night were dark, owing to the cutting and destruction of the electric wires; the working men were out of employment and had not been paid; hunger riots were in prospect; looting had already begun; and in the absence of police protection the uprising of the mob with all its attendant horrors seemed inevitable.

The cry on all sides among foreigners and Mexicans alike was, what can be done to save the situation? It was at this juncture that our American Ambassador rose nobly to the demands of the occasion, demonstrated his great efficiency and ability and brought the two contending generals together in a conference at the American Embassy, the place designated by them both as the only place in which they were willing to meet for conference. This conference lasted for several hours, and at various critical points in the discussion it seemed inevitable that it was destined to break up without reaching the agreement so necessary for putting an end to a situation replete with horrors. It is a fact of common knowledge that the skilful mediation of our Ambassador during these long hours of conference when everything hung in the balance, and the personal confidence which he inspired in both the opposing generals, finally brought about the agreement between them which was then and there reduced to writing, read before witnesses summoned for that purpose, signed by Generals Huerta and Diaz and delivered to the Ambassador for safe keeping.

This consummation so devoutly wished for by all the inhabitants of Mexico, constituted a diplomatic triumph of the first order for our Ambassador, not only by reason

of the immediate results obtained, which were the cessation of the combat, the immediate renewal of the policing
and municipal service of the city, the giving of an opportunity to the inhabitants who had left the city to return
thereto and take up their peaceful occupations, the opening up of ways and means to obtain food for the suffering
people, the opportunity for the burial of the dead which
had accumulated in such numbers as to threaten a pesti-
lence, and the alleviation of all the horrors resultant upon
the long-continued hostilities, but over and above all,
because the effective mediation of our Ambassador, and
the confidence which he inspired in Generals Huerta and
Diaz during the conduct of these negotiations, place him
in a unique position in connection with the solution of
all these difficulties and enable him, more than any other
man possibly could, to exercise a strong moral influence
upon all the parties to this agreement to carry it out in
all its expressed and implied terms.

If we are right in our deduction as above expressed, the
prestige which our Ambassador in Mexico now enjoys
with the parties in actual power and his personal acceptability to them and influence upon them render him indis-
pensable to the satisfactory solution of the Mexican situation and the maintenance of peace so long as the present
critical conditions in Mexico prevail.

It is a well-known fact in connection with the Mexican
character that it is extremely slow to give its confidence
to an individual, but that once an individual has obtained that confidence, it is given to him in full measure,
and carries with it a power to exercise influence which
cannot be transferred to a third party and is more potent
in its effect than any authority or power which may be

behind the personality. In other words, the personality and the personal equation are of the greatest importance in dealing successfully with the Mexican people.

The fact that Mr. Wilson has for over three years discharged the duties of American Ambassador in Mexico gives him an experience that is invaluable under the existing circumstances, and which entirely differentiates him from any new man, however able, who might succeed him at the present time. The great value of this experience is too patent to require further comment.

We pass with a word the facts of the Ambassador's long experience of over sixteen years in the American Diplomatic Service; his recognized ability and his fidelity and assiduity in the discharge of his duties, amply attested by his dispatches to the State Department; his character as a cultivated gentleman of broad sympathies; and his accessibility to all his countrymen; the refined and elevating atmosphere of the Embassy in Mexico; and the charming tact and social accomplishments of Mrs. Wilson.

The facts above set forth and our deductions from them constitute the basis of our sincere and earnest belief that the retention of Mr. Henry Lane Wilson as American Ambassador in Mexico, pending a satisfactory solution of the Mexican situation, will prove a most important factor not only in the protection of the lives and property of Americans and other foreigners in Mexico, but also in the continuance of the friendly international relations now existing between the two countries and the avoidance of any sudden and unfortunate event which might cause those relations to be strained or even ruptured, a contingency which would involve both countries in difficulties too painful to contemplate.

Since our arrival in Washington our attention has been called to certain charges against Ambassador Wilson published in the public press. Attached to this memorandum is a statement in which we set forth these charges and our replies thereto.

Mr. Secretary, in conclusion permit us to say that as American citizens resident in the Republic of Mexico, we highly appreciate the hospitality and good will of the Mexican people toward our fellow countrymen and ourselves personally, and recognize to the fullest extent the impropriety of our making any comment upon Mexican politics; and should anything we have said to you herein be susceptible of a construction contrary to such a view of the proprieties of the cases we expressly disclaim any intention to that end.

Permit us to convey to you our thanks for your kind reception and attentive hearing.

*   *   *

The facts in connection with the rebellion of February, 1913, which resulted in the overthrow of the government of President Madero by General Felix Diaz, are now historical, and are herein set forth .

The conduct of the American Ambassador, the Honourable Henry Lane Wilson, throughout the period of these revolutionary troubles was such as to win for him the highest praise not only from the Americans in Mexico but also from the nationals of other foreign countries resident in Mexico and the Mexicans themselves.

The universal appreciation of the undoubted fact that Ambassador Wilson, by his skilful and efficient handling of a most difficult situation, had been instrumental in bringing about a termination of the bombardment in the City of Mexico, thereby saving life and avoiding a continuation of the destruction of property, resulted in a call, issued by the President of the American Colony, for a mass meeting of American citizens in Mexico. This mass meeting was the largest and most enthusiastic of any similar meeting ever held by Americans in Mexico, and after many eulogies upon the conduct of affairs by the Ambassador during the bloody ten days of the bombardment, appropriate and laudatory resolutions were unanimously passed, as are hereto attached.

In harmony with the same spirit which led to the call for the mass meeting, another call was issued to over fifty of the leading American citizens in Mexico City asking them to meet for a conference with a view to determining what action should be taken by them for the purpose of conserving the interests of the Americans in Mexico, and the mutual welfare of that good feeling between both peoples (Americans and Mexicans).

In pursuance to this call some fifty American citizens met for conference, and after a prolonged discussion it was the unanimous opinion of this conference that it would be "highly conducive to the interests of Americans in Mexico and to the continuance of the extremely cordial relations now existing between the American and Mexican nations, if the Honourable Henry Lane Wilson were to be continued in the position of American Ambassador near the Mexican Government, which position he has filled with such marked efficiency and with such great honour to his country." This opinion was embodied in a resolution which was unanimously adopted and is hereto attached.

For the purpose of giving effect to the wishes of this

conference, an executive committee of eighteen was appointed with power and with instructions to proceed in such manner as it might deem best to accomplish the object desired. The names of the Committee are hereto attached.

This executive committee at once prepared and sent the President of the United States a cablegram setting forth the views and wishes of the American citizens in Mexico in regard to the retention of the present Ambassador, and likewise named a special delegation to proceed to Washington and lay before President Wilson and Secretary of State Bryan the view of the American citizens in Mexico on this subject, and their reasons therefor. The names of the delegation which came to Washington are hereto attached.

Respectfully submitted,
GEORGE W. COOK.—Chairman.

APPENDIX V (d)

RESOLUTIONS OF MASS MEETING OF THE AMERICAN COLONY PASSED ON FEBRUARY 28, 1913

WHEREAS: During the ten days from February 9th to 18th, this city was the theatre of a bitter strife between contending forces. The lives and property of Americans and other foreigners, as well as of Mexican residents, were gravely imperilled by shot and shell, several Americans being killed and wounded. Under the existing conditions Americans naturally looked to their national representative for aid and protection, and they were not disappointed.

Our Ambassador, the Hon. Henry Lane Wilson, caused

headquarters for the colony to be established at the American Embassy, and in concert with his staff of faithful assistants was untiring in his devotion to the best interests of not only his own countrymen but of the many foreigners of other nations who came to the Embassy for aid and comfort.

In recognition of those efforts, which undoubtedly saved the lives of many defenseless Americans, be it

RESOLVED: That the American Colony recognizes the fact that to the American Ambassador, Hon. Henry Lane Wilson, it owes a debt of gratitude, the magnitude of which cannot be expressed in words, but which will be retained as a cherished memory of the noble and patriotic services rendered under most trying conditions, which stamp him as an American of whom his countrymen may well feel proud, and to whom the American Colony extends this humble token of its appreciation:

RESOLVED: That a copy of these resolutions be engrossed and presented to Hon. Henry Lane Wilson, Ambassador of the United States, and that a copy also be sent to the State Department at Washington.

APPENDIX V (e)

RESOLUTIONS PASSED BY CONFERENCE OF FIFTY LEADING AMERICAN CITIZENS IN MEXICO CITY

WHEREAS: Fifty or more American citizens in the City of Mexico, irrespective of political affiliations, have met this day to confer in regard to matters of great import to Americans and American interests in the Republic of Mexico; and

WHEREAS: The unanimous opinion of this gathering is

that it will be highly conducive to the interests of Americans in Mexico, and to the continuance of the extremely cordial relations now existing between the American and Mexican nations, if the Honourable Henry Lane Wilson be continued in the position of American Ambassador near the Mexican Government, which position he has filled with such marked efficiency and with such great honour to his country, Now, therefore, be it

RESOLVED: That this gathering, embodying as it does many of the representative American men and interests in Mexico, believes that the record for patriotism and efficiency made by Ambassador Wilson during his incumbency justifies and demands that he be continued in this high office, and hereby pledges itself to work vigorously to that end.

APPENDIX V (f)

RESOLUTIONS FROM AMERICAN CLERGYMEN OF MEXICO CITY

Mexico City, March 15, 1913.

THE HONOURABLE HENRY LANE WILSON,

The United States Ambassador,

Mexico City.

DEAR SIR:

At a meeting of American clergymen of the City of Mexico held this day our attention was called by different members of the body to articles recently appearing in certain American newspapers, which very seriously and unjustly reflected upon your character and official conduct during the trying and tragic ordeal through which we all passed in the month of February.

Therefore, we, the undersigned, desire to express our

[362]

surprise and indignation at the tenor of such unjustifiable attacks, since it was known to us that you put forth extraordinary efforts to save the lives of the late unfortunate president and vice-president of this republic; that you offered your own home as a place of refuge to several branches of their respective families; that within four hours after the fall of the Madero government you summoned to the Embassy Generals Huerta and Diaz, chiefs of the forces contending in the city, and succeeded in bringing them to an agreement which produced an immediate cessation of hostilities and the speedy restoration of guarantees of life and property in the city; that during the combat you used your best influences to secure the establishment of a neutral zone and the cessation of hostilities within the city limits; that you, with the aid of the diplomatic corps, secured an armistice of twelve hours; and furthermore that you established within the embassy a bureau for the assistance of refugees; an automobile service for the removal of non-combatants from the most dangerous sections of the city, branches of the cable and post-office, a temporary bank, an emergency hospital, a bureau of supplies for your own country people, which good offices greatly alleviated the sufferings not only of Americans, but of many other foreigners and not a few Mexicans; and that in all this humanitarian and Christlike work you were patiently and efficiently aided by Mrs. Wilson.

We are also aware that your conduct in all these matters has won for you the general and high appreciation of the American colony at large, to which we particularly desire to hereby add our expression of sincere gratitude and highest esteem.

We are sending copies of this letter to the President of the United States, the Sun Bureau, Hearst papers, the Associated Press and the Mexican Herald.

Faithfully yours,

(Signed) John W. Butler, District Superintendent Methodist Episcopal Church; R. C. Elliot, presiding elder Methodist Episcopal Church, South; R. A. Carhart, missionary, Methodist Episcopal Church; Rev. John A. Reis, pastor San Lorenzo Catholic Church; Geo. H. Brewer, superintendent Baptist Mission; J. P. Hauser, district superintendent Methodist Episcopal Church; Sidney M. Conger, pastor Union Evangelistic Church, member of the Presbytery of Otsego; Rev. Edmund A. Neville, M. A. (Oxon.) rector Christ Church; Rev. F. E. McGuire, pastor Trinity Methodist Episcopal Church.

APPENDIX V (g)

RESOLUTIONS OF BRITISH COLONY

Mexico, February the 21st, 1913.

HIS EXCELLENCY, HENRY LANE WILSON,
U. S. Ambassador,
Mexico.

The undersigned members of the British Colony in Mexico, beg to express their appreciation for the able manner in which Mr. Wilson, U. S. Ambassador, handled the delicate situation created by the recent disturbances in the City of Mexico, and to thank him most sincerely for the help afforded to all foreigners by the Embassy, without distinction of nationality, and more especially to all Britishers:

(sgd.) A. W. Donly
" J. S. Campbell
" Robert A. H. Watson
" O. R. Shapp
" W. S. Crombie
" C. N. Mowag
" H. Hensy
" S. W. Goddard
" R. P. Easton
" Harwood H. Simpson
" A. H. Hewet
" Mr. Turner
" C. B. Knocker
" W. Hogg
" A. J. Stuart
" B. Voupy
" Syd. J. Smith
" A. Chermside
" C. H. Lloyd
" F. Woodcock

(sgd.) D. Bankhart
" D. Muirhead
" P. C. Proveny
" R. Rymer
" H. J. Alexander
" W. H. Gleadell
" R. V. Gray
" Hubert Earle
" L. M. B. Bullock
" Jas. F. Macnabb
" Sebbon D. Baker
" W. Chas. Price
" F. W. Green
" Arthur Williams
" Jas. McKinlay
" W. S. Brooks
" E. G. Aily
" Harmer C. Sandifer
" E. Wankeger
" O. H. Harrison
" J. W. S. Turner.

APPENDIX V (h)

RESOLUTION OF YOUNG MEN'S CHRISTIAN ASSOCIATION

RESOLUTION adopted by the Board of Directors of the Young Men's Christian Association of the City of Mexico, at their regular meeting on Thursday, April 10th, and recorded in their minutes:

"That WHEREAS it is the sense of this meeting that the attitude of the Hon. Henry Lane Wilson, Ambassador of the United States to this Republic of Mexico, always consistently maintained and especially during the recent period of keen and critical tension in this city, has been wise, patriotic and unselfish and has been such in our judgment as to belie certain uncharitable and unfair attacks of which he has been, and is being, made the victim, be it unanimously

RESOLVED that the members of this Board cordially sympathize with the Ambassador in the premises and that an expression of their renewed confidence be extended to him.

Be it RESOLVED, also, that copies of this RESOLUTION be sent to His Excellency, the President of the United States, to Hon. Henry Lane Wilson and to the press."

Signed:

Thomas Philips, President
Luis Alvarez Leon,
      Sec. de actas
J. E. Dennison
W. A. Price, Treasurer
R. Williamson
Dr. Antonio Orozco
A. Aldasoro

Guillermo B. Puga,
      Vice President
S. W. Rider
R. M. Raymond
P. H. L. King
W. W. Blake
G. J. Babcock, Gen. Sec'y.

APPENDIX V (i)

On Friday
February 21, 1913.

RESOLVED: that the MEXICO SOCIETY OF NEW YORK offers its congratulations to the HON. HENRY LANE WILSON, American Ambassador to Mexico, upon the ability, patience and courage he has shown in the discharge of the difficult duties imposed upon him during the recent crisis in Mexico.

RESOLVED: That the Society extends its heartfelt sympathy to the Mexican people and to those patriots who are fighting to establish and maintain a Constitutional Government, and expresses the hope that a stable Government, the necessary precedent to peace and prosperity, may soon be established by the people of Mexico.

RESOLVED: That copies of this resolution be sent to the State Department at Washington and to the Ambassador at the City of Mexico.

APPENDIX V (j)

AFFIDAVIT OF THE STAFF OF THE EMBASSY AND MR. TENNANT'S LETTER

We, the undersigned members of the staff of the Embassy of the United States of America at Mexico City, do hereby certify that one of our number was constantly on duty, both night and day, at the Embassy during the bombardment within the city, which lasted from February ninth to February eighteenth, 1913, and also

[367]

thereafter until the fall of President Madero's administration and the establishment of the present provisional government; that one of our number was present at all interviews between the Ambassador and messengers from President Madero and, later, at interviews between him and General Huerta and Felix Diaz; that all correspondence and notes of every kind were either dictated directly to one of us, or, when dictated to volunteer clerks, passed under our observation; that there was never the slightest indication of any understanding between Ambassador Wilson and General Huerta and Felix Diaz, excepting in regard to matters pertinent to the safety of the American and other Foreign Colonies within the City of Mexico; and that Ambassador Wilson's energies were directed throughout the bombardment to the saving of human life, to the bringing about of a cessation of hostilities and, after the fall of President Madero, to the restoration of order and peace within the City of Mexico and throughout the Republic.

We would also add that we have knowledge of the active efforts of the Ambassador to render aid to various members of the Madero family and especially to the deceased Ex-President.

We voluntarily make this statement in view of the unjust attacks upon Ambassador Wilson by certain American newspapers and by some Mexicans of the late administration, whose characters in this Republic are not above reproach.

HENRY F. TENNANT
Second Secretary of Embassy

LOUIS D'ANTIN
First Clerk of Embassy

W. W. BURNSIDE
Military Attaché

CHARLES B. PARKER
Second Clerk of Embassy

Embassy of the United States of America
Mexico City, April 14, 1913.

I, Nelson O'Shaughnessy, Secretary of the Embassy of the United States at Mexico, Mexico, do hereby certify that the signatures of Henry F. Tennant, Louis d'Antin, Charles B. Parker and W. A. Burnside above annexed, are their true and genuine signatures, made and acknowledged in my presence and that the said Henry F. Tennant, Louis d'Antin, Charles B. Parker and W. A. Burnside are known to me to be the persons they claim to be. In witness whereof I have hereunto set my hand and affixed the seal of the Embassy of the United States at Mexico, the day and year next above written, and of the Independence of the United States the One Hundred and Thirty-Seventh.

NELSON O'SHAUGHNESSY
Secretary of the Embassy of the United States
Mexico City.[1]

MR. TENNANT'S LETTER

May 26, 1926.

HONOURABLE HENRY LANE WILSON
Indianapolis, Indiana
DEAR MR. WILSON:

Your letter of the 17th was forwarded to me here. My memory of this matter is this:

I went to see Huerta and asked him, in your name, to place at liberty Madero's Cabinet, and especially mentioned Mr. Pedro Lascurain. Mr. Huerta returned and replied quickly, "*Que se pongan en libertad todos.*"

---

[1]This affidavit was drawn by Mr. O'Shaughnessy and signed by the staff without my knowledge.

Immediately afterwards, someone who was standing alongside, tapped him on the shoulder and said something to him; then Huerta turned and said that he would let them all go with the exception of Madero and Pino Suarez, as he feared that if he let them loose trouble would immediately start again. At the time I was at the Palace, all the Ministers, including Madero and Pino Suarez, were sitting around in another room, in chairs, with guards at the door. I remember that I went to the door of that room when the Ministers were let free and brought Mr. Lascurain to his house in the car I had with me; you remember he lived near the Embassy.

I hope this covers the point, and with kindest regards to you and Mrs. Wilson, I remain.

Very sincerely yours,
HENRY F. TENNANT.

APPENDIX VI

LETTERS FROM DIPLOMATIC COLLEAGUES

From the British Minister

British Legation
Mexico
February 22, 1913.

MY DEAR MR. WILSON:

I wish to express to you my most cordial thanks for the aid rendered to British subjects during the recent disturbances by Your Excellency, as well as by the members of your embassy and their gallant assistants of the American Colony.

The British Legation was difficult of access owing to its exposed position, and its remoteness from the principal residential quarter, and the help afforded by the United States Embassy and those who worked with it was therefore of special value.

I remain, my dear Mr. Wilson,

Yours very sincerely,
FRANCIS STRONG.

From the German Minister

Kaiserlich Deutsche Gesandtschaft
Mexico.
March 8, 1913.

DEAR MR. AMBASSADOR:

It is with profound satisfaction that I read in this morning's paper the praises duly bestowed on you by the

State Department. As an eye witness of last February's events, I wish to congratualte you upon the official recognition of your merits. May I add a word for my part? That is to say that I want to thank you most heartily for your excellent advice and practical help proffered to this Legation during a rather trying situation. I was so delighted when reading the morning paper that I wanted to get up to congratulate you in person, but the doctor won't have it as this intestinal hemorrhage has repeated itself last Wednesday.

Believe me, dear Mr. Ambassador,

Yours very sincerely and devotedly,

Von Hintze.

From the Spanish Minister

Mexico, March 12, 1913.

My dear Mr. Ambassador:

On account of my interminable labours I failed to express to you my sincere thanks for the visit made to me in your name by Mr. O'Shaughnessy to show me the telegram you sent to the Secretary of State and the favourable reply thereto, relative to the Spaniards at Piedras Negras, advising me that they had asked protection of the American Consul during the hours of trial caused by the threats and demands of the rebels.

I avail myself of this occasion to say to you that I shall always remember the daily and constant communication in which we were during the tragic days, and will keep grateful recollection of the always efficacious and kind assistance and coöperation I had from you. I have been an eye witness of your valuable efforts to solve the problems and responsibilities of those trying moments, and to accomplish the pacification of the country, a matter we both had at heart on account of the great importance of our respective colonies.

I avail, etc.

B. J. COLOGAN.

From the Chargé d'Affaires of France

Mexico, March 11, 1913.

MR. AMBASSADOR:

At the moment in which my functions as Chargé d'Affaires have ended, on account of the return to Mexico of H. E., the French Minister, I consider it my duty to express to Your Excellency my deep gratitude for the cordial manner in which you received me during the course of two months in which I had charge of the French Legation and notably during the tragic days of the revolution of February last.

I shall always keep in memory the special courtesies you had the goodness to accord to me and I congratulate myself that the discharge of my duties, during the above-mentioned difficult moments, allowed me the privilege of dealing more directly with the eminent Dean of the Diplomatic Corps.

With assurances of my highest consideration, believe me your obedient servant

V. AYGUESPARSSE.

APPENDIX VII

PRESIDENT TAFT'S LETTER OF APPROVAL AND SECRETARY
KNOX'S TELEGRAMS OF APPROVAL

New Haven, Conn.
April 3, 1913.

MY DEAR MR. AMBASSADOR:

I have yours of March 10th. The suggestion you make would be impossible for me to carry out. The fact is that the State Department—and I followed the State Department in general—were of opinion that your views of the Madero government were too pessimistic, and that you did not quite sympathize as much as you might have done with the difficulties that Madero had to encounter. The truth is that the Department was mistaken, and you were right, in that as well as in reference to the moving of the embassy. If it had come into the line of fire between two contending forces, under the extraordinary conditions that existed in the city of Mexico, the question of what should be done would be a doubtful one. It is certainly very unwise for a foreign government to project into a heated controversy too much of its right to protection from the existing government when that government is struggling for its life; but in this case the result vindicated you, as it had before, when at your instance, or at least acting upon your information, I sent the division of 20,000 troops to the Mexican border, at a time when the actual volcanic condition in Mexico was but little known in the United States or elsewhere. Neither a proper regard and sense of loyalty to the Secretary of State and the Department, nor the facts, would justify my disavowing these telegrams to which you refer. They were not sent at my instance, but having been sent, in information that seemed reliable at the time, I would not alter them in any regard.

I congratulate you on the reputation that you have properly won in the very trying situation that you had to meet, and whatever may be said as to the differences in judgment between you and the State Department, certainly the end does not show any such interference with your discretion as to prevent a successful result.[1]

Sincerely yours,
WM. H. TAFT.

Hon. Henry Lane Wilson,
   American Ambassador,
     Mexico, Mexico.

Secretary Knox's Telegrams of Approval

Department of State

Washington, February 18, 1913, 4 P. M.

12. Your February 15, 11 P. M. Your six agreements with General Huerta and the President cause no less satisfaction to the Department of State than to the American colony in Mexico City; the Department congratulates you upon your excellent work; also upon

---

[1]There was no actual difference between the embassy and the Department of State. For a few days the Department could not visualize the actual situation but there was no interruption of good feeling and the mutual affection and respect existing between Mr. Knox and myself endured until he passed away.

initiating and carrying out the measures mentioned in the
latter part of your February 15, 7 P. M.

KNOX.

Department of State

Washington, February 18, 1913, 4 P. M.

11. Your February 16, 11 A. M. The Department
compliments you upon your success in arranging an
armistice and the prompt and efficient way in which
foreigners were removed from danger zones and arrangements were made for the transportation of American
women and children to the United States.

KNOX.

APPENDIX VIII

SECRETARY BRYAN'S LETTER[1]

The Department of State desires to give expression to its gratification at the very cool, capable and successful manner in which, throughout the recent difficult situation in the City of Mexico, United States citizens there, American organizations, and especially the United States Embassy and its staff have conducted themselves. The Department of State considers that had it not had such efficient and prompt coöperation on the part of the Embassy the conduct of the relations of the Governments of the United States and of Mexico throughout this trying time would have been less effective and successful.

WILLIAM JENNINGS BRYAN.

---

[1]Another telegram from Mr. Bryan which is published in *Foreign Relations* expressly denies that the Department of State was investigating charges made against me, "and all their inferences and implications."

APPENDIX IX

Indianapolis, Indiana.
August 28, 1913.

Hon. W. J. Bryan,
  Secretary of State,
    Washington, D. C.

Sir:

I have the honour to acknowledge the receipt of your note of August 14, 1913, transmitting a copy of a telegraphic instruction of the Department of State to the American ambassador in London, directing him to disclaim all responsibility on the part of this government for an interview published on August 14th, attributed to me. The closing paragraph of the instruction referred to states that "the President regrets exceedingly that a diplomatic official of this government should have been guilty of such an impropriety." The last paragraph of your note to me, with which this telegraphic instruction was transmitted, states that "the President does not go further at this time because he takes it for granted that the action which he has been obliged to take in the matter will be to you a sufficient reminder of your official obligations."

On August 18th, I placed a memorandum on file with you which in substance stated that on account of our delicate relations with Mexico, I should refrain from making

[378]

any comment on your instructions to our ambassador in London or on your letter transmitting the same to me, and that when I might feel called upon to do so, I would place the matter of present publicity under your control.

In further and formal answer to your communication I must respectfully decline to accept as definitive or just the action of the President, either in instructing in such manner and in such language the American ambassador at London, or in transmitting it to me thereafter with a note the tenor of which is more suggestive of a threat than an admonition. I yield to no one in official life in my respect and deference for the President of the United States, and in obedience to my superior officers. There is, however, a just limit to patient silence, and I shall not permit myself to be made the victim of a hasty and unmerited rebuke without placing on record with you my earnest and solemn protest. For the purpose of making clear my reasons for taking this step I have the honour to call your attention to the following considerations:

That on August 11, 1913, a London dispatch was published throughout the United States, in which it was stated that among the factors determining the recognition by the British government of the provisional government of Mexico was the congratulatory speech of the American ambassador on the occasion of the reception given by the provisional president to the diplomatic corps. As years of contact have made me familiar with the methods of procedure of the British government, I felt confident that it had given to the press no official expression, and that the telegram was the invention of some active and imaginative correspondent. I, therefore, decided to pay no attention to it, and to maintain the attitude of reserve which I had maintained since the President, at my request, accepted my resignation as ambassador to Mexico. I found, however, on the two succeeding days following the publication of this dispatch, notices throughout the press of the United States, evidently inspired from administration sources, containing expressions of the gratification of this government over the supposed propitiatory explanation of the government of Great Britain. It seemed apparent to me that this was the first evidence of your intention to publicly question my official acts, and I accordingly gave to the press the interview referred to. This interview could not possibly be construed as an expression of the views of this government, as the Secretary of State had given out a statement to the press some time prior, announcing my voluntary severance with the diplomatic service of the United States. It was intended to be and was solely for the personal defense of a public officer against a false statement published in a foreign newspaper, and was not discourteous to the government of Great Britain, although it did prove objectionable to you. Thereupon, with tempestuous haste, and apparently prompted by partisan zeal, you dispatched an instruction to the American ambassador in London, directing him to apologize for language uttered by me which was not in the least degree offensive, and was based entirely upon the assumption that the supposed expression of the British government was a malicious fabrication. You thus hastily proceeded without ascertaining whether the supposed expressions by the British government or my comment thereon were veritable; and, as has since been developed, your action caused the greatest possible surprise to the government of Great Britain, which did not know it had been offended and had no official knowledge of the views attributed to it. Thus, through pique, you have unjustly discredited a diplomatic officer of this government and coincidentally have exposed to the British foreign office the spirit of hazardous adventure which presides over the Department of State.

That the President of the United States, whom I know to possess high and patriotic ideals, and whose lofty purposes ought never to be questioned by any American citizen, should, upon totally unwarranted and since discredited sources of information, lend himself to the hasty criticism of an old and tried official of the government of the United States, convinced me that he has been badly advised. That you, Mr. Secretary, who have been identified with movements for higher and better things in this country, should find reason for the censure of a plain and truthful statement of fact relating to matters of record in the Department of State and probably of record in all foreign offices having diplomatic relations with Mexico, by assuming an attitude which involves the correctness of the official procedure of a diplomatic officer under your control, inspires me with serious doubts as to your future success in dealing with delicate international affairs.

When the administration of President Wilson came into office I had been seventeen years in the diplomatic service of the United States. During that long period of service, probably the longest in the history of our government, extending from the opening of the administration of President McKinley until the present hour, I have never been criticized for a single official act, and have been commended by all the Presidents and Secretaries of State under whom it has been an honour for me to serve. During these years, in transacting the business of this government, I have had to deal with some thirty ministers of foreign affairs and eight chief executives, and I have yet to learn that I did not part with them on terms of cordial friendship and esteem, or that any official attitude of mine was ever questioned.

If you will take the time to investigate the record, you will find that the work I have done through these long years was useful in humanitarian, commercial, and political ways; that its character was appreciated is evidenced not only by the testimony of thousands on the records of the Department of State, but by the generous and repeated approval of my superiors. Solely upon the record which I had made President Taft, when he came into office, after having informally tendered me two other embassies, finally sent me to Mexico, a post which I desired because the expenses of its charge comported with my meagre fortune. When chosen for the embassy at Mexico, I went there with the full expectation of a stormy official career. In the period which elapsed between that time and the assumption of office by the administration of President Wilson, three distinct revolutions occurred in Mexico, namely, the revolution against Diaz, the revolution against Madero, and the existing revolution against Huerta. As may be supposed, these abnormal conditions imposed a heavy burden of responsibility upon me. That I met them to the best of my ability, honestly and conscientiously, is the testimony of all Americans living in Mexico. Not for a day or an hour did I have any other thought than the discharge of my duties to this government and to my unfortunate fellow countrymen in Mexico. As the records of your department will show, my chancellery work extended from six in the morning until twelve o'clock at night, sometimes to the small hours of the morning, and nearly always included the Sabbath day. During this entire period the American embassy remained constantly aloof from Mexican politics. When the administration of General Diaz was in power I thought it was my duty as an official of a friendly government to coöperate with it in every possible way. When the Madero administration took charge of affairs, I took the same course until, finding that there was no intention of righting American wrongs and that the administration was controlled by anti-American influences, I ceased to make representations to it except in urgent cases involving the loss of life or property. Yet I never gave expression, except to the Department of State, to my lack of faith in the government and never abated in the least my friendly relations with it. One of the last acts of the unfortunate and misguided Madero was to address to me a letter, on file at the Department of State, in which he refers to me as a friend of the Mexican nation.

My relations with Huerta were brought about by the stress of circumstances, by the pressure of an appalling situation threatening the lives and property of American citizens and of all foreigners. In my dealings with him and with General Felix Diaz I had in view solely the saving of human life and the abatement of conditions in the city of Mexico which had become intolerable, and which, from all appearances, might lead to a still greater tragedy. By my course at that time, which has been approved by all of my diplomatic colleagues then present, by the American and British colonies, by all American organizations in the city and throughout the republic, by the American Protestant and Roman Catholic clergy, by the

Y. M. C. A. organizations, and by private letters from nearly every responsible American citizen in Mexico, I believe that I saved hundreds of human lives, and I know that I vastly mitigated the horrors and sufferings of that terrible situation. As I was acting upon my own responsibility and in representation not only of the American government but, by force of circumstances, other governments also, whatever action I took was the result of deliberate and conscientious consideration. Without in the least assuming to take from you or from the President the privilege of supervision and ultimate decision in these matters, I must say to you that your conclusions that my action at that time was an intrusion into the politics of the country are at variance with the belief and testimony of all living eye witnesses, and against the record on file at the Department of State, which is clear, comprehensive, and conclusive; and I must add that under similar circumstances I should deem it my duty, as one charged with the preservation of human life, and as a possible factor in the restoration of order, to take precisely the same course as was then taken.

On March 4th, with the advent of the administration of President Wilson, I offered my resignation in the usual form, and expected it to be accepted. This, however, was not done; whether because of the President's desire to avoid the issuance of new credentials or whether he was influenced by the delegation of American citizens which travelled 3,000 miles for the purpose of urging my retention until peaceful conditions could be restored, I am not advised; but I assume that the President's course was affected by both considerations.

This situation continued for some time, being illuminated upon frequent occasions by public statements that the administration was investigating the situation through unofficial sources. These public statements, repeated with disagreeable frequency, affected my official usefulness. I, therefore, called upon you for a denial of them and, after waiting some ten days for a reply, and receiving none, I again requested you to urge the acceptance of my resignation. In reply you stated that you had been away and that the telegram had not been brought to your attention, and by inference also clearly indicated your desire that I should remain at my post.

After seventeen years of connection with the diplomatic service, which I entered when I was broken in fortune and health and which I am now leaving without sufficient means to sustain me for a single year, I feel obliged, with the deepest reluctance, but under a sense of duty to say to you that my treatment by this administration, which was under no obligation of retaining me at my post, might at least have been kindlier in spirit, more generous and more considerate. Coming events, which are already casting shadows before, will soon lead you, Mr. Secretary, to the sad conclusion that an indefinite and drifting policy toward Mexico, contrary to my official advice and recommendation, is likely to impose even greater burdens on our relations with the neighbouring and friendly republic and promote additional hatred and suspicion through all Latin America, endangering the lives and property of Americans, and finally possibly bringing on intervention, a thing which I know is not desired by the President or by you and to which I am strongly opposed.

In what I have had occasion to say in this note I have been actuated solely by the public interest and have thus spoken frankly. I have for the President and for you all the respect and deference to which your high elective and appointive positions entitle you, and in this matter I am not seeking publicity, but that justice which presidents not less than kings must render. I do not desire in any way to embarrass the President's policy in Mexico. On the contrary I earnestly hope that his special mission may bring about good results. I have the profoundest commiseration for the situation of that unhappy country and its unfortunate people, and if any methods better than those I have suggested from time to time can bring about order and peace and the reëstablishment of good relations with this country I shall be not less pleased than the administration.

After due deliberation and in consideration of the circumstances herein recited, I feel that unless the President shall, through a sense of justice, feel disposed to revoke or modify his instructions of August 14th, to our ambassador in London, I must respectfully request you to again urgently present my resignation as ambassador to Mexico, to take effect on the date of the receipt of this communication.

I have the honour to be, sir, your obedient servant,
HENRY LANE WILSON.

APPENDIX X

New York City, March 8, 1913.

HIGHLY ESTEEMED AND DEAR FRIEND:

My wife has informed me that you were good enough to convey to us your sympathy upon the occasion of the disaster in the family which we recently suffered.

My first duty after placing myself at your orders, upon arrival at this city, is to forward you this letter which brings with it my sincere appreciation for your excellent favours and courtesies which I shall never forget.

I decided to leave Mexico and station myself in this city for a few months with the expectation of going later to Europe. I have deemed it more conformable to remain absent from the Republic in order to avoid trouble for the new government and also for myself, for, unfortunately in our country denunciations against honest people are frequent, and there will be no lack of those who will believe me implicated in political conspiracies to which I am a complete stranger. You know that I have never been a politician and that I have never cared for politics and if I served for two years as Minister of Agriculture, I did so at a personal sacrifice and with the single desire of doing a service to my country.

It is my sincere desire to see order reëstablished soon

---

[1]Uncle of President Madero, and member of his cabinet at the time of the revolution.

in the Republic and the end for all time of the fratricidal wars which have cost so many lives and which have brought to the inhabitants so much material harm.

With best wishes for your health, I remain, your affectionate friend and attentive servant

ERNESTO MADERO.

APPENDIX XI

New York City, April 12, 1916.

My distinguished Friend:

With genuine satisfaction I am addressing this letter to you, in compliance with the wish you expressed to me, that I should relate sincerely and loyally my personal impression relative to your course as ambassador of the United States in Mexico.

The official positions which I held from 1908 to 1913 and the personal relations which I maintained during the period with the highest authorities in the United States and Mexico, make it possible for me to comment with full knowledge concerning these matters.

Your work as representative of the United States in my country was inspired by sentiments of sincere sympathy toward Mexico and you understood how to harmonize the discharge of your official obligations with the duty of preserving the respect due to the national sovereignty and to the different governments which succeeded during your time.

During the régime of General Diaz you laboured to avoid all cause for friction between the two governments and did so without weakening your position. During my provisional government the best understanding existed between the two chancelleries, founded on mutual respect for the rights and interests of the two countries. No conflicts of opinion occurred during this time and you, with your tact and constant labour, contributed to this result so beneficial to both countries.

During the presidency of Señor Madero it was quite evident that you pursued the same course. The grave faults of this administration brought about its destruction; this, public opinion recognized as being the cause of an overthrow which had such serious consequences.

Although I had, as you know, no part direct or indirect in the Ciudadela agreements, I believe that the part that you played was in behalf of that peace which we all desired. Your attitude was, in general, one of aloofness from all internal politics; your diplomatic acts were not inspired by personal sympathies or antipathies, but had their inspiration in higher and purer ideals.

I do not wish to enter into details which I shall later relate in "Pages of the History of Mexico" which I intend to publish when I have in my hands all of the necessary documents and when the political passions shall be less vehement, permitting reason and justice to be heard.

Believing that this letter will perform the office which you desired, it only remains for me to express sentiments of sincere esteem and distinguished consideration.

Your sincere friend,
F. L. DE LA BARRA.

APPENDIX XII

LETTER FROM ENRIQUE CREEL, MEXICAN MINISTER OF FOREIGN AFFAIRS

Los Angeles, California,
May 25, 1916.

MY DEAR MR. WILSON:

Your favour of the 20th inst. duly received.

I regret very much to learn that you should have been attacked by the newspaper correspondent whose articles have been published in the *Harper's Weekly*. I have not had an opportunity to read the articles mentioned in your letter.

I consider any unfavourable criticism of the discharge of your official duties in Mexico as unfair and unjust. I know from my personal experience as Secretary of State under the Diaz Administration and also in my capacity as Ambassador of Mexico to the United States and as Governor of the State of Chihuahua that all your efforts were toward harmonizing and coöperating with the Mexican government to solve in a friendly and just way whatever friction or difficulties there might have arisen in the relations of the two countries.

I also know that among the Mexican community and the high officials of the Republic you enjoyed the confidence and the high regard to which you were entitled.

I do hope that the time may come soon when full justice may be done to your diplomatic career in Mexico.

With kind regards, I am

Very sincerely yours,
ENRIQUE CREEL.

APPENDIX XIII

Washington D. C., May 14, 1912.

MY DEAR MR. AMBASSADOR:

I take pleasure in informing you that I have assumed the duties devolving upon me as Mexican Ambassador near your Government, and was, on Friday last, received by your President, with whom I was charmed to a very special degree.

My attention has just been called to the enclosed clipping from the Washington *Post* of to-day's date. I hasten to express to you my warm appreciation for your kindness in making the emphatic denial, for, as you know, the whole thing, from beginning to end, is false; it seems to be only another sample of the yellow journalism of the worst type of which I have been made the victim, ever since my arrival in New York.

I have as yet been unable to present the letters of introduction you so graciously gave me, but shall not fail to do so at the earliest possible moment.

The recollection of our pleasant associations during my tenure of office as Minister of Foreign Affairs, is an earnest that they will be continued in my new sphere, where I

[392]

should deem it an honour to serve you in what lies in my power.

Pray accept, Mr. Ambassador, the renewed assurances of my high regard.

Sincerely yours,
MANUEL CALERO.

THE END

INDEX

INDEX

171

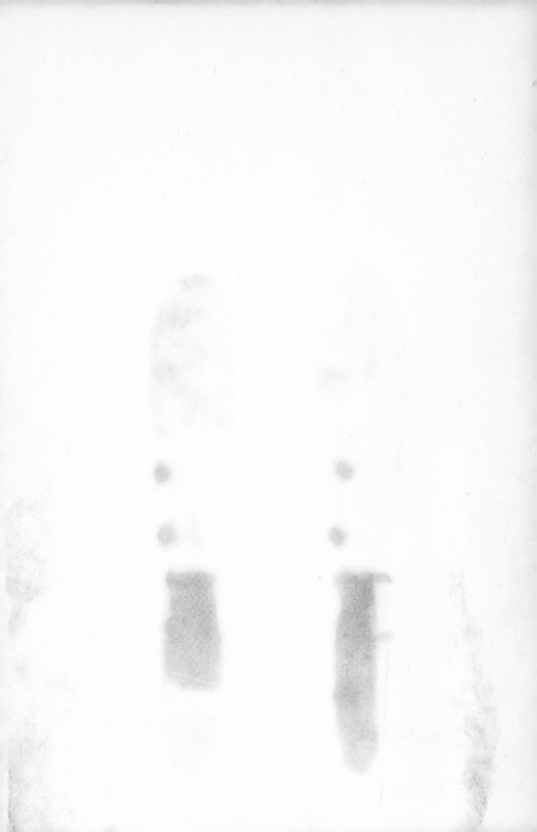